SIDREA Series in Accounting and Business Administration

This is the official book series of SIDREA - the Italian Society of Accounting and Business Administration. This book series is provided with a wide Scientific Committee composed of Academics by SIDREA. It publishes contributions (monographs, edited volumes and proceedings) as a result of the double blind review process by the SIDREA's thematic research groups, operating at the national and international levels. Particularly, the series aims to disseminate specialized findings on several topics – classical and cutting-edge alike – that are currently being discussed by the accounting and business administration communities. The series authors are respected researchers and professors in the fields of business valuation; governance and internal control; financial accounting; public accounting; management control; gender; turnaround predictive models; non-financial disclosure; intellectual capital, smart technologies, and digitalization; and university governance and performance measurement.This book series is indexed in Scopus.

Francesca Bernini
Editor

Creating Value Through Sustainability

An Interdisciplinary Perspective

Springer

Editor
Francesca Bernini
Department of Economics and Management
University of Pisa
Pisa, Italy

ISSN 2662-9879 ISSN 2662-9887 (electronic)
SIDREA Series in Accounting and Business Administration
ISBN 978-3-031-74291-0 ISBN 978-3-031-74292-7 (eBook)
https://doi.org/10.1007/978-3-031-74292-7

This Springer imprint is published by the registered company Springer Nature Switzerland AG
The registered company address is: Gewerbestrasse 11, 6330 Cham, Switzerland

Preface

Although the topic of sustainability has its roots in past decades, it is currently undergoing rapid growth. This phenomenon affects the lives of both people and companies. Driven by various incentives, firms can manage this shift in the social ecosystem or define new business models capable of including environmental, social, and governance (ESG) strategies.

This book fits fully into the current context, which is marked by a change in approach that drives companies to integrate ESG issues into their decisions, operations, and value-creation processes. The institutional context strongly promotes doing away with viewing sustainability and financial dynamics as distinct elements and, instead, urges companies to consider the impact of sustainability on their financial plans. Therefore, in light of recent developments in ESG reporting legislation (i.e., Corporate Sustainability Reporting Directive, 2022), companies are evaluating whether ethical-sustainable issues and economic-financial values are on separate tracks or have areas of overlap. Hence, understanding how sustainability influences the value-creation process leads to a reevaluation of the concept of value creation and affects several aspects of corporate life.

Adopting a multidisciplinary approach, this research spans several fields of study by examining the "sustainability–value creation" interaction through a macro lens.

From the firm's perspective, Chap. 1 investigates how ESG initiatives can enhance value creation. It uses a framework inspired by strategic cost management to trace the activities of the value chain, their drivers, and their contribution to sustaining the organization's strategy and, in turn, their value-creation potential. Within the strategy and activities, the chapter focuses on the integration of ESG initiatives with the general strategy of the organization. The research method combines case studies and conceptual argumentation. Findings suggest that integrating ESG initiatives into the competitive strategy affects the ESG activities that the company carries out, as well as their drivers and financial results.

The interplay between the company and its stakeholders is considered by investigating some ethical aspects of digital transformation, specifically by analyzing a new form of deliberately deceptive communication that aims to reassure stakeholders about companies' ethical behavior during the development of digital technologies, thus undermining value in stakeholders' network engagement processes. Following this premise, Chap. 2 analyzes the ethicswashing phenomenon, particularly the issue of the (ir)responsible use of artificial intelligence (AI), which may lead to corporate conduct not aligned with ethical principles. This is known as "digital ethicswashing," a strategy based on misleading reporting about AI use to gain stakeholder acceptance and loyalty. The research observes digital ethicswashing practices by investigating the reliability of disclosures related to the social aspects of AI use. Owing to the issue's novelty, the study develops an exploratory analysis to investigate how companies implement digital ethicswashing. Starting with a content analysis of external reporting, it proposes designing a dashboard to manage digital ethicswashing. Moreover, the study highlights the need to develop AI reporting audit tools to minimize such practices, thanks to the work of third-party experts.

Taking the firm's perspective, Chap. 3 examines the integration of ESG factors into risk management and performance measurement systems through the lens of management accounting change. This chapter presents a field study consisting of 12 interviews with four Italian companies that voluntarily disclose non-financial information and highlights the factors that either facilitate or hinder this process. Facilitating factors include changes to stakeholders' expectations and the regulatory landscape, while hindering factors include a lack of knowledge about ESG issues and inadequate information systems. The findings suggest that companies are increasingly aware of the need to implement ESG into their management systems, although the process is still in its early stages. This study adds to the literature on ESG-oriented management control systems and offers insights to companies seeking to initiate the ESG integration process.

These analyses demonstrate how sustainability is a wide-ranging concept that can engage the social sciences in various ways. Therefore, by adopting a juridical perspective, Chap. 4 proposes a "constitutionally oriented" reading of corporate sustainability. In 2022, the Italian Constitution was significantly revised. It established that the Republic "safeguard[s] the environment, biodiversity and ecosystems, also in the interest of future generations" (Art. 9) and that private economic enterprise may not be carried out in a manner that could harm health and the environment. Furthermore, the law shall determine appropriate programs and checks to ensure that public and private economic enterprise activities are directed and coordinated for social and environmental purposes (Art. 41). Considering this premise, Chap. 4 examines whether and to what extent adherence to ESG criteria—and, more generally, issues of corporate social responsibility (CSR)—is consistent with the new perspectives opened by the constitutional reform. The focus of the examination is to reconstruct the scope of the new constitutional provisions—especially concerning the "intergenerational" dimension—and to verify how the application of ESG criteria can be seen as an activity that is also "constitutionally qualified." In particular, the chapter reflects on the possibility of a "constitutionally oriented" reading of social responsibility principles and how companies adhering to ESG criteria might spontaneously conform their initiatives to the "function" of private initiative as envisioned by the new Art. 41 of the Italian Constitution.

In line with its multidisciplinary aim, the manuscript also includes the perspective of financial companies. Chapter 5 explores the role of administrative controls in fostering banks' commitment to sustainability. A single-case study conducted at a leading Italian bank sheds light on the approaches adopted to integrate ESG factors within administrative controls. This chapter extends prior research on sustainability in banking by examining the inter-organizational impact of sustainability with specific regard to administrative controls, a topic that is rarely explored. In addition, by identifying the approach followed by the bank in implementing administrative controls for sustainability, this chapter allows us to define best practices for integrating ESG factors into organizational and governance structures, as well as policies and procedures, as required by supervisory authorities.

The book's interdisciplinary approach extends to an analysis from an organizational perspective. Recent literature indicates that organizations must adhere to sustainability standards and ESG criteria to be eligible for financial resources. Although human capital plays a pivotal role in this corporate transformation, there seems to be a research gap regarding how human resource management (HRM) supports organizations in addressing the ESG criteria. To explore HRM's contribution to ESG strategies, Chap. 6 conducts a bibliometric analysis (activity indicators and bibliographic coupling) and a systematic literature review. The main finding of this review is that the three components of ESG strategies are essential and closely connected to sustainable HRM, despite the absence of specific and explicit literature on HRM and ESG integration. The governance aspects are very important for effectively implementing the environmental, social, and economic strategies and, by extension, achieving corporate sustainability. Integrating corporate governance into triple-bottom-line HRM and shifting to quadruple-bottom-line HRM is crucial for a more comprehensive assessment of corporate sustainability.

Chapter 7 focuses on the interplay between Corporate Social Responsibility (CSR) and tax avoidance. This issue has gained increasing attention in recent research on the ethical implications of taxation. Studies show that companies use tax avoidance strategies ranging from tax planning to more aggressive methods such as evasion and sheltering to reduce tax burdens. However, research on the relationship between tax avoidance and CSR presents a mixed picture, with some studies suggesting a negative relationship and others indicating a positive association. Theoretical frameworks like corporate culture theory, stakeholder theory, resource-based view, shareholder theory, legitimacy theory, and risk management theory offer different perspectives on this relationship, further complicating the understanding. This chapter aims to bridge this gap by exploring the nuanced relationship between tax avoidance and CSR across ESG dimensions. The study uses environmental, social, and governance scores to investigate how tax avoidance influences different components of CSR. Drawing on data from US firms listed on the NYSE and NASDAQ, the empirical analysis reveals that tax avoidance positively correlates with the environmental and social components of the ESG scores, with no significant association with governance. These findings suggest that taxation may influence corporate behavior in specific CSR dimensions, such as environmental initiatives and social or philanthropic activities. Furthermore, the study underscores the need for further exploration into the mechanisms through which CSR influences tax avoidance and vice versa.

Chapter 8 examines a new legal business model introduced by Italian Law 208/2015, in force from 2016: the "*Società Benefit*." This corporate form aims to balance profit distribution to owners with one or more common benefit purposes by aligning the interests of shareholders with those of other stakeholders. The research adopts stakeholder theory and uses the instrumental approach to analyze, through empirical research, the effect of this corporate model on default risk, estimated by calculating the default spread. To this end, a statistical analysis was carried out on a sample comprising a group of *Società Benefit* and a group of comparable profit companies, which revealed a significant negative relationship between being a *Società Benefit* and the risk of default. In other words, lenders perceive benefit companies as less risky than comparable profit companies.

I would like to thank all the authors who, by bringing their diverse perspectives, have contributed to enriching the originality of the research on a topic that is both novel and fundamental today.

Pisa, Italy
June 10, 2024

Francesca Bernini

Funding This work is supported by the University of Pisa under the "PRA—Progetti di Ricerca di Ateneo" (Institutional Research Grants)—Project no. PRA_2022_6 "Creazione di valore e strategie ESG: un approccio multidisciplinare" (PRA_2022–2023_).

Contents

Chapter 1
Analyzing the Link Between ESG Initiatives and Shareholder Value Creation Through the Value Chain Lens: A Qualitative Approach

Francesca Bernini, Cristina Campanale, and Riccardo Giannetti

1.1 Introduction

The recent global evolution in the legislation and stakeholder culture regarding CSR (corporate social responsibility) has made environmental, social, and governance (ESG) goals a crucial issue for companies. Both academics and practitioners recognize ESG metrics as an expression of companies' commitment toward sustainability issues (Bernini et al., 2024; Atkins et al., 2023), both of which evidence the relationship between ESG initiatives and performance (Rajesh & Rajendran, 2020).

Owing to the pressures that the institutional context exerts, companies are strongly motivated to comply with the ESG fields' ethical and legal rules. Simultaneously, firms' involvement in ESG initiatives is crucial for their success and survival (Eccles et al., 2014; Ortiz-de-Mandojana & Bansal, 2016) and for gaining a competitive advantage or improving theirs (Bini et al., 2018).

The pressure that companies face to adhere to ESG rules goes hand in hand with the need to understand ESG initiatives' financial impact, thereby guaranteeing their economic sustainability.

In this respect, European legislation's development regarding mandatory sustainability disclosure (European Commission, 2022; EFRAG, 2023) has given the codification of certain relationships between ESG practices and financial performance a strong impetus. It is also an incentive for defining paths to measure sustainability efforts' effects on corporate value. According to the Corporate Sustainable Reporting Directive (European Commission, 2022), companies are, in keeping with specific rules and requirements, required to consistently report the impacts, opportunities, and risks related to sustainability (Sanchez et al., 2023).

F. Bernini (✉) · C. Campanale · R. Giannetti
Department of Economics and Management, University of Pisa, Pisa, Italy
e-mail: francesca.bernini@unipi.it; cristina.campanale@unipi.it; riccardo.giannetti@unipi.it

F. Bernini (ed.), *Creating Value Through Sustainability*, SIDREA Series in Accounting and Business Administration,
https://doi.org/10.1007/978-3-031-74292-7_1

The concept of double materiality came into play, pushing companies to disclose information regarding the link between ESG practices and financial performance.

This new reporting perspective is a strong incentive for companies to not only regard sustainability issues as issues that have to be fulfilled or as a competitive lever but to also regard sustainability as capable of impacting a company's financial performance.

In terms of ESG initiatives' financial impact, the International Valuation Standards Council (IVSC) highlights important problems with quantifying ESG initiatives' impact on shareholders' value. A particularly difficult problem is identifying a rational connection between the costs for which ESG investments are responsible and the related benefits as well as establishing a way of measuring these. Moreover, invisible assets' growing importance in the value creation process contributes to the increasing difficulty of tracing each investment's contribution to improving the company's profitability. Although significant progress has been made regarding incorporating environmental risks into valuation processes (i.e., A4S Essential Guide to Valuations and Climate Change), including ESG effects into financial metrics and business valuation still seems to be a difficult undertaking. Among other things, this is due to many ESG investments' uniqueness.

The literature also reveals contradicting research on ESG activities' financial effects, underlining the need for further investigation. Currently, the linkages between sustainability, financial performance, and shareholder value cannot be determined, therefore leading to heated discussions (Lee & Raschke, 2023; Li et al., 2023; Aouadi & Marsat, 2018). Furthermore, while literature is focused on investigating the cause and effect relationship between ESG initiatives and financial results, there is a dearth of research on how this relationship evolves.

Given the above premises (the need to measure ESG initiatives' financial impact, the difficulty of doing so, the conflicting results in terms of previous research, and the lack of research on how ESG strategies affect financial results), a willingness to understand ESG strategies' financial impact motivates this research in support of companies, which the context to pursue sustainability compels to shed light on their ESG investments' financial impact.

The motivations described above stimulate this research to study how ESG initiatives are involved in shareholder value creation (SHVC).

This research's focus is not on studying whether ESG creates values but rather on how ESG can create value. In order to help achieve this aim, this research focuses on ESG activities and how they are developed. A specific framework was developed that traces the value chain's ESG activities, their drivers, and their impact on SHVC. Subsequently, this framework was applied to empirical materials. Unlike previous research, this research does not focus on defining a precise cause and effect relationship between ESG and SHVC but investigate how this relationship works.

Strategic cost management (SCM) (Shank & Govindarajan, 1993) inspired the elaborated framework and recognized ESG activities' underlying role in SHVC. In fact, activities and how they are done may determine the financial and economic results (Cooper & Kaplan, 1999).

This research focuses specifically on activities that the ESG goals impact most. The analysis therefore examines ESG activities by considering their capacity to contribute to organizations' goals. In this respect, Schmeltz (2014) undertook similar reach focused on integrating core values, sustainability values, and stakeholders' involvement, finding that companies might experiment with integrating different degrees of corporate social responsibility values into the strategy, which vary from the caring and strategizing stages to the core values stage.

This research's primary contribution is by providing literature on the relationship between ESG initiatives and SHVC. Further, unlike previous research, this research is focused on the how by shedding light on this relationship's complexity. The research also offers a secondary, methodological contribution and, specifically, a framework that combines the SCM with the ESG initiatives. Finally, it suggests what the financial results will be.

The chapter is structured as follows: Sect. 1.2 analyzes the recent literature on this topic; Sect. 1.3 provides the research framework; Sect. 1.4 describes the research method and Sect. 1.5 the results. Finally, Sect. 1.6 discusses the findings and their implications.

1.2 Literature Background

Over time, scholars often regarded sustainability as a compliance action with evolving regulations more than a competitiveness lever. Since they considered sustainability a parallel scenario, it is possible to hypothesize that companies did not know how ESG efforts could create or destroy value and did not investigate their impact on the financial or risk parameters. Next, the evolving context integrated ESG practices into a competitive strategy by allowing companies to estimate ESG issues' impact on financial statements, risk, and the company value (Zioło et al., 2023; CRSD, 2022; EFRAG, 2023).

On the one hand, companies increasingly emphasize the mapping of relevant issues in the ESG field (e.g., the matrix for detecting ESG practices' impact materiality). Furthermore, the ESG concept has moved from being a parallel activity to being a strategy that is strictly interrelated with companies' core activities and which can generate financial evidence.

According to the evolution involving ESG disclosure's regulation as well as corporate perceptions and behaviors, the academic literature has also exhibited a growing focus on the relationships between ESG practices, financial parameters, risk, and value. This has led numerous scholars to recognize that commitment to sustainability has a strategic value (El Ghoul et al., 2016). Below we provide a literature review of the relationship between ESG activities and SHVC.

Sustainability impacts companies' lives, gradually, shifting from a formal to a substantial perspective. At first, sustainability was regarded as a required compliance with regulations necessitating increasing commitment to sustainability reporting. The gradual inclusion of ESG issues into companies' business models changes these efforts into substantive commitment.

Consequently, the literature is devoted to both ways in which sustainability might contribute to SHVC.

1.2.1 ESG Initiatives' Disclosure and SHVC

Certain researchers investigate the mediating role that ESG disclosure plays in SHVC. The recent improvements in ESG disclosure regulations contributed to academic literature's improved focus on the effects that ESG disclosure have on stakeholders' perception (Bernini & La Rosa, 2024; Fatemi et al., 2018), on the corporate reputation, the financial performance, and, ultimately, on SHVC (Chen & Xie, 2022). Following this research stream, the literature explored the possible determinants and effects of strategies aimed at improving SHVC through a symbolic or misleading ESG disclosure (Walker & Wan, 2012; Seele & Gatti, 2017; Zharfpeykan, 2021; Torelli et al., 2020; Wu et al., 2020; Cho & Patten, 2007).

Scholars regard sustainability disclosure as a tool for legitimizing (Deegan et al., 2002) a company's behavior, thereby impacting stakeholders' perception, the company's reputation, and, ultimately, its value. This new perspective invites business operators and researchers to rethink the value concept by considering ESG reporting not only a possible tool for facilitating value drivers' identification but also as a possible value lever. Companies could adopt different behaviors when faced with changes in the environment in which they operate. For exactly this reason, there are various ways in which ESG issues could fuel the paths leading to the creation (or destruction) of value. Companies might adopt sustainable management and define new business models that actually include sustainability in their strategies or they could just adopt symbolic behaviors by using misleading communication about ESG initiatives or impacts. The latter behavior provides benefits in the context of dystopian scenarios, where stakeholders reward "bad companies." Consequently, the literature recognizes disclosure of moderating's role as revealing ESG commitment's possible strengths and weaknesses (Fatemi et al., 2018; Cohen, 2023).

1.2.2 ESG Initiatives, Financial Performance, and Risk: A Link Worth Exploring Further

Certain researchers investigate the relationship between ESG initiatives and financial performance directly, providing a picture comprised of contrasting results. Fatemi et al. (2018) showed that earlier research regarded sustainability as a value-destroying investment. In particular, Friedman (1970) regarded sustainability efforts exceeding the minimum legal requirements as a source of additional company costs.

Kim and Lyon (2015) stated that firms only make ESG investments under compulsion, because they do not think they are necessary.

Subsequent studies showed different results. There was, for example, in terms of firms' value and stock returns evidence of a positive (D'Agostini et al., 2017; Cohen, 2023) or non-negative (Xie et al., 2019) relationship between, on the one hand, ESG engagement and sustainability and commitment and financial performance on the other hand (Mercereau et al., 2022).

Moreover, some researchers analyzed the role that ESG practices play in risks. ESG practices could help firms become more resilient by preparing them emerging issues' impact and helping them maintain their robust governance, risk management, and controls (KPMG, 2022; CNDC, 2022), although ESG management is also a source of risk (Stewart, 2015). In addition, since companies with higher social performances are perceived as less risky than others, ESG investments (Aouadi & Marsat, 2018) or certification (Wong et al., 2021) could impact firms' value positively, because they could help reduce the capital costs. In keeping with these findings, Cohen (2023) states that since investors are more attracted to ESG-compliant companies, this commitment impacts competitiveness in capital markets. It could therefore improve firms' value by decreasing the cost of debts and equity and through the possibility of a more convenient leverage. Consistent with this perspective, some scholars consider that firms engaging in sustainability and CSR regard ESG commitment as a value-relevant activity that could lower the cost of capital (Dhaliwal et al., 2011). Several studies analyzed the relationship between sustainability and companies' value. Notwithstanding this research's mixed results, most of the researched identified a non-negative link between the two (Brooks & Oikonomou, 2018; Eng et al., 2022).

Additional research shows that financial performance has a mediating role in the positive relation between ESG performance and firms' market value (Zhou et al., 2022). Other studies argue that the correlation between ESG practices and resilience's financial performance is complex and mediated by customer satisfaction, long-term shareholders, and stakeholders' value (Avery & Bergsteiner, 2011). Conversely, through their operations' maturity model (which included corporate sustainability, economic capital, societal capital, human capital, and natural capital measures), Balugani et al. (2020) found that profitability does not have a significant relationship with sustainability.

Other studies focused on the institutional context's role. Showing that ESG performance has a positive effect on corporate value, Chang and Lee (2022) clarify that the institutional context's features could mediate this relationship.

From a complementary point of view, other studies investigated ESG controversies' impact on firm value. Servaes and Tamayo (2013) found that sustainability problems impact firms' value negatively, while Aouadi and Marsat (2018) provided evidence that although ESG concerns harm firms' financial performance per se, they impact stakeholders' perception in a way that ultimately improves the relationship between sustainability and market value.

Observing capital markets, Cohen (2023) emphasizes that sustainability's effect considers both the positive and negative attitudes of ESG commitment. He specifically reveals that investors prefer investing in companies that are sensitive to these issues, in order to reduce their sustainability risk, but that investors simultaneously prefer to limit funding for companies that do not respect the principles underlying sustainability.

According to the International Valuation Standards Council (IVSC), ESG initiatives' impact on value is due to invisible assets being improved. Based on this, the IVSC identifies three stages of ESG value creation's life cycle, which is in line with its analysis of investments in intangibles. Direct assets are those intangibles that benefit directly from ESG investments. In turn, indirect assets are the intangibles that could benefit from an increase in direct intangibles' value. Finally, scalable value creation is the last phase of the life cycle's last phase and results from its interconnection with other intangible assets.

Scholars could investigate the relationship between ESG commitment and corporate value in the light of a wide, theoretical framework comprising several theoretical perspectives in the business economics field.

From the resource-based view's perspective, resources are a key determinant of firms' competitive advantage (Barney, 1991; Wernerfelt, 1984), meaning that firms' ability to gain distinctive resources fosters higher performance (Peteraf and Barney, 2003). According to this viewpoint, companies' commitment to sustainability contributes to improving managerial skills, attracting a qualified workforce (Fatemi et al., 2018; El Ghoul et al., 2016), and fostering firms' reputation and, ultimately, their value creation potential (Bernini & La Rosa, 2024).

Stakeholder theory might also motivate the way companies approach sustainability and their ESG commitment's possible effects (Freeman, 1984). The theory focuses on stakeholders' engagement, which could have a dual purpose. It aims to fulfill societal norms' ethical requirements as well as endeavoring to manage relational capital strategically (Edvinsson & Malone, 1997; Stewart, 1997). Both these purposes are instrumental for a competitive advantage (Cennamo et al., 2009; Seele & Shultz, 2022). Moreover, according to this perspective, sustainability enables companies to meet stakeholders' interests and, therefore, to boost contracting's efficiency, which enhances the likelihood of growth and could reduce the risks (Fatemi et al., 2018).

From legitimacy theory's perspective (Deegan et al., 2002), socially accepted values characterize the context in which, in keeping with the perception of the social environment's actors, corporate actions are considered appropriate. Within legitimacy theory, scholars therefore framed ESG strategies as a search for legitimacy. Moreover, by adopting institutional legitimacy theory's lens (Suchman, 1988), scholars' increasing awareness of sustainability's importance could be considered a form of adaptation to comply with stakeholders' perception and to achieve advantages in SHVC terms. Conversely, early studies framed in the shareholder theory perspective (Friedman & Miles, 2004; Friedman, 1970) argued that sustainable actions could be detrimental to profitability and value creation. On the other hand, the more recent instrumental stakeholder theory's perspective views sustainability as a tool for achieving stakeholders' support, and, ultimately, for improving the invisible assets that nourish relational and reputational capital (Barney, 1991; Porter

& Kramer, 2006). Scholars regard the latter as strategic for gaining a competitive advantage (De Castro et al., 2006) and for improving a financial performance by enhancing environmental responsibility and by, ultimately, creating value (Bernini & La Rosa, 2024).

Following a different perspective, other studies (El Ghoul et al., 2016) regarded ESG efforts as resulting from agency conflict (Jensen & Meckling, 1976). Consequently, sustainability could be regarded as the outcome of management decisions aimed at creating relationships with specific stakeholders.

1.3 The Research Framework

Many value-based models could be adopted to measure and manage SHVC (e.g., Ittner & Larcker, 2001).

In this research, we propose the approach of the strategic cost management (SCM) framework to investigate the value creation process and, specifically, how ESG initiatives could create SHVC. Scholars define SCM as an "analysis of ways to decrease costs and/or enhance [the] differentiation of a firm's products, through exploiting linkages in the value chain and optimizing [the] cost drivers" (Lord, 1996, p. 438). Within this definition, Tomkins and Carr's (1996) work, which drew on Shank and Govindarajan's (1992, 1994) studies, provides a link between strategy formulation, value chain analysis, and cost driver analysis. Their model conceived a cost driver analysis to support competitive strategy development by either reducing the costs or through differentiation.

Specifically, SCM can both evaluate the coherence between the strategies' value creation objective and manage the value drivers. It might be useful if this research could investigate how value is created and what the drivers of value creation are.

In order exploit SCM, namely, identifying the strategy, the value chain, and the cost/differentiation (or uniqueness) drivers, we need to address certain elements.

Cost leadership and differentiation are the basic competitive strategies that scholars adopted to sustain a competitive advantage (Porter, 1985). Costs are important in both strategies. In fact, although companies pursuing differentiation can rely on higher prices, they need to cover the differentiation costs. Analyzing costs by means of the value chain involves an analysis of the value chain activities, which includes the following steps.

The first step is identifying the value chain and related costs (in this research, the activities' costs were not mapped, because they were not part of the analysis). Costs could be the operating costs and the investment costs (both the current and previous ones). Operating costs are attributed to activities within which they are incurred, while investment costs are allocated to activities using the underlying assets.

The second step is an analysis of the cost drivers (cost leadership strategy) and the differentiation drivers (differentiation strategy) (Porter, 1985). Drivers are factors that determine or influence activities. Cost drivers affect an activity's costs (in the case of cost drivers), because they determine the resources allocated to an activity and, therefore, the consequent costs. If a company pursues a cost leadership strategy, it should focus the innovations that allow it to reduce the costs or redesign its products in such a way that this will reduce their cost but will not impoverish the company excessively. Differentiation drivers relate to items that allow products and services to develop distinctive characterizations that differentiate them from other products and services. Cost drivers need to be understood, because it is important to know the origins of costs and differentiations, of their evolution, and for identifying strategies to act on these. According to Porter (1985), cost drivers are economies of scale, learning, the use of capacity, connections, inter-relationships, vertical integration, timing, discretionary policies, geographical location, and institutional factors. Differentiation drivers (Porter, 1985) are discretionary policies, connections, inter-relationships, vertical integration, timing, geographical location, institutional factors, and economies of scale. Differentiation drivers contribute uniqueness to the company's value proposition. Furthermore, these drivers might also mean a company suffering high costs (Porter, 1985). Summing up, the way activity driver impacts how activities are carried out and their output's characteristics all affect the company's costs, revenues, investments, and riskiness.

Shank and Govindarjan (1992) provided another classification for cost drivers, which we can integrate with that of Porter (1985) and which is also structural and operative drivers' classification. Organizational structure and investment decisions determine structural cost drivers and a company's cost structure. The efficiency and efficacy with which activities are carried out determine executional cost drivers (Shank & Govindarajan, 1992, 1994).

This classification is useful for evaluating how specific cost drivers, such as technology, quality, and product configuration, impact value creation. Structural drivers concern the strategic choice and comprise the:

1. Scale economies
2. Field of activity
3. Experience
4. Technology
5. The complexity in terms of the number of products and services

Operational drivers concern the company's capacity to be successful and comprise the:

1. Employees' involvement
2. Quality
3. Capacity use
4. Efficiency with which assets are used
5. Product configuration
6. The development of relationships with customer and suppliers

Consequently, when the value chain analysis that the SCM framework proposed is integrated into the differentiation drivers that Porter (1985) proposed, it supports competitive strategy's translation in terms of the cost/differentiation drivers and value chain activities. In turn, these variables allow a more likely estimate of the

SHVC's main monetary drivers, namely, the sales growth and the operating margin, investments in current and non-current assets, the competitive advantage's sustainability, and, therefore, the expected results' variability (riskiness).

In the case of cost leadership, SHVC acts by minimizing costs by means of taking actions that the cost drivers finalized to make value chain activities more efficient. For example, low prices might support an increase in revenues, while economies of scale could support an increase in the operating margin. In turn, minimizing cash transactions or reducing the time taken to collect money from customers could reduce investments in current assets; investments in non-current assets could also support value creation by increasing fixed assets' use or by buying assets more efficiently.

In the case of differentiation leadership, maximizing customer value perceptions by taking action regarding differentiation drivers could achieve SHVC. For example, a service company could implement this strategy by exploiting scale economies, but without intending to minimize the cost incidence per service unit, but rather offering the customers a better service than the competitor can (e.g., a car rental company represented in all of a country's airports/towns). The differentiation activity drivers impact SHVC's financial drivers as previously explained in respect of the cost drivers. However, in this case, the effect on the main drivers mentioned above (sales development, operating margin, investments, and riskiness) is mainly derived from the premium price related to the value proposition's uniqueness, rather than being derived from the lowest cost.

Finally, regardless of the competitive strategy type, the capital invested in the value chain activities affects the cost of capital. The cost of capital is one of the main SHVC drivers, while value chain activities could impact it in different ways. From an operational perspective, investments made in value chain activities and in ways of performing them determine the operational risk affecting the interest rate, which conveys the cost of capital (in percentage). From a financial point of view, capital (fixed and working) invested in value chain activities requires funds, which could influence the company's financial structure and, ultimately, the financial risk included in the rate used to express the cost of capital.

Figure 1.1 illustrates the framework that we will adopt to investigate empirical evidence. Figure 1.1 shows the framework's underlying linkages: specific drivers impact ESG activities (the primary and support ones), which, in turn, have an impact on SHVC. We will deepen the ESG activities to investigate what they impact (i.e., primary or support activities). Our research therefore involves identifying (in logical succession):

1. The competitive strategy (cost leadership and differentiation leadership)
2. The ESG initiatives' role in the competitive strategy
3. The ESG value chain activities, i.e., the primary and support activities that ESG initiatives impact
4. The cost/differentiation drivers impacting the ESG value chain activities
5. The ESG value chain activities' impact on the SHVC's financial value drivers (the sales growth, operating margin, risk drivers, and the invested capital)

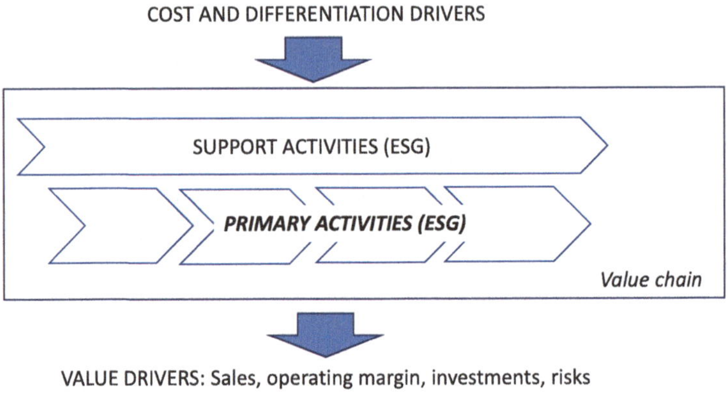

Fig. 1.1 The framework of analysis

By providing the details of ESG activities and their drivers and by identifying their impact on a SHVC, this framework is useful to gain a view of how the relationship between an ESG initiative and a SHVC evolves. Secondly, being familiar with such activities and drivers is useful for managing this relationship.

1.4 The Research Method

1.4.1 Research Method and Steps

The method adopted in this research is based on the interplay between conceptual and empirical analyses.

In the first phase, the research elaborated a framework for investigating how ESG's impact on SHVC works, because the research was conceptual in this phase. In this part, integrating value-based models' financial side into the SCM framework allowed us to elaborate it (Porter, 1985; Shank & Govindarajan, 1992, 1994). With regard to the SCM framework, it is worth mentioning that many proposals from different backgrounds identify the determinants of shareholder value based on value chain/process concepts and on their cost-value drivers (e.g., Rappaport, 1986, 1998; Young & O'Byrne, 2001; Banker & Johnston, 2007). This research adopts an approach that Porter (1985) inspired and which Shank and Govindarajan (1992, 1994) integrated into the framework. SCM's emphasis on cost analysis from a strategic perspective, which is associated with considering both non-monetary and monetary performances, motivated our choice of SCM. We believe that this approach could effectively investigate the link between SHVC and sustainability. Furthermore, given the model's specific characteristics, it lends itself to future developments by integrating, of cost and performance measurement tools.

The research framework was elaborated through the concerned researchers' discussions and logical arguments. The researchers also decided to only focus on the activities that the ESG impacted, and not on all of the value chain's activities, which focused the research on the topics of interest.

In the research's second phase (April and June 2023), researchers developed and held semi-structured interviews with the CEOs of the two organizations involved in this research. For the following reasons, the organizations were significant for this research's aim. First, they are both involved in ESG initiatives, making them relevant for this research. Second, they have different motivations for performing ESG initiatives, because they have very different core businesses. Case A is a company undertaking activities that have a low impact on the environment, while Case B is a company undertaking activities that could have a high impact on the environment. The results might therefore provide meaningful insights for interpreting how different ESG activities, and integrating ESG activities' differently into the business might have a different impact on the SHVC. Each interview lasted approximately 1 hour. Semi-structured interviews guarantee adherence to a codified research protocol but simultaneously provide the researcher with the flexibility required to analyze each situation's peculiarities (Yin, 2014). To facilitate both flexibility and adherence to the protocol, we defined specific guidelines for the interviews, which referred to evidence from the literature and practice protocols. The interviews were designed according to the following themes, which we considered suitable for answering our research question:

1. The meaning that the company attributes to sustainability
2. Sustainability initiatives' goal
3. The developed sustainability initiatives (a description and the specific goal)
4. Sustainability's expected impact on SHVC drivers

1.4.2 Cases' Description

Company A

Company A was founded in 2010 and is unlisted. It operates in the advanced technology and design sector and does not carry out activities with a direct environmental impact, because its value proposition is not primarily aimed at reducing pollution. In Table 1.1, we present the main financial data.

The year 2021 shows higher income measures and indicators. These indicators show a clear decline in 2022. The net financial position is passive and particularly high in 2022, when there is also an increase in the level of debt.

Sustainability goals are not part of the company's core business but could be a way to perform its business. Growth in sustainability is therefore voluntary and an indirect consequence of the other strategies.

Table 1.1 Financial statement report (company A) (source: AIDA Bureau Van Dijk)

	2022	2021	2020
Revenues	2,627,731	2,725,978	1,716,446
EBITDA	741,295	680,285	242,629
Net income	118,441	184,219	105,899
Total asset	6,060,316	5,219,351	3,566,174
Equity	1,361,185	937,743	753,525
Net financial position	2,685,968	2,028,950	1,387,040
ROS (%)	8.13	11.16	8.24
ROA (%)	4.29	6.62	4.32
ROE (%)	8.70	19.64	14.05
Debt/equity ratio	2.09	2.74	1.86

Table 1.2 Financial statement report (company B) (source: AIDA Bureau Van Dijk)

	2022	2021	2020
Revenues	12,300,508	11,060,034	7,085,789
EBITDA	3,954,558	4,352,696	2,253,341
Net income	1,651,850	2,251,369	1,068,068
Total asset	35,116,471	20,346,447	17,273,085
Equity	27,545,768	12,589,887	10,738,514
Net financial position	−17,374,995	−3,993,461	−699,074
ROS (%)	17.50	26.79	17.96
ROA (%)	6.27	15.14	7.66
ROE (%)	6.00	17.88	9.95
Debt/equity ratio	0.06	0.27	0.38

In respect of company A, we can categorize the competitive business strategy as "differentiation through innovation." According to information on its website, this company aims to:

> Provide solutions and technologies to support customers, guaranteeing internal control of the entire supply chain from the idea/project to the physical realization of the product/system. The company operates in 2/3D, hydraulic, electrical, electronic design, structural and fluid dynamic modelling and simulation, and software design and development. It can physically create demonstrators and/or prototypes, including the industrialized product in [the] pre-series; it creates complete special machines for trials and tests, stations for industrial automation, and robotization. (Translation from the company website)

From this statement, it is clear that the company provides customers with tailored solutions, and that is proactive in the research and development of innovative solutions.

Company B

Company B was founded in 1985 and has been listed since 2022. It operates in the hydrogen production sector and is greatly interested in environmental issues.

In Table 1.2, we present its main financial data.

Company B is a larger company than company A, and its financial situation is stable; consequently it does not indicate any financial risks.

The year 2021, which was the year before the listing, shows higher income measures and indicators. The active net financial position, which was particularly high in 2022, is the data that seems to be most relevant. The active net financial position indicates many financial activities and a high financial independence, which makes the company less risky from a financial point of view.

The sustainability goals are part of the company's core business devoted to supporting environmentally friendly solutions. The green economy mission is perfectly consistent with the company's mindset. We can categorize company B's competitive business strategy as sustainable innovation.

The information reported during the interviews and on its website reveals that sustainability is part of this company's competitive strategy, because its competitive advantage is based on a sustainability-focused differentiation strategy. It actually produces machinery based on sustainability-enabling technology. Environmental issues affect this company's activity and output specifically, since it is committed to producing hydrogen. A declaration on the website underlines that the sustainability concept is strongly rooted in this company, which has been committed to environmental protection for many years, even before sustainability was a known concept:

> Our company works with hydrogen, is active in the production of electrolyzers, and is therefore aimed at a green economy. Sustainability is important to us. Moreover, sustainability is an important strategy, because having the label allows us to approach important companies, which in turn also have the label, and they are happier when they contact companies with the label. (Manager, company B)

> In 1985, three guys developed one of the first calculators for electronic automation. One of the most innovative applications concerned the world of hydrogen. When no one was talking about sustainability, these three guys understood the importance of renewable energy and the great prospects of this business. Another young man joined them … and together they designed a new technology to produce energy with hydrogen. (From company B's website)

In respect of company B, ESG issue emerges as being embedded within the competitive strategy, which means that the company is committed to delivering something (a technology) that can improve sustainability, especially environmental sustainability.

1.5 Findings

1.5.1 ESG Activities and Competitive Strategy

In terms of company A's primary activities, we find the ESG activity "Production: development of ad-hoc projects." This production activity was developed during the pandemic to pursue social sustainability objectives. The aim was to improve the company's image.

> Then the most significant case for us was when we felt morally driven to participate in an initiative related to the Covid pandemic in its entirety. We made all our 3D printers available, free of charge of course, to produce valves required for the adaptation of Decathlon diving masks to hypertensive patients' forced respirators (…). We went to the newspapers, which meant it was something that also made the outside world talk about us. This certainly had a positive effect on our reputation at that moment. (Manager, company A)

In terms of ESG support activity, this company has three activities. The first one is "Company infrastructure: Production of solar energy through photovoltaic systems." This activity consisted of installing a photovoltaic system aimed at generating energy savings and is summarized in the sentence below:

> The photovoltaic system had two main purposes. First, we aimed to create cost-saving opportunities. Thereafter, our attention was also on sustainability in terms of the use of resources, energy, and so on. We mention this, because we are not a company that has a significant impact on the microenvironment around us. (Manager, company A)

The second ESG support activity is "Company infrastructure: waste sorting," directed, as summarized in the sentence below, at environmental sustainability:

> We have no problems with the company's impact on the environment in respect of the current community and future generations. For example, we have started managing our material in a differentiated way, using dedicated material storage sites. We also have a waste disposal company. This is because we were aware that we couldn't continue, for example, throwing paper in bins. (Manager, company A)

The third ESG support activity is "Human resources management and company infrastructure: organizational well-being activities (non-reflective LED lights, smart working)," directed at social sustainability (a better environment for the employees), environmental sustainability (reducing energy consumption), and reducing costs, as summarized in the sentence below:

> Things that outline this aspect are certainly that, here, we do not require marking systems during a person's working hours, and that we are open to the possibility that our collaborators can work at home one day a week, two days every ten days or one afternoon a week. (Manager, company A)

> No distinctions are made between male and female collaborators. In our front line, there are male project managers, and the coordinator of the project managers, who is a female engineer. There is free access to responsibility functions; it is open. (Manager, company A)

It is possible to detect company B's following primary and secondary ESG activities:

In terms of primary ESG activities, there is "Research and development: green production." This activity is part of this company's core business and deals with the identification of systems producing clean energy and reducing carbon emissions. It is therefore an activity devoted to environmental sustainability:

> We are a company working with hydrogen, and active in the production of electrolyzers; we therefore aim to achieve a green economy. Sustainability is important to us. In the meantime, we have started implementing some, let's call them, rules. [He refers to acquiring future certifications.] (Manager, company B)

> Talking about carbon footprint, this will allow us to reduce CO_2 emissions even if we produce very little CO_2. In 2015, we even made an exhale system; that is, a system that was a project. But we also delivered a plant with which to make synthetic biomethane, therefore capturing the CO_2 present in the biomethane and producing it again, throwing in hydrogen, making biomethane, which is synthetic at that point, completely pure, which allows us to reduce that CO_2 to very, very high values. (Manager, company B)

The support activities are "Activities required for certification." These activities are related to both environmental sustainability and social sustainability. They are part of this company's core business. Below we report sentences that support the above claims:

> We are already implementing this here, and we have also started with UNI ISO 14064, which will allow us to evaluate the total quantity of greenhouse gas emissions that we produce, both directly and indirectly, from all the production activities that we carry out in our factories, because we have more than one production site. (Manager, company B)

> This has always been our goal, as has 14001/2015, which we are implementing to integrate the currently existing and certified 9001, 45001, and 13485 management systems. This is therefore an environmental management system that is compliant with standard 14001/2015. (Manager, company B)

> We have 25 certifications and each certification clearly costs, I won't say sweat and effort, but it costs time, it costs people, and every year we have confirmation audits. In my opinion, they are essential to be able to work and present ourselves. (Manager, company B)

Another ESG support activity is "Human resources management: Activities to improve the internal climate." Here, it is possible to find activities directed toward social sustainability and, in particular, toward improving the internal climate, which the sentences below support:

> I created a company in which the employees are all crucial. Some employees, little by little, were put in positions of control, depending on their attachment to the company. For us, employees are truly at the heart of the company. We have started awarding a welfare bonus; this is already the fifth year that we will award one. That's also something we do to keep us close to our employees. We established flexible working hours to give, above all, those who have commitments in the morning or in the afternoon an opportunity to adapt their working hours in keeping with their commitments; that is, we have always tried to meet people's needs. (Manager, company B)

1.5.2 The Activity Driver Analysis

This section examines the activity drivers that the two companies exploited to support their competitive strategies. The labels used for the drivers are tailored to the company's specificity. Drivers are classified according to Porter (1985) and Shank and Govindarajan (1992). Regarding the classification of structural and operational cost drivers, we included those drivers involving investment in long-term infrastructure into structural drivers' classification. Drivers' classification of differentiation and costs is based on their immediate effect (i.e., their capacity to distinguish the company proposal from competitors or reduce costs); however, the distinction is nuanced, because differentiation drivers may also have an impact on cost reduction and vice versa.

Tables 1.3 and 1.4 show the list of drivers (classified as described above) and indicate how those drivers impact the activities identified in Sect. 1.5.1. Table 1.3 refers to company A, while Table 1.4 refers to company B.

In the case of company A, it is possible to identify drivers that support primary and support activities and to identify the "differentiation through innovation" competitive strategy. It is important to note here that although company A does not pursue a cost strategy, it intends to invest in the development of drivers that can reduce costs. Therefore, differentiation, innovation, and cost drivers all co-exist in this company. As the description below underlines, although the drivers may appear to be ESG inspired, they were developed and managed to benefit the company directly and to support its innovative capacity in order to increase its revenues and reduce its costs.

In terms of discretionary policies, the driver "Promotion of a company's image that pays attention to environmental and social issues" is relevant for this company, because it attracts customers and employees. For example, the company has a panel in the hall showing that energy consumption is useful regarding supporting a good company image and attracting new customers:

> A customer arrives in the hall and sees the monitor that indicates how much we produce during the day, the progress we have made, and, since we installed the photovoltaic system, how much less carbon dioxide we have emitted into the environment. In short, these things obviously support our image. (Manager, company A)

On the other hand, during the pandemic, the company contributed its valve-producing competences, which it considered an important activity that would contribute to improving its image.

In terms of technology, the driver "Efficiency through photovoltaics and energy-saving systems" is also important regarding allowing all of the company's activities to become more efficient, to support a better climate, to improve the work conditions (e.g., by allowing the employees to recharge their cars), and, simultaneously, to reduce the costs (see the sentences about photovoltaic systems in Sect. 1.5.1):

> Another of the things that we implemented when, for example, producing solar energy, was offering our employees a free connection to recharge their hybrid or electric cars. In turn, our employees benefit from this green production that powers the cars of those who have already switched to an electric car. (Manager, company A)

> We also work better at the organizational level. For example, to reduce consumption, we fitted LEDs, which don't create reflections on the technical office's desks, because they are regulated depending on the natural light intensity. Then they are dimmed depending on how much natural light there is. Moreover, the window openings and the thermal insulation optimized the natural light. These things were all done in compliance with the law, but also to make people work efficiently—that's it. (Manager, company A)

In terms of discretionary policies, the driver "Sustaining personnel initiatives (e.g., flexible working hours, and a balanced personal and working life") clarified

Table 1.3 ESG activities and drivers (company A)

	Drivers impacting activities			Activities			
	Classification)	*Description of the driver*	*Cost/ differentiation (r)*	Production: development of ad hoc projects (primary activity)	Company infrastructure: producing solar energy through photovoltaic systems (support activity)	Company infrastructure: waste sorting (support activity)	Human resources management and company infrastructure: organizational well-being activities (support activity)
Structural	Discretionary policies	Promotion of a company's image that pays attention to environmental and social issues	Differentiation	The image has the capacity to attract new jobs comprising environmental and social aspects	The image supports the company's capacity to sell its photovoltaic systems	The image stimulates employees to contribute to waste sorting	The image supports the company's capacity to attract and retain personnel
	Technology	Efficiency through photovoltaics and energy-saving systems	Cost	Reduction of energy costs	Reduction of energy costs		Possibility to recharge employees' cars
Executional	Discretionary policies	Sustaining personnel initiatives (e.g., flexible working hours and a balanced personal and work life)	Differentiation	The innovation results' expected improvement	The innovation results' expected improvement	Motivated personnel's expected contribution to waste sorting	The capacity to attract highly skilled personnel, which, in turn, stimulates innovation
	Connection (between the activities)	Activities are connected to the circular economy's rationale	Cost	The production activities' efficiency improvement	The production activities' efficiency improvement	Reduction of waste and costs	

Table 1.4 ESG activities and their drivers (company B)

	The driver's impact on the activities					
	Classification	*Description of the driver*	*Cost/ differentiation*	Activities required to gain certification (support activity)	Production, research, and development: green production (primary activity)	Human resources management: activities to improve the internal climate (support activity)
Structural drivers	Field of activities	Electrolyzer production	Cost and differentiation	The production experience helps with gaining certification	The production experience supports the green production	
	Experience	Skills accumulated over the time	Cost and differentiation	The production experience helps with gaining certification	The experience supports improvements in effectiveness and efficiency. The relevant accumulated skills impact the products' features	
	Discretionary policies	Security	Differentiation/ costs	Security investments support safe, efficient, and effective production processes. It avoids production delays due to potential accidents	Security investments support safe, efficient, and effective production processes. It avoids production delays due to potential accidents	Work security improves the climate, because the employees feel safe in their workplace and are more innovatively productive

	The driver's impact on the activities					
Executional drivers	Employee involvement	Favorable contexts (cleanliness, internal climate, etc.)	Differentiation			Employees feel better when working in a clean, safe environment and are more innovatively productive
		Internal climate and gender equality	Differentiation			Employees feel better when working in an environment that favors equality and are more innovatively productive)
	Discretionary policies (focus on quality and environmental management)	Mechanisms and rules are useful for managing quality and the environmental impact, which are necessary to gain certain certifications	Differentiation (associated with cost containment)		Rules adopted to gain certification also improve green production	Rules adopted to gain certification also improve the internal climate

the importance of attracting qualified personnel who can support this company's innovation effectively.

In terms of "the connections between activities," the "study of the circular economy and its implementation" is another driver that, through the company's continuous innovation and efficiency, could help reduce waste, which the sentence below underlines:

> For example, other things that we are increasing are additive printers with which we create things at the prototype or production level for ourselves. We purchased a system that allows us to recycle waste, recompose it into raw materials in order to essentially reuse them in the printing processes. (Manager, company A)

In the case of company B, it is possible to identify the following drivers that support primary and support activities. The company is aware of the importance of cost containment and efficiency, but only as the long-term outcomes of ESG sustainability. In this company, it is therefore possible to identify differentiation, sustainability, and cost drivers. Table 1.4 shows the activities and their drivers. As shown in Table 1.3, the same driver may have an impact on different activities.

Regarding the activity field, the company's focus on "Electrolyzer production" supports its capacity to identify the production and achieve efficiency in terms of the costs.

The focus on a specific field and the accumulated experience also support the capacity to be innovative and efficient in terms of costs.

In terms of a discretionary policy, "the "security" of the personnel is another important driver. The manager is aware that an investment in security is costly, but also that it is a way to contain future costs:

> We are always very attentive to safety. We make machines safe. The accidents that we have had in 23 years have been very few and very similar; that is, people perhaps have an accident on their way to work. We have always paid 100% attention to safety. Inside, I have always bought ladders specifically Even stairs step ladder that seem safe are not completely safe.. And ladders that cost 3–4 thousand euro don't actually cost two lire. (Manager, company B)

Regarding the employees' involvement, when the company adopts the driver "Favorable context" and "Internal climate and gender equality," it also adopts a long-term vision. The intention to invest in order to improve the internal climate, to stimulate the working environment's effectiveness, and to improve the image is a matter of priority. The awareness that this investment might have long-term positive impact on profitability is a second priority:

> It (the good and clean organizational environment) also increases the processes' effectiveness, because, as I told you before, when you work in a welcoming, clean, comfortable environment, you work better. (Manager, company B)

Caring about its image is also important for Company B, because this can help the company sell products, although caring about its image can be costly:

> The first thing I look at when I enter a company is whether they have a well-kept garden, whether the ground is clean, if, when I go to the bathroom, it is clean, because this tells me that my customer is calm and is able to take care of those aspects that might perhaps not

> give him a profit, but which are important for … And this tells me that this is a calm customer and I can also be assured that he will certainly pay off. If I go to a poorly maintained environment, I believe the company has so many problems that cleaning the bathrooms is the least of its priority. (Manager, company B)

Finally, regarding discretionary policies, the development of "Activities required to gain certification" is key a success factor for differentiation and efficiency:

> Therefore, this (the environmental certification) will serve as an initial assessment of the company's impact on climate change, but it also allows us to identify any inefficiencies in the production process. (Manager, company B).

> It will therefore allow us to move in the direction of energy efficiency and will reduce the environmental impact. The results will then form the basis for obtaining environmental product certifications, such as the EPD (Environmental Product Declaration). This is clearly something that cannot be achieved in three days, but we are moving toward achieving this goal. (Manager, company B)

> Having a company certified in this way, allows us to approach large, already certified companies. Consequently, it places us in a privileged situation compared to other, non-certified companies. (Manager, company B)

1.5.3 The Impact of ESG Activities on SHVC

In this sub-section, we discuss how activities impact the main financial value drivers. The discussion is based on a conceptual argument that the researchers developed and has not as yet been empirically tested.

In terms of the impact on SHVC drivers (the sales growth, operating margin, investments in current and non-current assets, the risks depending on the operations, and the financing strategies), we observed the differences between two companies.

Company A had established a strategy of "differentiation through innovation," paying particular attention to profitability. The company is, therefore, focused on sustaining drivers that can support the company's ability to be innovative and, simultaneously, efficient. Commitment to ESG initiatives impacts the way activities are carried out to improve efficiency, rather than integrating sustainability within the value proposition in order to retain some of the service/product's uniqueness. Consequently the company's intention was, first, for most of the ESG activities to have a rather immediate impact on the financial SHVC by reducing the costs. The second intention was for these activities to have a more long-term effect on the revenues by increasing/stabilizing them by improving the corporate image. The third intention was for the activities to make an expected personnel contribution derived from the policies that the company had adopted.

The company, for example, installed a photovoltaic system that increased not only the fixed capital but also the operating margin by increasing the revenue gained through the company's improved image and by reducing the costs by saving energy:

> The photovoltaic system had two main purposes. First, we aimed to create opportunities for cost saving. The latter also impacted our sustainability in terms of the resources we used, the energy, and so on. (Manager, company A)

The investments in qualified staff and internal climate were aimed at improving the company's efficiency and effectiveness. The organizational well-being (increased by installing non-reflective LED lights and smart working) impacts the value drivers by increasing their efficiency, productivity, and innovation as well as by reducing the IT risks.

Company B established a strategy of "differentiation through sustainable innovation" as its core business. Consequently, it is devoted to nurturing drivers that primarily support sustainability and innovation. The company's intention is therefore for the majority of the drivers to have a relevant impact on sustainability and a long-term important impact on value drivers such as the revenues, costs, and invested capital. The latter is due to sustainability, in this case, being embedded in the competitive strategy (the company produces an enabling technology to ensure sustainability) and in the way the company's value propositions are delivered.

For example, the company's market listing alongside its environmental certification is a way in which the company can increase its capital in the long term. The company is aware that obtaining certification is costly in the short run, while achieving benefits from it in terms of increased revenues and saving will require some years. The sentences below refer to ESG activities, which are:

> [a] future way of containing company costs, because you initially spend to achieve these things. But, in the long run, they give an exceptional result, in terms of the well-being of those who work and financial results. (Manager, company B).

The same can be said in relation to investments in the personnel's' security:

> Always work safely, because if you get hurt, you've perhaps saved five minutes, but then you're at home for a month. Where's your good profit then?

Investments in security and the internal climate affect the company's operating margin in the long run. Reducing the costs and the investments in environmental sustainability in the short run will decrease the operating margin. However, can this have a positive impact on the operating margin in the long run by increasing the sales (based on the company's improved image) and reducing the costs (due by the company's greater efficiency):

> The advantages for the company will be that it will demonstrate its commitment to the gender equality issue, which will strengthen the corporate image and reputation, contribute to achieving its objectives, which the 2030 Agenda and the National Plan for Resilience set, thereby possibly allowing companies access to tax relief, and, subsequently, allowing them to access rewards for participating in both Italian and European tenders, which will allow them to plan their future improvements. (Manager, company B)

The analysis of the two companies suggests an opportunity to adopt an entrepreneurial mentality capable of developing a dual valuation logic of sustainability's impact on the SHVC. In addition to adopting an as is valuation logic, it seems appropriate to also follow a potential valuation logic. The first valuation logic captures the value drivers that verify the ESG initiatives' impact on the company's current strategic and operational setting. The latter valuation logic recognizes and quantifies the value drivers emerging from the assumptions based on the strategic breakdowns and the changes in the entrepreneurship formula. This formula determines the value creation, which is mainly based on the activities that the company is expected to carry out differently in the future than it does at present (Guatri & Bini, 2009).

1.6 Discussion and Conclusion

This research analyzed how the relationship between ESG commitment and SHVC evolves. The research did so by preliminarily developing a framework that the SCM's framework inspired. This second framework traces the relationship between ESG commitment and the SHVC, which has also been used to interpret the empirical material. Since ESG commitment is moving from being a parallel activity to being a part of the competitive strategy, the ESG initiatives deepen as activities directly involved in pursuing a competitive strategy. In this respect, this research has also interpreted the role that ESG activities play in a competitive strategy in order to provide evidence that could have a possible impact on the SHVC.

First, a willingness to understand ESG strategies' financial impact better motivated this research. In fact, previous studies on these relationships use heterogeneous research designs that provide contrasting results (Hang et al., 2019). The results require further investigation into the links between sustainability, financial performance, and shareholder value, which are currently undetermined and lead to heated debates (Lee & Raschke, 2023; Li et al., 2023; Aouadi & Marsat, 2018). The second motivation was that there are still scant studies on the possible relationships between ESG commitment and firm value's three directions. Finally, ESG issues' introduction to corporate strategies suggests a fundamental change in business valuation methods and procedures. As the IVSC recognized, the latter methods and procedures require a framework to map the value creation and surmount the limitations of the evaluation of the value that the ESG commitment created.

The still unclear understanding of the relationship between ESG commitment and SHVC occurs in a context in which the European legislation on mandatory sustainability disclosure (CRSD, 2022; EFRAG, 2023) strongly stimulated the codification of the relationships between ESG practices and financial performance. This codification brought the double materiality concept into play.

Unlike previous research, which investigated the ESG's impact on the SHVC, this research focuses on how the relationship between ESG commitment and the SHVC works. In order to analyze this relationship, this research focuses on the value chain's ESG activities.

However, to investigate the relationship between ESG commitment and the SHVC, we first needed to identify the competitive strategy and ESG commitment's integration into it. Second, we identified the value chain's ESG activities involved in achieving the strategy and the drivers that impact these activities. Finally, using previous evidence, we make suggestions regarding the relationships between the activities and the financial SHVC.

Our findings underline ESG commitment's degree of integration into the competitive strategy and how value chain activities can affect the way ESG initiatives impact the SHVC.

First, the role that ESG commitment plays in the competitive strategy determines the order of magnitude of the ESG commitment's impact on the SHVC.

Findings suggest that the ESG commitment's level integration into the strategy may affect the ESG activities' impact on the SHVC. Specifically, when the ESG commitment is integrated into the strategy, its impact on the SHVC is long-term oriented. On the other hand, when ESG commitment only acts as collateral in respect of the main strategy, but is not integrated into the competitive strategy, its impact on the SHVC is short-term oriented.

In company A's case, the empirical findings suggest that ESG activities are considered a way of acting on the SHVC's financial drivers and are not motivated by a profound willingness to offer customers (and society) benefits that integrate sustainability commitment into its value proposition. In this case, ESG values are not part of a competitive strategy but are instrumental in achieving other aims, such as increasing profits efficiently. In these cases, we expect a positive relationship between ESG commitment and financial performance (D'Agostini et al., 2017), although other variables, such as the validity of the innovative proposals that the company staff formulate, modulate and mediate this positive relationship. More generally, we also expect the value proposition, which does not focus on sustainability as a primary variable, to be competitive in order to capture potential customers' attention.

On the other hand, company B's willingness to be sustainable motivates it profoundly, while its product makes sense due to society's emerging sustainability and because this product is produced sustainably. In this case, the ESG commitment's impact on the SHVC is of a different magnitude. The impact on the financial shareholder value drivers (e.g., the operating profits, etc.) and on the SHVC value drivers is considered of secondary importance, although the company does recognize these impacts. Further, in this case, company B experiences the moderating variables of this impact, such as people's ability to execute a strategic plan in which ESG activities play a primary role or they translate company climate effectively into improved productivity and innovation. However, this case is in line with studies arguing that the correlation between ESG practices and financial performance is complex and mediated by other elements (Avery & Bergsteiner, 2011; Balugani et al., 2020), such as the ESG strategy's integration into the competitive strategy.

Researchers investigating the relationship between ESG initiatives and financial performance directly provide contrasting results. There are proof of an increase in costs due to ESG investments (see, e.g., Fatemi et al., 2018; Kim & Lyon, 2015) and proof that these investments have a positive impact on the financial results (D'Agostini et al., 2017; Cohen, 2023; Xie et al., 2019; Mercereau et al., 2022).

In term of risks, ESG practices have been found to reduce risks (KPMG, 2022; CNDC, 2022; Aouadi & Marsat, 2018; Wong et al., 2021).

Our research, however, does not confirm or disregard findings from previous research but, unlike previous research, recognizes that a precise cause and effect relationship cannot adequately summarize the relationship between ESG practices and the SHVC's complexity. Instead, the ESG activities' mediating role and its integration into the competitive strategy need to be investigated. This should offer deeper insights into and an understanding of how ESG practices are involved in the SHVC. Our research sheds some light by underlining that the ESG initiative and the SHVC's contrasting results might depend on the competitive strategy, activities, the activities' strategic drivers, and the ESG initiatives' integration into the competitive strategy. Furthermore, this research has another value in that the use of this framework not only provides insights into the how of the relationship between the ESG initiatives and the SHVC but also provides knowledge of the activities and their drivers, which, in turn, provides opportunities to affect the abovementioned relationship.

The findings suggest that by developing activities to commit the company to the ESG goals and by underlining these activities' aims, these might allow the complexity of the relationship between ESG commitment and the SHVC to be investigated and managed. Although the elaborated framework is functional in terms of interpreting the empirical material, it could be regarded as an additional research output and could be employed and further refined in other studies.

Finally, this research allowed us to verify that it is possible to investigate issues concerning double materiality by integrating models and approaches usually investigated separately. In this research, we proposed carrying out a strategic analysis by using the SCM framework and integrating it into the ESG and SHVC models.

Future research and improvement are required, of course, while many aspects should also be deepened. First, the framework should be applied to other cases in order to refine and enrich the conclusion developed in this research and to elaborate the framework further. Second, the empirical cases only deal with sustainability's environmental and social side, because the governance side is still underdeveloped in the companies we investigated. Third, the relationship between ESG initiatives and SHVC drivers has only been elaborated from a theoretical and qualitative point of view and has not been tested empirically. In this respect, it would be interesting to also undertake multiple and longitudinal case studies to verify the activities' costs and these activities' impact on the value drivers.

References

Aouadi, A., & Marsat, S. (2018). Do ESG controversies matter for firm value? Evidence from international data. *Journal of Business Ethics, 151*, 1027–1047.

Atkins, J., Doni, F., & Gasperini, A. (2023). Exploring the effectiveness of sustainability measurement: Which ESG metrics will survive COVID-19? *Journal of Business Ethics, 185*(3), 629–646.

Avery, G. C., & Bergsteiner, H. (2011). Sustainable leadership practices for enhancing business resilience and performance. *Strategy and Leadership, 39*(3), 5–15.

Balugani, E., Butturi, M. A., Chevers, D., Parker, D., & Rimini, B. (2020). Empirical evaluation of the impact of resilience and sustainability on firms' performance. *Sustainability, 2020*, 12.

Banker, R. D., & Johnston, H. H. (2007). Cost and profit driver research. In S. C. Chapman, A. G. Hopwood, & M. D. Shields (Eds.), *Handbook of management accounting research* (Vol. 2, pp. 531–556). Elsevier.

Barney, J. B. (1991). Firm resources and sustained competitive advantage. *Journal of Management, 17*(1), 99–120.

Bernini, F., & La Rosa, F. (2024). Research in the greenwashing field: Concepts, theories, and potential impacts on economic and social value. *Journal of Management and Governance, 28*, 405–444.

Bernini, F., Ferretti, P., Gonnella, C., & La Rosa, F. (2024). Measuring machine washing under the corporate digital responsibility theory: A proposal for a methodological path. *Business Ethics, the Environment and Responsibility* (a).

Bini, L., Bellucci, M., & Giunta, F. (2018). Integrating sustainability in business model disclosure: Evidence from the UK mining industry. *Journal of Cleaner Production, 171*, 1161–1170.

Brooks, C., & Oikonomou, I. (2018). The effects of environmental, social and governance disclosures and performance on firm value: A review of the literature in accounting and finance. *The British Accounting Review, 50*(1), 1–15.

Carr, C., & Tomkins, C. (1996). Strategic investment decisions: The importance of SCM: A comparative analysis of 51 case studies in U.K., U.S. and German companies. *Management Accounting Research, 7*(2), 199–217.

Cennamo, C., Berrone, P., & Gomez-Mejia, L. (2009). Does stakeholder management have a dark side? *Journal of Business Ethics, 89*, 491–507.

Chang, Y. J. & Lee, B. H. (2022). The impact of ESG activities on firm value: Multi-level analysis of industrial characteristics. *Sustainability, 14*.

Chen, Z., & Xie, G. (2022). ESG disclosure and financial performance: Moderating role of ESG investors. *International Review of Financial Analysis, 83*.

Cho, C. H., & Patten, D. M. (2007). The role of environmental disclosures as tools of legitimacy: A research note. *Accounting, Organizations and Society, Elsevier, 32*(7–8), 639–647.

CNDC. (2022). *Finanza sostenibile e fattori ESG: stato dell'arte, sviluppi futuri e opportunità.*

Cohen, G. (2023, May). The impact of ESG risks on corporate value. *Review of Quantitative Finance and Accounting, Springer, 60*(4), 1451–1468.

Cooper, R., & Kaplan, R. S. (1999). *Design of cost management systems* (2nd ed.). Prentice Hall.

D'Agostini, M., Goncalves Tondonlo, V. A., Camargo, M. E., & Russo, S. (2017). Relationship between sustainable operations practices and performance: A meta-analysis. *International Journal of Productivity and Performance Management, 66*(8), 1020–1042.

de Castro, G. M., López, J. E. N., & Sáez, P. L. (2006). Business and social reputation: Exploring the concept and main dimensions of corporate reputation. *Journal of Business Ethics, 63*, 361–370.

Deegan, C., Rankin, M., & Tobin, J. (2002). An examination of the corporate social and environmental disclosures of BHP from 1983–1997: A test of legitimacy theory. *Accounting, Auditing and Accountability Journal, 15*(3), 312–343.

Dhaliwal, D. S., Li, O. Z., Tsang, A., & Yang, Y. G. (2011). Voluntary nonfinancial disclosure and the cost of equity capital: The initiation of corporate social responsibility reporting. *The Accounting Review, 86*(1), 59–100.

DIRECTIVE (EU) 2022/2464 OF THE EUROPEAN PARLIAMENT AND OF THE COUNCIL of 14 December 2022.

Eccles, R. G., Ioannou, I., & Serafeim, G. (2014). The impact of corporate sustainability on organizational processes and performance. *Management Science, 60*(11), 2835–2857.

Edvinsson, L., & Malone, M. (1997). *Intellectual capital*. Harper Business.

EFRAG. (2023). *European sustainability reporting standards.*

El Ghoul, S., Guedhami, O., & Kim, Y. (2016). Country-level institutions, firm value, and the role of corporate social responsibility initiatives. *Journal of International Business Studies, 1–26*, 360–385.

Eng, L., Fikru, M., & Vichitsarawong, T. (2022). Comparing the informativeness of sustainability disclosures versus ESG disclosure ratings. *Sustainability Accounting, Management and Policy Journal, 13*(2), 494–518.

European Commission. (2022). Directive (EU) 2022/2464.

Fatemi, A., Glaum, M., & Kaiser, S. (2018). ESG performance and firm value: The moderating role of disclosure. *Global Finance Journal, 38*, 45–64.

Freeman, R. E. (1984). *Strategic management: A stakeholder approach*. Pitman.

Friedman, M. (1970). The social responsibility of business is to increase its profits. *New York Times Magazine*, 13 September, 26–32.

Friedman, A. L., & Miles, S. (2004). Stakeholder theory and communication practice. *Journal of Communication Management, 9*(1), 95–97.

Guatri, L., & Bini, M. (2009). *Nuovo trattato sulla valutazione delle aziende*. Egea.

Hang, M., Geyer-Klingeberg, J., & Rathgeber, A. W. (2019). It is merely a matter of time: A meta-analysis of the causality between environmental performance and financial performance. *Business Strategy and the Environment, 28*(2), 257–273.

Ittner, C. D., & Larcker, D. F. (2001). Assessing empirical research in managerial accounting: A value-based management perspective. *Journal of Accounting and Economics, 32*(1–3), 349–410.

Jensen, M., & Meckling, W. (1976). Theory of the firm: Management behavior, agency costs, and ownership structure. *Journal of Financial Economics, 3*, 305–360.

Kim, E. H., & Lyon, T. P. (2015). Greenwash versus brownwash: Exaggeration and undue modesty in corporate sustainability disclosure. *Organization Science, 26*, 705–723.

KPMG. (2022). *ESG: Addressing greenwashing in financial services*.

Lee, M. T., & Raschke, R. L. (2023). Stakeholder legitimacy in firm greening and financial performance: What about greenwashing temptations? *Journal of Business Research, 155*, 1–11.

Li, W., Li, W., Seppänen, V., & Koivumäki, T. (2023). Effects of greenwashing on financial performance: Moderation through local environmental regulation and media coverage. *Business Strategy and the Environment, 32*(1), 820–841.

Lord, B. R. (1996). Strategic management accounting: The emperor's new clothes? *Management Accounting Research, 7*(3), 346–366.

Mercereau, B., Melin, L., & Lugo, M. (2022). Creating shareholder value through ESG engagement. *Journal of Asset Management, 23*, 1–17.

Ortiz-de-Mandojana, N., & Bansal, P. (2016). The long-term benefits of organizational resilience through sustainable business practices. *Strategic Management Journal, 37*(8), 1615–1631.

Peteraf, M. A., & Barney, K. B. (2003). Unraveling the resource-based tangle. *Management and Decision Economics, 24*(4), 309–323.

Porter, M. E. (1985). *Competitive advantage: Creating and sustaining superior performance*. The Free Press.

Porter, M. E., & Kramer, M. R. (2006). Strategy & society: The link between competitive advantage and corporate social responsibility. *Harvard Business Review*, December, 79–92.

Rajesh, R., & Rajendran, C. (2020). Relating environmental, social, and governance scores and sustainability performances of firms: An empirical analysis. *Business Strategy and the Environment, 29*, 1247–1267.

Rappaport, A. (1986). *Creating shareholder value. The new standard for business performance*. The Free Press.

Rappaport. (1998). *Creating shareholder value* (Revised and Updated ed.). The Free Press.

Sanchez, D. G., Heintges, S., Mazzeo, P., Villacorta, V., & Trouvain, E. (2023). *Implementation guidance for the materiality assessment*. EFRAG.

Schmeltz, L. (2014). Identical or just compatible? The utility of corporate identity values in communicating corporate social responsibility. *International Journal of Business Communication, 51*(3), 234–258.

Seele, P., & Gatti, L. (2017). Greenwashing revisited: In search of a typology and accusation-based definition incorporating legitimacy strategies. *Business Strategy and the Environment, 26*(2), 239–252.
Seele, P., & Shultz, M. D. (2022). From greenwashing to machinewashing: A model and future directions derived from reasoning by analogy. *Journal of Business Ethics, 178*, 1063–1089.
Servaes, H., & Tamayo, A. (2013). The impact of corporate social responsibility on firm value: The role of customer awareness. *Management Science, 59*, 1045–1061.
Shank, J., & Govindarajan, V. (1992). Strategic cost management: The value chain perspective. *Journal of Management Accounting Research Fall, 4*, 179–197.
Shank, J. K., & Govindarajan, V. (1993). *Strategic cost management—The new tool for competitive advantage*. The Free Press.
Shank, J. K., & Govindarajan, V. (1994). Measuring the "cost of quality": A strategic cost management perspective. *Journal of Cost Management, 8*, 5–17.
Stewart, T. A. (1997). *Intellectual capital*. The new wealth of nations.
Stewart, L. S. (2015). Growing demand for ESG information and standards: Understanding corporate opportunities as well as risks. *Journal of Applied Corporate Finance, 27*(2), 58–63.
Suchman, M. C. (1988). *Constructing an institutional ecology: Notes on the structural dynamics of organizational communities*. Paper presented at the annual meeting of the American Sociological Association, Atlanta, GA.
Torelli, R., Balluchi, F., & Lazzini, A. (2020). Greenwashing and environmental communication: Effects on stakeholders' perceptions. *Business Strategy and the Environment, 29*, 407–421.
Walker, K., & Wan, F. (2012). The harm of symbolic actions and green-washing: Corporate actions and communications on environmental performance and their financial implications. *Journal of Business Ethics, 109*, 227–242.
Wernerfelt, B. (1984). A resource-based view of the firm. *Strategic Management Journal, 5*(2), 171–180.
Wong, W. C., Batten, J. A., Ahmad, A. H., Mohamed-Arshad, S. B., Nordin, S., & Adzis, A. A. (2021). Does ESG certification add firm value? *Finance Research Letters, 39*, 1–7.
Wu, Y., Zhang, K., & Xie, J. (2020). Bad greenwashing, good greenwashing: Corporate social responsibility and information transparency. *Management Science, 66*(7), 3095–3112.
Xie, J., Nozawa, W., Yagi, M., Fujii, H., & Managi, S. (2019). Do environmental, social, and governance activities improve corporate financial performance? *Business Strategy and the Environment, 28*, 286–300.
Yin, R. K. (2014). *Case study research: Design and methods* (5th ed.). Sage.
Young, S. D., & O'Byrne, S. F. (2001). *Eva® and value-based management. A practical guide to implementation*. McGraw-Hill.
Zharfpeykan, R. (2021). Representative account or greenwashing? Voluntary sustainability reports in Australia's mining/metals and financial services industries. *Business Strategy and the Environment, 30*, 2209–2223.
Zhou, G., Liu, L., & Luo, S. (2022). Sustainable development, ESG performance and company market value: Mediating effect of financial performance. *Business Strategy and the Environment, 31*(7), 3371–3387.
Zioło, M., Bąk, I., & Spoz, A. (2023). Theoretical framework of sustainable value creation by companies. What do we know so far? *Corporate Social Responsibility and Environmental Management, 30*(5), 2344–2361.

Chapter 2
Artificial Intelligence's (AI's) Responsible Use: How to Manage Digital Ethicswashing

Francesca Bernini, Paola Ferretti, and Fabio La Rosa

2.1 Introduction

Artificial intelligence's (AI's) (ir)responsible use might lead to corporate conduct that fails to align with its ethical principles. This is known as digital ethicswashing, which identifies firms' strategy that is based on misleading reporting of AI's responsible use and aimed at gaining corporate stakeholders' acceptance and loyalty (Schultz et al., 2024).

Focusing specifically on the centrality of AI's social aspect use, this study aims to analyze the possible (negative) ethical impact that advanced technology might have on society and, ultimately, on the economy.

The existing literature shows the need to further investigate AI reporting's ethical use, especially concerning AI's social profile. To fill this research gap, our study develops an exploratory analysis to investigate how companies implement digital ethicswashing. We focus on the disclosure of AI use's social aspects and provide a twofold contribution.

A dashboard's design, which is useful for managing digital ethicswashing, is an important contribution. Identifying tools suitable for managing digital ethicswashing is crucial in the current context, which is characterized by advanced technology's wide dissemination. To this end, we also highlight the need for AI auditing tools, which, thanks to third-party experts' work, will minimize misleading practices.

F. Bernini (✉) · P. Ferretti
Department of Economics and Management, University of Pisa, Pisa, Italy
e-mail: francesca.bernini@unipi.it; paola.ferretti@unipi.it

F. La Rosa
Department of Law, University of Catania, Catania, Italy
e-mail: fabio.larosa@unict.it

F. Bernini (ed.), *Creating Value Through Sustainability*, SIDREA Series in Accounting and Business Administration,
https://doi.org/10.1007/978-3-031-74292-7_2

The study is structured as follows: Sect. 2.2 provides an overview of the current context in terms of AI's ethical perspective. Section 2.3 focuses on AI's theoretical background, its increasing relevance, and its relationship with ethics. Section 2.4 describes the research design and the methodological approach that we followed when running the analysis. Section 2.5 shows the study's results, and Sect. 2.6 suggests a dashboard for managing digital ethicswashing. Lastly, Sect. 2.7 describes AI auditing's role in mitigating misleading practice.

2.2 Artificial Intelligence's (AI's) Ethical Perspective in the Current Context

In the current economic context, the development-innovation mix is increasingly affirmed as a key factor for firms' growth in any industry (e.g., financial and non-financial industries) and, consequently, for the national and international economies' growth. Specifically, advanced digital innovations' use (artificial intelligence, the Internet of Things (IoT), Big Data, etc.) is one of the most crucial driving forces for improving competitiveness on a global level (Felicetti et al., 2024; Wang & Esperança, 2023; Si et al., 2023).

This is confirmed both by the many provisions of benefits (first of all, the tax ones) on digital transformation and the principles enunciated by the National Industry Plan - NIP - 4.0, based on the interconnection and automation of production processes. The underlying paradigm is technological and allows an improvement in efficiency.

However, the great centrality of NIP 4.0 should be now considered in extensive terms, to overcome its prevailing techno-economic vision. We could do so by also including environmental and social factors based on a holistic approach. This lies within NIP 5.0's scope, which is aimed at placing innovation beyond a higher business level efficiency's grasp, as NIP 4.0's main focus. Consequently, NIP 5.0 could also be the lever that economies should use to achieve social and environmental goals (Xu et al., 2021). In other words, NIP 5.0 considers NIP 4.0's approach in a broader context by offering the business a regenerative purpose, which is, consequently, also oriented toward people's well-being, and not only toward the shareholders' benefits. This implies including different dimensions, such as a social one, aimed at focusing on the employees' well-being, social inclusion, and the adoption of technologies. The latter should not be used as a substitute for human capabilities but rather be used to integrate them. Another dimension is linked to promoting a virtuous interdependence with the natural systems (the environmental dimension). All of this suggests that the two NIPs should be considered closely, to adequately balance the orientation to technology with the value orientation. This could form the basis for creating a system in which the technology is the enabling tool for achieving the goals linked to social needs. This means that the many enabling technologies that NIP 4.0 provides could contribute to achieving the NIP 5.0 objectives. These technologies could do so by establishing a virtuous human-machine interaction in the business processes during which, among other things, machines are used for repetitive tasks and humans are exploited for their creative skills.

To ensure business development, we should promote everyone's transitioning to an age of sustainable wellness as an essential step for a future business strategy. The latter should therefore be based on NIP 5.0's distinctive features regarding promoting economically based behaviors, which should simultaneously be focused on the human person's centrality, sustainability, and resilience.

An approach exclusively oriented toward profit is currently considered unsustainable, because it disregards the costs and the benefits for society and the environment. In contrast, responsible innovation should not only be focused on operational efficiency (cost reduction and/or profit maximization) but also on improving all of the stakeholders' prosperity: that of investors, employees, customers, and authorities to name just a few. In this regard, NIP 5.0 assigns businesses the role of achieving social goals, which go beyond economic growth and employment, and the responsibility of being a resilient source of prosperity. Consequently, NIP 5.0 endeavors to consider employees' well-being and stakeholders' expectations as the priorities of the firm's activities. Technology use should therefore fit human needs, not vice versa, by enhancing social capital's centrality (among others, Ali & Anwar, 2021; Ballestar et al., 2022).

Our study addresses social capital's relevance (that of employees, customers, the community, etc.) regarding artificial intelligence (AI) systems' use and endeavors to analyze the possible (negative) ethical impact that advanced technology, such as AI, might have on society and, ultimately, on the economy.

Such use might indeed cause problems for humans on different levels (Meske et al., 2022). There might even be automation bias, which means the possibility of not recognizing errors in an automated decision-making process (Goddard et al., 2012). Moreover, the problem might be related to employees' potential deskilling, which is in turn linked to humans' possible inadequate reliance on AI (Herse et al., 2018). At the same time, AI misuse might be a risk (Schneider et al., 2020; Xiao et al., 2020). In this regard, therefore, it is well known that AI might be used in a distortive way, creating negative and unethical effects (Haenlein & Kaplan, 2020; Haenlein et al., 2022). Some examples of these are the impact on employment (robots replacing humans), threats to transparency and privacy, the creation of algorithms fostering discrimination, etc. All of this is linked to the possible (un)ethical use of digitalization, specifically AI, and to the implications for society and the relationships between companies and their stakeholders.

On the other hand, many endeavors illustrate the positive effects that AI use produces. This is a key point, particularly in light of the abovementioned transition from NIP 4.0 to NIP 5.0 and their convergence. Firms could, among others, improve their stakeholder engagement by sharing information and experiences (Okazaki et al., 2020; Viglia et al., 2018). Furthermore, firms might even develop value-creation processes in digital contexts, thereby gaining the potential to engage with their stakeholder networks. The latter is important, especially given the complexity of the models and algorithms underlying the AI. In addition, this complexity is a black box, as it is not fully comprehensible (Meske et al., 2022).

Currently, the empirical evidence shows that certain industries, such as the financial one, play a significant role in AI's use. Projects based on AI have grown in terms of their total expenditure, mainly due to their digital lending applications. More generally, these applications give the financial sector opportunities to achieve time and cost savings by using AI, to make decisions based on all the available information and thereby mitigate information asymmetries, and to improve its customer service offers by shortening the response time. These are some of the positive reasons that encourage financial intermediaries to use AI-based models. Nevertheless, at the same time, it is important that these intermediaries should assess the related risks adequately (Siani, 2022). In other words, AI shouldn't replace the final decision-makers, but it should support the decision-making process in the best possible way.

Ultimately, therefore, understanding if firms' use of AI has real and only positive impacts on stakeholders—including the ethical effects—is relevant. In other words, firms often, more or less deliberately, provide stakeholders with information about their virtuous and responsible AI use, although this cannot actually be verified. Hence, by reporting, companies could become aware of misleading behavior, also from an ethical perspective, producing negative effects on their stakeholders and contributing to the spread of some disclosure-based strategies (Bernini et al., 2024).

Specifically, the question arises whether the (ir)responsible use of AI might lead to corporate conduct not aligned with ethical principles. This is known as digital ethicswashing, i.e., when firms' strategy is based on misleading reporting on responsible AI use aimed at gaining their stakeholders' acceptance and loyalty (Schultz et al., 2024). When firms intend to show a digitally ethical approach, this leads them to create a gap between their ethical principles and practices as well as between their goals and their means, with misleading impacts on their stakeholders. The analogy between ethicswashing and greenwashing is quite intuitive (Khan et al., 2021; Bernini et al., 2023), with the latter specifically related to environmental practices. There are, however, important differences between these two phenomena. A greater intangibility and lower visibility linked to AI models' complexity and opacity characterize ethicswashing. Additionally, in the context of AI models' constant evolution, AI's use is strongly associated with the use of technical jargon (Seele & Schultz, 2022).

The existing literature highlights gaps in the analysis of AI reporting's ethical use. Specifically, there is still little research on addressing AI's social profile. To this end, we endeavor to fill the gap by considering digitalization's ethical aspects when ESG topics' social dimension acts as a proxy for them. Our goal is therefore to observe digital ethicswashing practices by investigating the reliability of their disclosure, specifically with regard to AI use's social aspects, which we call social digital talk. We believe that such an analysis could be useful for understanding firms' misleading approach and for subsequently identifying a dashboard that could contribute to digital ethicswashing's management. It is, in fact, crucial to identify tools suitable for managing digital ethicswashing. Consequently, we believe that due to third-party experts' work, AI auditing could make an important contribution to doing so, as it might help minimize such practices. These experts are called to audit the disclosed information and reduce firms' possibly misleading approaches and their impacts on ethics.

2.3 Theoretical Background

AI applications' increasing development over recent years has highlighted several opportunities for companies and stakeholders as well as various potential risks (Camilleri, 2023; Bonsón et al., 2021a). AI technologies could be used to facilitate inclusion and customer service or even act as a substitute for humans doing dangerous tasks. On the other hand, as mentioned, AI could be a threat to the workforce, who might be replaced by automation. Furthermore, due to the consequence of AI's use, other issues could arise, such as threats to people's privacy.

2.3.1 Artificial Intelligence and Sustainability

In respect of all possible perspectives regarding AI's business and society implications, interest has recently increased in AI's potential in the context of environmental, social, and governance (ESG) commitment to companies (Pierli et al., 2023). Specifically, awareness of AI's possible impacts on sustainability has moved the focus to the ethical impacts. Consequently, institutions and academic literature (Bonsón et al., 2021a, b; Bonsón & Bednárová, 2022) have shown increased interest in the requirements that AI should meet to be considered trustworthy, i.e., ensuring safety, cybersecurity, privacy, fundamental rights, diversity, non-discrimination and fairness, and its societal and environmental well-being, which includes its social impact, society, and democracy (European Commission, 2019). Since AI currently impacts several human activities widely, particular attention is paid to a social approach to AI (Brusseau, 2022; Bernini et al., 2024; Shultz et al., 2024) in terms of employment (Shen & Zhang, 2024), knowledge sharing, decision-making processes (Telkamp & Anderson, 2022), and stakeholder engagement (Okazaki et al., 2020; Viglia et al., 2018). Given the moral foundation theory, Telkamp and Anderson (2022) state that people regard AI use as ethical if it aligns with these people's and societies' moral basics. From an internal company perspective, a human-centered AI effort drives AI ethics (Kartajaya et al., 2021). Further, in light of the European Commission (2019), AI approaches need to be oriented toward human life and society. Companies and researchers should therefore always take a holistic approach to AI impacts involving both technologies and human actors belonging to the social ecosystem (Bonsón et al., 2021a, b).

Academic studies have investigated several aspects of ethical AI technology applications, paying attention to different AI implications, such as particular technological aspects, accounting and auditing (Gunz & Thorne, 2020; Munoko et al.,

2020), decision-making (Vakkuri & Abrahamsson, 2018), human work and activities (Wright & Schultz, 2018), and other concerns.

The increasing attention paid to the specific issue of social ethical approaches to AI leads to disclosure of this issue likewise gaining increasing importance. With the European Union encouraging AI innovation regulation, companies have demonstrated a growing interest in reporting their activities related to AI and its impact on human capital and society (Bonsón et al., 2021a). Certain scholars (Sætra, 2022; Bonsón et al. 2021a, b) also underline the strong connection between AI and sustainability in general and digital technologies' impact on human activities and society. Sætra (2022) specifically underlines the crucial role that awareness of AI technology's impact on people plays in respect of good corporate governance and in virtuous decision-making processes.

2.3.2 Artificial Intelligence and Digital Ethicswashing

Notwithstanding the abovementioned importance of awareness of AI's possible effects, the literature informs (Bonsón et al., 2021a, b) readers about the lack of a shared approach toward AI impacts' assessment of and reporting on sustainability's ethical-social dimension. All standards reflect AI-related reporting's transparency; consequently, AI's disclosure depends on each company's discretion and varies according to its perception. According to Sætra (2023), none of the current reporting frameworks is capable of defining appropriate disclosure, which is related to AI impacts on sustainability and, particularly, on the social dimension and human capital. The abovementioned disclosure is therefore voluntary and made at a company's discretion. The Sætra studies (2023, 2022) contribute to the existing literature by defining a framework and a protocol for developing disclosure of the AI-ESG relationship.

Bonsón and Bednárová's (2022) study reveals that voluntary AI disclosure is scant and limited to the financial, technology, and telecommunications industries. This study promotes a path for structuring AI-related information and for fostering its transparency, also regarding the development of artificial intelligence reporting standards.

Furthermore, Bonsón et al. (2021b), exploring the non-financial disclosure of AI that Spanish IBEX 35 listed companies released, found that despite the growing interest in AI technologies, and the reporting related to these, the information is disclosed in an unstructured way. Moreover, the study reveals that using ethical methods to approach AI is still at a very embryonic stage.

Exploring AI ethical approaches by analyzing the reports of 200 companies listed in Germany, Sweden, Finland, France, Spain, and Italy, Bonsón et al. (2021a) found that the capability of disclosing AI compliance with ethical principles depends on the industry and the country. Specifically, technology and telecommunications as well as Northern firms are more prone to report their compliance with ethical principles in terms of AI technologies. Bonsón et al.'s study (2021a) contributes to literature development by suggesting the use of certain topics and a taxonomy in research devoted to understanding AI's ethical approach.

This current situation fosters companies' lack of interest in understanding the consequences of using AI technology and in reporting its negative effects. This is true especially if we consider that the reporting regarding AI's impact on human capital appears as a mysterious issue for most stakeholders due to the language, terms, or jargon used (Seele & Schultz, 2022; Bernini et al., 2024). Specifically, certain scholars (Bonsón et al., 2021a; Bonsón and Bednárová, 2022; Seele & Schultz, 2022; Van Maanen, 2022; Schultz et al., 2023, 2024; Bernini et al., 2024) highlight the risk of disclosure's misleading use for strategic purposes and to illustrate company behavior that seems to be compliant with AI's ethical use. Hagendorff (2020) mentions that, to date, the ethical approach to AI has failed. He specifically asserts the need for a reinforcement procedure, since the current lack of compliance with the existing code of ethics has no consequences. An ethical approach therefore seems to be rather similar to a marketing strategy.

Starting from these premises, we focus on the literature strand that deals with the ethicswashing concept, which, as previously mentioned, comprises producing misleading disclosures aimed at communicating ethical behavior that substantial real actions do not support (Seele & Schultz, 2022; Schultz et al., 2023, 2024; Bernini et al., 2024). In digital technologies' specific context, the risk of providing intentionally misleading reporting on AI's ethical use is increasing. This provides the possibility that the AI-sustainability binomial might be useful for implementing the scope for disclosure-based strategies, such as greenwashing or ethicswashing. The latter arises when the misleading approaches' target is sustainability's social and governance dimensions. Specifically, the studies devoted to digital ethicswashing contribute to machinewashing research's development. To the best of our knowledge, the first theoretical contribution is that by Seele and Schultz (2022), which defines a conceptual framework that compares the use of misleading reporting on AI's responsible use (machinewashing) with environmental (greenwashing) fields' antecedents and their outcomes.

Along with this theoretical contribution, other studies have also developed this issue by means of a literature review. Schultz et al. (2023) provide a review to illustrate CSR communication's and ethicswashing's set of features. Schultz et al. (2024) undertook a literature review and an assessment in various fields of study on digital ethicswashing aimed at defining a multidimensional framework, which they structured according to the process–perception–outcome dimensions. Bernini et al. (2024) contributed to this line of research by analyzing machinewashing according to the corporate digital responsibility theory's theoretical lens. In addition, they contributed empirically with a pioneering study aimed at providing a first methodology to assess machinewashing evidence. Specifically, these authors proposed an original methodological path based on an exploratory content analysis of reporting on Italian-listed companies in order to identify the machinewashing strategies for which the gap between information capacity and the information reliability acted as a proxy.

The existing literature informs on evident gaps relating to AI disclosure's ethical use in general and to its social dimension in particular.

First of all, although AI ethics have been widely investigated, studies of AI's impact on sustainability (Venuesa et al., 2020) are still scarce (Sætra, 2022; Verhoef et al. 2021). Moreover, although such studies take the connection between AI and ESG into account, only one of them (Bernini et al., 2024) develops a tool for evaluating AI disclosure's impacts on ESG, while a few of them provide a protocol for reporting ESG-relevant AI issues (Sætra, 2023, 2022). Notwithstanding the abundance of research on ESG disclosure, only a few studies report on an ethical approach to AI and provide useful tools for evaluating this kind of disclosure (Bonsón et al., 2021a). The gap appears wider in terms of studies focusing specifically on ethicswashing, while it appears all-encompassing regarding those focusing on AI's social dimension. Research on AI technologies' ethical implications is still in the first embryonic stage and predominantly theoretical (Bonsón et al. 2021a, b). Consequently, scholars suggest that authors should develop an empirical analysis based on companies' reporting. Moreover, Vakkuri and Abrahamsson (2018) called for improved research able to change the existing theoretical framework into ethics' true involvement in AI systems' applications.

Ethicswashing strategy might not be fully analyzed without taking a suitable theoretical framework into consideration that supports and explains firms' behaviors and disclosure's role as the main tool for realizing the above strategies.

Business economics studies take theories arising from various social science disciplines into consideration in order to understand human and corporate behaviors as well as to define the framework for studying such behaviors.

The theoretical framework we defined for understanding ethicswashing takes both theories—commonly referred to as non-financial and voluntary disclosure studies—into consideration. These are legitimacy theory (Oliver, 1991), signaling theory (Mahoney et al., 2013), stakeholder theory (Freeman, 1994), and other theories belonging to the corporate governance field, such as agency theory (Jensen & Meckling, 1976), and to the CSR field, such as digital social responsibility (Elliott et al., 2021; Herden et al., 2021).

In keeping with the legitimacy theory perspective, the socially accepted rules or values represent the setting in which the perceptions or judgments of this social setting's actors consider whether corporate behaviors are appropriate (Suchman, 1995). According to legitimacy theory, companies and stakeholders are linked by a contract (Deegan et al., 2002; Deegan & Unerman, 2011). Consistent with this perspective, firms are required to behave properly, while stakeholders legitimize companies considered compliant with social rules (Zharfpeykan, 2021) and gain opportunities to achieve resources and a competitive advantage (Walker & Wan, 2012; Seele & Gatti, 2017). Digital ethicswashing strategies can be observed through this theory's lens, since ethics and sustainability are currently an important source of legitimacy (Seele & Gatti, 2017; Hahn & Lülfs, 2014), although scholars refer to them as the novelty that AI technologies introduced. In keeping with the above perspective, disclosure strategies could therefore be viewed as a type of search for legitimacy based on misleading disclosures (Seele & Schultz, 2022).

Ethicswashing might, however, be more strictly concerned with the pragmatic development of legitimacy theory, which regards ethicswashing as a strategy for improving (Cho et al., 2022) or for rebuilding legitimacy (Laufer, 2003; Deegan et al., 2002). In the above perspective, legitimacy is considered a resource that companies could obtain from the external social environment (Suchman, 1995). Moreover, scholars can analyze ethicswashing from the perspective of institutional studies devoted to legitimacy. In this view, the increasing awareness of the impact of AI technologies' relevance and of the related disclosure could be considered a form of the company behavior's adaptation to comply with the stakeholders' perception (Hahn & Lülfs, 2014).

Stemming from voluntary disclosure theory (Clarkson et al., 2008), signaling theory (Mahoney et al., 2013) considers disclosure a corporate value driver due to its power to reduce information asymmetries (Berrone et al., 2017; Michelon & Parbonetti, 2012). According to signaling theory, AI-related disclosure is a tool to inform stakeholders about the firm's approach when using AI. Consistent with the above interpretation of AI disclosure, firms choose to only report information that signals a positive image of their behaviors (Li et al., 2023), thereby improving their reputation. Since scholars consider AI technologies capable of improving sustainability efforts' effectiveness and corporate value, voluntary disclosure devoted to this issue might be manipulated to signal companies' ethical behaviors and to, among other things, attract financial resources (Bonsón et al., 2021a).

Stakeholder theory is based on the stakeholder engagement concept and attributes a dual goal to the relationship between the company and its stakeholders, namely, realizing the society's ethical norms and fostering the relational and reputational capital (Bernini & La Rosa, 2024). Ethicswashing could also be considered an answer to the increasing stakeholder pressure related to AI's impact on social capital (Seele & Schultz, 2022).

The above theories define a framework for understanding ethicswashing that regards disclosure as the key driver of signaling companies' ethical use of digital technologies and of generating stakeholders' awareness of this, therefore improving their engagement in companies' strategies and, consequently, legitimizing their behaviors.

Since mandatory disclosure is improving, but it is still scarce, voluntary disclosure could be an important tool for fostering ethicswashing strategies. Consequently, legitimation and stakeholders' engagement draw from information asymmetries that originate from misleading disclosure.

From the ethics in reporting perspective (Adams & Abhayawansa, 2022), disclosure of AI technologies' social impact should be a way to generate accountability. However, in order to be accountable, a report should strive to disclose all if AI's material impacts honestly and indicate its compliance with ethical responsibilities (Adams, 2004). However, since such disclosure is frequently found to be misleading, uncertain, and, ultimately, unreliable, corporate digital responsibility (CDR) is an adequate theoretical framework that allows untrustworthy AI-related disclosures to be identified (Seele & Schultz, 2022; Bernini et al., 2024). Wade (2020) defines CDR as a set of practices and behaviors that helps an organization use data and digital technologies in a way that is socially, economically, technologically, and environmentally responsible. Consequently, CDR takes an ethical perspective in respect of digital transformation. Like CSR, CDR is related to engagement with social issues.

Finally, agency theory's perspective analyzes ethicswashing through corporate governance's lenses (Ghitti et al., 2023). Misleading disclosure could be a lever for promoting managers' reputation at the expense of the owners or of other stakeholders. Moreover, from the agency conflict perspective of the relationship between the control owner and the minority stakeholders, ethicswashing could be a tool to generate an entrenchment effect output (Bennedsen & Nielsen, 2010), resulting in opportunistic behaviors that majority stakeholders and managers pursue, but which compromise minority and other stakeholders (Bernini & La Rosa, 2024).

AI's impact on business ethics as well as its influence on internal and external stakeholders' decision-making process makes corporate communication related to AI technologies' use value relevant (Sætra, 2022). Supporting this evidence, Bonsón et al. (2021a, b) found that the use of AI technologies leads to the widespread use of AI disclosure. However, currently, annual reports do not have a section dedicated to AI communication, nor is the AI disclosure structured.

Disclosing AI technologies' use could therefore create a growing risk resulting in digital ethicswashing. This risk requires a regulation that clearly defines the relevant information and ethical principles with which AI needs to comply (Bonsón et al. 2021a, b). Further, the lack of a mandatory AI-related disclosure helps companies issue discretionary information in order to achieve specific strategic intents. In support of this, Bonsón et al. (2021a, b) found that firms only tend to report positive information to ensure that they gain legitimacy from the social ecosystem and to signal their superiority to their stakeholders.

Despite the recent struggles that the European Union promoted, Sætra's (2023, 2022) studies revealed that current standards do not define an adequate protocol for evaluating AI technologies' social impacts. In 2019, the EU Commission introduced the issue of accountability, which included auditability, the minimization and reporting of negative impacts, trade-offs, and the redressing of AI disclosure (European Union ethical guidelines, 2019). Moreover, as Sætra (2022) points out, the UE (EU AI Act, 2022) promulgated a more aggressive regulation on AI, calling for more transparency and risk management. The EU AI Act, which is not yet in force, regulates AI and classifies AI systems into potential risk categories.

Notwithstanding the abovementioned efforts, certain scholars question the UE Acts' actual effectiveness regarding constraining potential strategies based on misleading AI-related disclosure. Specifically, Shultz et al. (2024, Section 1) state that the current EU AI Act of 2022, which was a pioneering act, was nevertheless heavily criticized for its watered-down definition of AI, while the AI Act of 2019, with its controversial notion of "trustworthy AI," led the philosopher and panel member, Thomas Metzinger, to challenge the panel's legitimacy. He subsequently referred to the decision-making process as "ethicswashing" and to the industry's efforts as "ethicswashing machine[s]."

AI's growing importance and the subsequent stakeholders' expectations relate to it empowering digital ethicswashing approaches. It is therefore necessary to monitor companies' attitudes toward ethicswashing to manage this kind of strategy.

2.4 Research Design and Methodology

Our aim was to contribute to the nascent study field dedicated to the observation of ethicswashing behaviors. In turn, the investigation was aimed at providing instruments for detecting digital ethicswashing (DEW) strategies through an analysis of reporting's reliability in terms of the social aspect of AI's use, termed social digital talk (SDT). Specifically, we captured AI's ethical use by detecting and analyzing the content related to ESG issues' social dimension. In respect of each company that we analyzed, we defined the SDT's intensity, which we called the talk level (TL). We identified a low TL when the SDT comprised less than 50 text units; a medium TL when the SDT comprised more than 50 text units but less than 100; and a high TL when the SDT comprised more than 100 text units.

According to this perspective, a greater level of reporting unreliability tends to highlight a higher intensity of misleading approaches and, therefore, of DEW strategies.

Given the DEW topic's novelty, current literature provides very few consolidated methodologies to identify and analyze these (Bernini et al., 2024; Bonsón et al., 2021a). Consequently, this calls for an analytical investigation.

In order to provide such an investigation, we started with previous studies dedicated to greenwashing and, given the conceptual analogy between greenwashing and ethicswashing issues, carried out a similar content analysis (Seele & Schultz, 2022; Guix et al., 2022). We specifically aimed to observe how companies realize strategies based on misleading communication that depends on AI use's ethical implications.

Since this work is aimed at observing a new problem's nature, we developed an exploratory analysis to investigate how companies implement DEW strategies, starting with their disclosure (Easterby-Smith et al., 2021). Specifically, this study is aimed at proposing a methodological dashboard that can identify and manage DEW strategies.

Sample

We study a sample of five Italian-listed companies belonging to different industries that we observed during the period 2020–2022.

The sample was defined by first identifying ten different industries based on the Industry Classification Benchmark level 2 (i.e., basic materials, consumer goods, consumer services, financials, healthcare, industrials, oil and gas, technology, telecommunication, and utilities). In respect of each industry, we selected a company with the largest market capitalization. In order to have sufficient content to analyze, and starting with this group of ten, we selected those with an average (across the 3 years) of at least 100 text units referring to the ESG topic's social dimension. Ultimately, we selected a sample of five companies (which we anonymized for confidentiality reasons) operating in the following industries: basic materials (A), industrials (B), financials (C), utilities (D), and consumer goods (E).

Content Analysis

The content analysis approach collects and codifies data into specific categories. The classification is instrumental for describing the data facts (Krippendorff, 1980). Literature suggests that corporate report content is usually examined in research on sustainability in order to identify ethical issue disclosures (Bonsón et al., 2021a, b; Kumar & Firoz, 2019). Moreover, the content analysis literature considered the companies' Annual Reports and Non-financial Statements the main information sources (Campbell et al., 2010; Cabrita et al., 2017). We therefore developed our content analysis on the basis of the Annual Report and Non-financial Statements of the five companies participating in our exploratory study.

Content analysis-based research assumes that the disclosure of a specific issue indicates a company's commitment to that issue (Mention, 2011; Krippendorff, 1980). Consequently, a wider SDT could signal that greater attention is being paid to AI's ethical use, therefore concealing possible misleading reporting strategies at the stakeholders' expense.

We undertook the content analysis by means of a two-step approach. The first step started with identifying the text units referring to AI's use.

Following a semi-objective approach to content analysis, we selected the contents that we had to code and classify ex ante, based on a top-down approach (Humphreys & Jen-Hui Wang, 2018; Beattie et al., 2004). We collect the AI-related text units by defining a set of keywords that could individuate the contents. We derived the set of keywords from literature (Hossnofsky & Junge, 2019) and from the "Piano Nazionale Industria 4.0" (2017–2020) report that the Italian Ministry of Economic Development issued.[1]

A keyword's presence signaled the presence of at least a text unit on AI's use. We extracted each text unit with a keyword presence, considering each text unit a coding basis that had to be classified. To improve our understanding of the information report in each text unit, we considered the entire paragraph to which these text units belonged.

Starting with this set of text units, we developed another selection aimed at collecting those units referring to digitalization's ethical aspects and proxied by the ESG topics' social dimension. We specifically considered the shape of the ESG rating indicators' construction (Refinitiv, 2022; Dempretic et al., 2020), which classified the social dimension into Workforce (S1), Human Rights (S2), Community

[1] For more information regarding the content selection and the selection of the contents, please see Bernini et al. (2024), Table 2.3.

Table 2.1 Unreliability signals

Type of claim	Description
Vague and misleading	Broad statements without specific meaning
Inaccurate	Incorrect or invented statements or data
Jargon	Statements using language, terms, or jargon that do not resonate with the interested parties (especially customers)
Irrelevant	Statements that emphasize a trivial ethical aspect, while the remaining business practices are contrary to ethical or environmental standards
Exaggerations	Claims that make the organization or its products look better than they are
	Exaggerated claims that go far beyond the possibilities of the organization's product or capabilities

Source: Seele and Schultz (2022)

Table 2.2 Scale of reporting's degree of unreliability

Number of signals	Score	Unreliability degree
1	5	Lightly unreliable (LU)
2	4	Modestly unreliable (MU)
3	3	Significantly unreliable (SIU)
4	2	Strongly unreliable (STU)
5	1	Fully unreliable (FU)

Source: authors' elaboration

(S3), and Product Responsibility (S4). In this way, we defined the definitive information set.[2]

Following Seele and Schultz (2022), who identify five signals of information unreliability in DEW practices (i.e., "vague and misleading claims," "inaccurate claims," "jargon claims," "irrelevant claims," and "exaggerations") (Table 2.1), we assigned one or more of these signals to each text unit. This attribution was based on a pilot analysis that the research group repeated and validated. By doing so, we measured the degree of information unreliability, which is intuitively higher when the number of signals increases.

The presence of the DEW strategies is hypothesized when one or more unreliability signals are detected. The misleading approach becomes stronger as the number of signals for each text unit increases. On this basis, we designed a scale for measuring SDT's unreliability degree (Table 2.2).

The content analysis allowed us to classify the collected text units according to their information content (S1, S2, S3, and S4), the types of claims they make (Table 2.1), and their degree of unreliability (Table 2.2). In this way, it was possible

[2] Since the contents to be analyzed were complex, the classification was realized by developing a human code. To ensure the methodological validity of the analysis (Weber, 1985), we formalized the coding process by defining some specific coding rules. To nurture the coding uniformity and the reliability of the process (Beattie & Thomson, 2007), we realized a pilot analysis before developing the entire coding process. To have a more detailed description of the coding process, see Bernini et al. (2022, 2024), Text and Appendix.

to systematically analyze the contents, the type of claims, and each text unit's unreliability degree.

2.5 Results

In this section, we first present the results of each selected firm's analysis, as follows: We present the evidence starting with the firm with less SDT, subsequently moving to the others. We additionally organized our findings according to a TL indicator: from a low talk level to a medium and high talk level.

To better understand each company's possible misleading behavior, we considered not only the total SDT but also the way companies split this into different content types (CT), which are S1, S2, S3, and S4. This choice is appropriate for showing the methods that companies mostly use to pursue digital ethicswashing goals.

In general, the content analysis evidence is described according to different investigation profiles. We therefore organized the data into tables aimed at showing the various features of firms' behaviors related to digital ethicswashing. As mentioned above, we started by splitting the SDT into different content types. Thereafter, we considered unreliability's impact on SDT, that is, the unreliable information's weight in respect of the total reporting for each CT. This is useful for understanding which CT unreliability affects most. The analysis needs to be done truly in depth to help achieve our study's goal. We therefore proceeded to focus on each CT's unreliability degree with the aim of linking unreliable information to the frequency with which these claims occur, regardless of their nature (vague, inaccurate, etc.). We then included the type of claims in the analysis. Specifically, we studied the relationship between unreliable information and each CT's claim category. This helped us understand DEW's qualitative evidence. Lastly, we linked the types of claims with their frequency in order to show the types of unreliability claims occurrence according to the unreliability degree.

All the analyses were carried out over 3 years, from 2020 to 2022. Where it is relevant, we comment on the results, also taking the time horizon into account.

Company A

Although the sector to which the firm belongs could push it toward paying some attention to digitalization's impact on the social sphere, its SDT is quite limited. Consequently, company A can be defined as a low-talk-level firm.

The analysis shows established disclosure of community-related (S3) contents, although their percentage decreases over the 3 years in favor of product responsibility (S4). On the other hand, there were no disclosures about human rights (S2) in any of the years.

The unreliability impact on the SDT suggests that the unreliable units' weight is rather high (Table 2.3). However, company A's low talk level does not allow any generalization, but its analysis contributes to a holistic view of the phenomenon when compared to other firms' analyses.

Despite the relatively high unreliability degree, company A does not present full unreliability (FU) cases nor strong unreliability (STU) ones. The light unreliability (LU) cases predominate, while the remaining modestly unreliable (MU) and significantly unreliable (SIU) are almost absent. Our analysis's construction and the processing of data allowed us to assess the contents' (S1, S2, S3, and S4) unreliability degree. Again, company A's low talk level does not allow any generalizations (Table 2.4).

The prevalent unreliability types are the vague and misleading claims, and the jargon claims, as the percentages of these assertions are higher and continue across the 3 years (Table 2.5).

In terms of the unreliability type's occurrence per unreliability degree, the analysis shows that vague and misleading claims are specifically present in LU cases. This could suggest that these assertions are the prevalent tool in cases with light DEW intent. On the other hand, the MU cases are associated with exaggerations, which therefore take on a strengthening function. In 2022, exaggerations, together with vague and misleading claims, resulted in a MU case (Table 2.6).

In this respect, the following is an example related to product responsibility talk content (TC) (S4).

"The concluded contracts allowed a corporate culture to be created, oriented toward all of the external stakeholders' greater involvement (*exaggerations*) and toward some projects being started (*vague and misleading claims*) in order to help the start-ups test some (*vague and misleading claims*) of their technologies."

Company B

Company B could be defined as a medium-talk-level company.

The overall analysis of the 3 years clarifies that also company B, just like the previous one, mainly reports on the community (S3), followed by the workforce (S1). Although with lower percentages than the other sub-categories, human rights (S2) are also present as a TC.

The unreliability impact on SDT is high in respect of all TCs, especially for S2, followed by S3. Based on the aforementioned statements, it is possible to comment on S2. In general, the human rights contents are less disclosed but have a higher unreliability impact, although only a slight one (Table 2.3).

The unreliability degree's analysis reveals the absence of full unreliability (FU) cases, while there are strong unreliability (STU) cases. The most prevalent cases are those labeled LU and MU (Table 2.4).

Human rights (S2) TCs exhibit the highest unreliability degree compared to the medium severity, that is, the significantly unreliable (SIU) cases. The workforce TC (S1) exhibits a moderately balanced distribution of text units across the various unreliability degrees. On the other hand, community (S3) and product responsibility's (S4) TCs exhibit a higher concentration of content on such analysis profiles (Table 2.5).

Table 2.3 Unreliability impact on social digital talk per content

	A			B			C			D			E		
Y	2020	2021	2022	2020	2021	2022	2020	2021	2022	2020	2021	2022	2020	2021	2022
S1	100%	50%	66%	37%	33%	28%	47%	33%	83%	63%	71%	50%	71%	85%	83%
S2	0%	0%	0%	11%	2%	4%	100%	91%	67%	33%	89%	75%	65%	74%	87%
S3	50%	80%	66%	35%	38%	52%	70%	84%	83%	83%	85%	86%	67%	83%	76%
S4	50%	100%	66%	17%	26%	16%	53%	79%	82%	76%	86%	80%	73%	75%	57%

Table 2.4 Unreliability degree per content (quantitative evidence of number of unreliability signals)

	S-type	LU			MU			SIU			STU			FU		
		2020	2021	2022	2020	2021	2022	2020	2021	2022	2020	2021	2022	2020	2021	2022
A	S1	50%	0%	17%	0%	11%	0%	0%	11%	17%	0%	0%	0%	0%	0%	0%
	S2	0%	0%	0%	0%	0%	0%	0%	0%	0%	0%	0%	0%	0%	0%	0%
	S3	33%	44%	33%	0%	0%	0%	0%	0%	0%	0%	0%	0%	0%	0%	0%
	S4	17%	33%	17%	0%	0%	17%	0%	0%	0%	0%	0%	0%	0%	0%	0%
B	S1	43%	43%	22%	43%	43%	20%	7%	7%	40%	7%	7%	0%	0%	0%	0%
	S2	67%	0%	5%	0%	0%	0%	33%	100%	50%	0%	0%	0%	0%	0%	0%
	S3	14%	47%	44%	43%	23%	44%	28%	29%	20%	14%	0%	4%	0%	0%	0%
	S4	86%	25%	28%	14%	42%	14%	0%	25%	14%	0%	14%	0%	0%	0%	0%
C	S1	43%	100%	100%	57%	0%	0%	0%	0%	0%	0%	0%	0%	0%	0%	0%
	S2	100%	100%	100%	0%	0%	0%	0%	0%	0%	0%	0%	0%	0%	0%	0%
	S3	58%	89%	64%	32%	4%	24%	10%	7%	12%	0%	0%	0%	0%	0%	0%
	S4	78%	87%	67%	22%	13%	18%	0%	0%	15%	0%	0%	0%	0%	0%	0%
D	S1	42%	35%	18%	25%	29%	28%	33%	35%	28%	0%	0%	0%	0%	0%	0%
	S2	50%	37%	33%	50%	12%	67%	0%	0%	0%	0%	0%	0%	0%	0%	0%
	S3	42%	47%	29%	35%	26%	42%	23%	26%	29%	0%	0%	0%	0%	0%	0%
	S4	35%	45%	46%	32%	46%	42%	32%	16%	12%	0%	0%	0%	0%	0%	0%
E	S1	35%	25%	36%	25%	7%	25%	0%	0%	100%	0%	0%	0%	0%	0%	0%
	S2	15%	14%	13%	25%	14%	0%	0%	0%	0%	0%	0%	0%	0%	0%	0%
	S3	32%	36%	27%	25%	50%	33%	0%	100%	0%	0%	0%	0%	0%	0%	0%
	S4	19%	25%	24%	25%	29%	42%	0%	0%	0%	0%	100%	100%	0%	0%	0%

Note: Tot. unreliable S (for each S-category and unreliability level) on tot unreliable S

Table 2.5 Qualitative evidence of DEW attributes

			Vague and misleading claims			Inaccurate claims			Jargon claims			Irrelevant claims			Exaggerations		
			2020	2021	2022	2020	2021	2022	2020	2021	2022	2020	2021	2022	2020	2021	2022
Signals-unreliability (SU)	A	S1	33%	100%	50%	0%	0%	0%	100%	100%	100%	0%	50%	50%	0%	0%	0%
		S2	0%	0%	0%	0%	0%	0%	0%	0%	0%	0%	0%	0%	0%	0%	0%
		S3	100%	50%	100%	0%	0%	0%	0%	50%	0%	0%	0%	0%	0%	0%	0%
		S4	100%	100%	100%	0%	0%	0%	0%	0%	0%	0%	0%	0%	0%	0%	50%
	B	S1	78%	71%	20%	7%	0%	40%	50%	64%	30%	21%	21%	10%	21%	28%	50%
		S2	67%	100%	100%	0%	0%	0%	67%	100%	50%	33%	0%	50%	0%	100%	0%
		S3	86%	59%	80%	7%	0%	4%	64%	76%	48%	36%	35%	28%	50%	12%	36%
		S4	57%	67%	43%	0%	8%	0%	43%	58%	71%	14%	42%	0%	0%	42%	28%
	C	S1	71%	0%	20%	0%	0%	0%	28%	0%	40%	43%	100%	20%	14%	0%	20%
		S2	17%	20%	50%	17%	10%	0%	17%	50%	0%	33%	20%	0%	17%	10%	50%
		S3	53%	15%	64%	5%	4%	0%	21%	0%	16%	47%	15%	48%	26%	37%	20%
		S4	44%	40%	74%	11%	20%	100%	22%	27%	18%	33%	13%	33%	11%	7%	15%
	D	S1	58%	70%	100%	25%	12%	0%	33%	59%	43%	42%	18%	0%	33%	18%	57%
		S2	50%	75%	33%	0%	12%	12%	50%	50%	33%	50%	0%	0%	0%	12%	33%
		S3	70%	76%	46%	2%	3%	0%	56%	53%	55%	19%	12%	16%	35%	12%	19%
		S4	58%	62%	46%	6%	0%	0%	64%	70%	37%	32%	11%	4%	35%	22%	29%
	E	S1	37%	68%	50%	13%	0%	3%	3%	11%	10%	53%	32%	43%	13%	14%	17%
		S2	62%	47%	10%	0%	12%	0%	38%	47%	30%	8%	6%	8%	9%	24%	8%
		S3	42%	44%	43%	0%	7%	4%	8%	13%	12%	46%	27%	23%	12%	42%	15%
		S4	57%	40%	3%	0%	10%	13%	0%	10%	6%	38%	43%	88%	19%	23%	31%

Note: Tot. unreliable S (for each S-category and type of signals) on tot unreliable S (for each S-category)

Table 2.6 Incidence of unreliability type per unreliability degree

		2020					2021					2022				
Type of claim		LU	MU	SIU	STU	FIU	LU	MU	SIU	STU	FIU	LU	MU	SIU	STU	FIU
Vague and misleading	A	66%	0%	0%	0%	0%	71%	50%	33%	0%	0%	75%	0%	33%	0%	0%
Inaccurate		0%	0%	0%	0%	0%	0%	0%	0%	0%	0%	0%	0%	0%	0%	0%
Jargon		33%	0%	0%	0%	0%	29%	50%	33%	0%	0%	25%	0%	33%	0%	0%
Irrelevant		0%	0%	0%	0%	0%	0%	0%	33%	0%	0%	0%	0%	33%	0%	0%
Exaggerations		0%	0%	0%	0%	0%	0%	0%	0%	0%	0%	0%	100%	0%	0%	0%
Vague and misleading	B	50%	46%	33%	25%	0%	29%	39%	25%	25%	0%	55%	39%	30%	25%	0%
Inaccurate		6%	4%	0%	0%	0%	0%	0%	0%	12%	0%	0%	3%	12%	0%	0%
Jargon		3%	27%	33%	25%	0%	53%	29%	25%	25%	0%	33%	18%	21%	25%	0%
Irrelevant		6%	11%	17%	25%	0%	6%	16%	17%	12%	0%	11%	5%	12%	25%	0%
Exaggerations		6%	11%	17%	25%	0%	12%	16%	7%	25%	0%	0%	18%	24%	25%	0%
Vague and misleading	C	30%	42%	33%	0%	0%	37%	50%	33%	0%	0%	51%	53%	33%	0%	0%
Inaccurate		4%	8%	0%	0%	0%	4%	33%	17%	0%	0%	2%	0%	5%	0%	0%
Jargon		19%	12%	17%	0%	0%	23%	0%	0%	0%	0%	10%	5%	19%	0%	0%
Irrelevant		30%	29%	33%	0%	0%	14%	17%	17%	0%	0%	19%	37%	33%	0%	0%
Exaggerations		19%	8%	17%	0%	0%	21%	0%	33%	0%	0%	17%	5%	9%	0%	0%
Vague and misleading	D	43%	31%	32%	0%	0%	46%	0%	32%	0%	0%	37%	39%	41%	0%	0%
Inaccurate		0%	3%	5%	0%	0%	0%	0%	1%	0%	0%	0%	0%	0%	0%	0%
Jargon		37%	31%	25%	0%	0%	28%	35%	30%	0%	0%	50%	39%	41%	0%	0%
Irrelevant		8%	15%	17%	0%	0%	10%	0%	21%	0%	0%	8%	9%	18%	0%	0%
Exaggerations		11%	19%	21%	0%	0%	15%	65%	16%	0%	0%	12%	13%	0%	0%	0%

(continued)

Table 2.6 (continued)

		2020					2021					2022				
Type of claim		LU	MU	SIU	STU	FIU	LU	MU	SIU	STU	FIU	LU	MU	SIU	STU	FIU
Vague and misleading	E	39%	50%	33%	0%	0%	41%	36%	33%	25%	0%	78%	25%	0%	33%	0%
Inaccurate		3%	6%	17%	0%	0%	21%	7%	13%	0%	0%	0%	0%	0%	0%	0%
Jargon		9%	0%	17%	0%	0%	16%	11%	3%	25%	0%	22%	50%	0%	33%	0%
Irrelevant		40%	25%	17%	0%	0%	21%	25%	23%	25%	0%	0%	0%	0%	0%	0%
Exaggerations		9%	19%	17%	0%	0%	20%	21%	27%	25%	0%	0%	25%	0%	33%	0%

As mentioned before, human rights content features less frequently than all the other TCs. However, its disclosure reveals all of the unreliability types' presence, with the exception of inaccurate claims and with vague and misleading claims as well as jargon claims all peaking.

Together with jargon claims, vague and misleading claims are the most frequent unreliability types in respect of the low unreliability degrees (LU and MU) during the period. When the unreliability degree shifts toward that of the other claims, it means that the other types also have an effect regarding making the reporting misleading. Consequently, the relative weight decreases in favor of more balanced percentages (Table 2.6).

In this respect, we provide an example of S1-related TC with three unreliability types.

"The D&I Index's progress to 115% is due to the confirmation of some (*vague and misleading claims*) of the key projects' positive results, aimed at increasing the share of women managers and young talents, and at improving employees' participation in upskilling and reskilling (*jargon claims*) programs. The increase in the number of organizational units that have implemented smart working policies and action plans in respect of disability, is also extremely positive (*exaggerations*)."

Company C

Company C could be defined as a medium-talk-level company.

The analysis shows that the most commonly disclosed issue is related to community (S3) in both 2020 and 2021; in 2022, product responsibility (S4) is the most common content. This company shows that SDT takes all the TCs into consideration, even though the workforce (S1) and human rights (S2) contents are less reported (Table 2.3).

With the exception of S1 in 2021, the other TCs do not generally provide fully reliable text units.

Company C does not display full and strong unreliability degrees. On the other hand, a significant concentration of text units, characterized by light unreliability (LU), emerges. The relationship between the unreliability degree and the categories demonstrates that the abovementioned concentration is particularly evident in respect of S2 and, to a lesser extent, of S1 (Table 2.4).

However, S3 and S4, which are the TCs with larger percentages across the period, display a greater distribution of the different unreliability degrees. Specifically, S3 exhibits more MU cases, but also some SIU cases.

Vague and misleading claims, as well as irrelevant claims, mainly impact S1. There is no steadily prevailing claim over the entire period. Although it has lower percentages, S2 presents the same claims as S1, but there are also others, such as exaggerations. Further, in this case there is no steadily prevailing claim in any of the years, although the unreliability types are more distributed across the various TCs. S3 presents mainly vague and misleading claims as well as irrelevant ones. Unlike S1 and S2, the claims related to S3 are less concentrated. Lastly, the company uses all the S4 claims to realize DEW. However, in respect of 2022, the vague, misleading, and inaccurate claims are more relevant (Table 2.5).

In respect of the occurrence of the unreliability types per unreliability degree, the analysis points out that vague and misleading claims appear most frequently in LU and MU cases. This might suggest that vague and misleading claims are the DEW tool that company C uses most often. In this respect, it is possible to add other unreliability types that contribute to increasing the disclosures' overall unreliability degree. However, the claims that comprise the vague and misleading ones are not always the same, which means that those claims that differ from the vague and misleading ones have a higher variability (Table 2.6).

We illustrate company D's misleading approach by mentioning an example of S3-related CTs characterized by the most frequent claims (vague and misleading) and accompanied by another type of claim, namely, an exaggeration.

"The electrification of mobility, logistical efficiency, and intelligent data-usage are other challenges that lie ahead (*vague and misleading claims*), but to which we hope to provide new answers soon, and to develop innovative opportunities to create value for the community in which we live (*exaggerations*)."

Company D

Company D could be defined as a high-talk-level company.

The most disclosed TCs are related to S3 and S4. On the other hand, in line with what we observed regarding the other companies, S2 is the less disclosed topic. No relevant changes emerge over the period, except for a strong SDT decrease in 2022, which applies to all the categories.

Unreliability's impact on SDT is high. On average, the most disclosed topics are associated with the highest impact. Conversely, the unreliability degree of the less disclosed topic (human rights—S2) increases strongly over the period (Table 2.3).

The unreliability degree's analysis illustrates the absence of full unreliability (FU) cases and strong unreliability cases (STU). Compared to the other companies, company D indicates a higher presence of significantly unreliable cases (SIU). Besides S2, which exhibits low unreliability degrees, there are also various other gradations of unreliability (Table 2.4).

The vague and misleading claims are the most frequent unreliability type, followed by the jargon claims. All the sub-categories are involved, with the exception of S2, which is less impacted (Table 2.5).

Vague and misleading claims do not occur in respect of all the unreliability degrees. As mentioned, they are frequently found, but are not an absolute majority compared to the other claims. On the other hand, exaggerations usually seem to be the unreliability type, which mostly occurs in MU cases and which is accompanied by at least one other type of claim. Contrary to the other companies, the exaggerations here do not necessarily go well with vague and misleading claims. The latter therefore lose their ever-present characteristic, thereby, for example, benefitting the jargon claims.

Jargon claims are prominently present in all of unreliability's gradations, also in the case of LU (Table 2.6).

The following is an example of a S4 topic impacted by jargon claims and exaggerations.

"Company D could be considered a global leader (exaggeration) in such technologies. It is also busy with the third generation of smart meters, known as open meters (jargon claims), in which cutting-edge technologies allow features that go beyond the traditional concept of simple measurement."

Company E

Company E could be defined as a high-talk-level company.

The SDT analysis shows that there is a more balanced distribution of the text units regarding all the TCs over the entire period. S1 is the most disclosed topic in two of the years and S3 in one.

This company has a generally high unreliability impact on SDT, which is widespread across all the categories. The peak of S2 occurred in 2022, although this category is the less disclosed one (Table 2.3).

Company E generally exhibits LU cases and MU cases, but with the latter being less intense. It is not possible to establish a significant link between the different TCs and the unreliability degrees (Table 2.4).

As in previous companies, the most frequent unreliability types are vague and misleading claims and irrelevant claims, especially regarding S1, S3, and S4. In addition to vague and misleading claims, S2 also presents jargon claims (Table 2.5).

Vague and misleading claims are the unreliability type with the most impact on the LU cases. In more severe cases, the vague and misleading claims mainly accompanied irrelevant claims in 2020 and 2021. In 2022, vague and misleading claims were linked with jargon claims (Table 2.6). In this respect, we next report an example of an S1 TC.

"Podcasts and videos are integrated into internal communications channels' wider ecosystem (*vague and misleading claims*), and incorporated into an editorial plan channeled through Yammer and an internal digital signage circuit (*jargon claims*)."

Our analysis's second step focuses on the opportunity to highlight evidence relevant to all the companies in order to understand whether the DEW approach has common features.

On examining SDT, the community-related topics (S3) are generally the most reported ones and human rights (S2) the least disclosed ones. Sometimes, the latter are absent. The low S2 disclosure could be due to the companies' human rights commitment (a projected moral aspect) being perceived as less impacted by artificial intelligence. Although this topic is less disclosed, it appears to be subjected to firms' manipulative ploys. Consequently, questions arise regarding whether companies perceive this category, although not much disclosed, as the one most instrumental to realizing the DEW approach.

The SDT related to S4 follows S3, especially with regard to non-financial firms. This insight might be due to such firms considering product responsibility the driver most likely to be sensitive to digitalization's ethical impact. On the other hand, the financial institution considers digital ethics more important for the workforce (S1), because digitalization impacts a commercial offer less.

All of the firms' unreliability degree is high, around 50%, even reaching 100% at times.

The unreliability severity is almost equally light and modest (in LU and MU). Significant unreliability (SIU) exhibits a low frequency and strong unreliability (STU) even less. There is no full unreliability case.

Firms mostly realize DEW via vague and misleading claims, together with jargon claims and irrelevant claims. In this respect, it is worth noting that the other two types of unreliability's (exaggerations and inaccurate claims) low frequency do not necessarily mean they are not relevant, but rather that some claims are more difficult to detect.

Vague and misleading claims are always present, which helps us understand LU cases' frequency. In this respect, it is worth noting that such claims are the unreliability type that is easiest for firms to make and for researcher to detect.

2.6 A Dashboard for Detecting the DEW Approach

The previous empirical analyses offered information providing evidence of a potentially misleading approach. This forms a basis for further investigations. We can organize and finalize the information to build a tool that will not only provide a systematic vision of the emerged evidence, but which will also form a basis for identifying and managing DEW.

In line with this goal, the previous empirical analysis defined a model for identifying a DEW dashboard in a multi-step process (Fig. 2.1). This process aims to explore the empirical evidence emerging from the content analyses of the companies' reporting and to provide a holistic vision of the ethicalwashing approach.

We develop the process by integrating several steps logically. During the process, the previous step feeds each following step, which, in turn, feeds the next one in terms of the information capacity required to define the DEW approach. Each of the process's steps has an informative value and contributes to the process's advancement. Consequently, each step has an incremental explicative power and contributes to the entire process's enhancement.

The first label identifies the company on the basis of the TL–TC combination.

The second label provides evidence of the information areas (S1, S2, S3, and S4) that companies use most to implement DEW strategies. This label could, per se, be an indicator of DEW strategies, but when it is considered in isolation, it is unable to offer a complete representation of the company's attitude, thereby producing a distorting opinion. It is a necessary, but not sufficient, representation of the reality. The model therefore uses this result as incremental input for the subsequent step.

The second label's converging into the third allows us to understand not only the number of unreliable text units (second label) but also the severity of each sentence's unreliability. As mentioned, the unreliability degree increases with the increasing number of claims in respect of each text unit. At this level, the dashboard shows which contents a higher level of unreliability affects and consequently shows

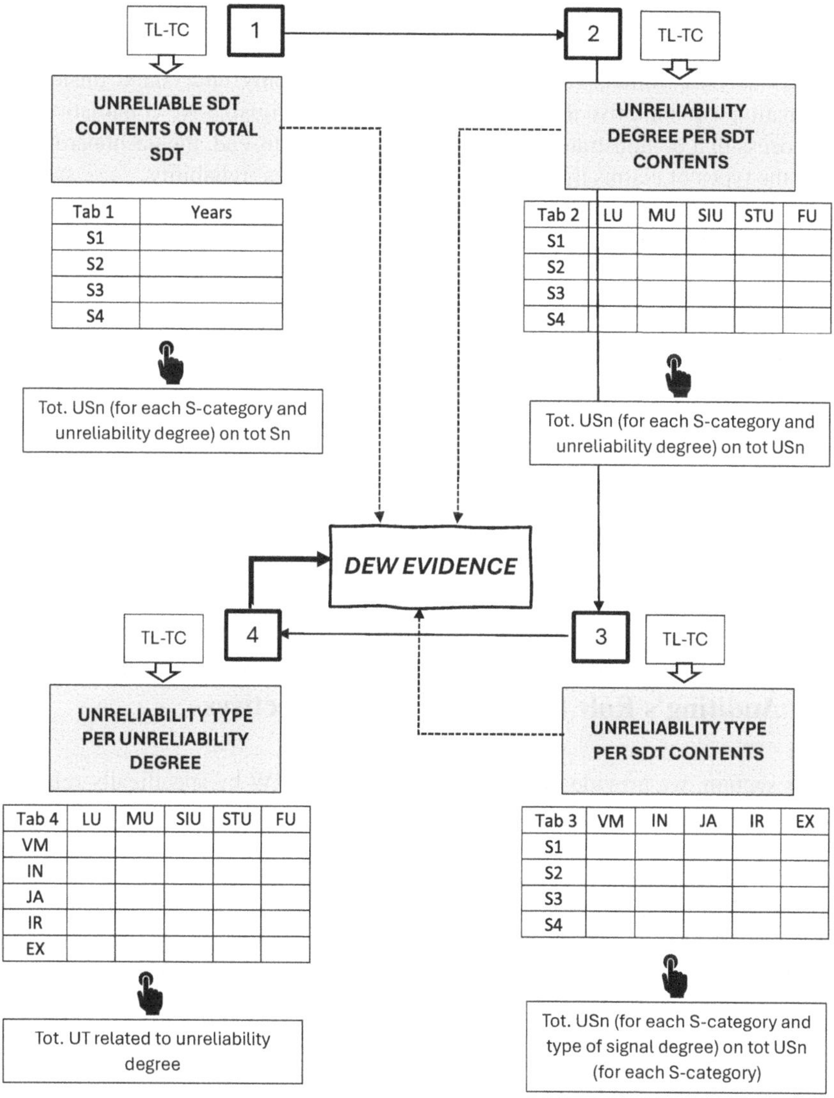

Fig. 2.1 Dashboard for detecting the DEW approach. Source: authors' elaboration. *USn* unreliable text units for S1, S2, S3, S4, *Sn* text units for S1, S2, S3, S4, *UT* unreliability type, *TL* talk level, *TC* talk content

the content areas that lead to a greater DEW intention. As pointed out before, this label also just represents information, but, at the same time, it is required to further refine the model.

The dashboard path's other two steps systematize more complex variables for detecting more DEW peculiarities.

The fourth label introduces a qualitative vision into the DEW model. This step specifically highlights the attributes of misleading information that overcome quantitative analyses' limits. The dashboard aims to not only understand misleading information's quantitative dimension but also include a qualitative connotation into the process that demonstrates the DEW approach. To this end, the dashboard highlights the types of claims that undermine SDT categories' reliability.

The final label links the unreliability degree claims, completing the information path aimed at providing evidence of the DEW approach. This level of analysis systematizes the previous ones, becoming essential for defining the approach.

The dashboard underscores certain relevant issues, which are also related to the analysis's theoretical shape. Some obstacles emerge when attempts are made to recognize digital ethicswashing. This is mainly due to the difficulties that an external analyst encounters with identifying the use of unreliable claims.

The dashboard is a useful tool for helping insiders and auditors detect and manage DEW strategies. However, the levers of action should also be delegated in order to control procedures and interventions, such as the possibility of acting in terms of an information audit. Further, the possibility of using this tool should also be understood in the light of the current critical issues affecting AI disclosure.

2.7 Preventing Digital Ethicswashing: Insights into AI Auditing's Role from Different Perspectives

In this section, we provide insights into preventing DEW by specifically referring external auditors' role. Instead of waiting for a major AI scandal with disastrous implications (Schultz & Seele, 2023), it is vital to anticipate, prevent, and manage DEW practices. For example, when using algorithmic processes to make decisions about humans, such as their hiring and assessing their workplace productivity or educational performance, these processes' opacity could seriously compromise public trust and accountability, especially when their benefits have been misallocated. Similarly, social media algorithms could accelerate the spread of harmful information in terms of relational capital (Goodman & Trehu, 2022).

AI ethics concern issues such as responsibility, transparency, auditability, incorruptibility, predictability, and machines' morality (Bostrom & Yudkowsky, 2014). Seele and Schultz (2022) recognize that external objective observers find it difficult, or even impossible, to assess DEW practices. Consequently, even voluntarily transparent firms are unlikely to share their algorithmic code with the public, due to their interest in protecting their business models. Seele and Schultz (2022), however, suggest a more practical solution—an independent third-party verification undertaken by an auditing firm. Algorithm auditing is defined as "the research and practice of assessing, mitigating, and assuring an algorithm's safety, legality, and ethics" (Koshiyama et al., 2021). In this regard, external ethical auditing is a key component of any form of operationalized AI ethics (Rahwan, 2018; Morley et al., 2021).

Adopting a third-party team comprised of industry experts to audit the information that the company disclosed and to reduce public skepticism about the disclosed information could therefore minimize DEW behavior (Bernini et al., 2024), given that AI is still a relatively unknown topic for investors (Minkkinen et al., 2024).

Different approaches could be considered in an attempt to shape external auditing's role in respect of AI. For example, both Goodman and Trehu (2022) and Selinger et al. (2023) pose a set of basic audit questions regarding the who, what, why, when, and how of an AI audit. We, on the other hand, follow La Rosa and Caserio's (2013) framework on auditors' interest in XBRL, and we adopt the lens of different perspectives to investigate AI auditing.

Specifically, one or more of the following contribute to the understanding of AI auditing:

1. The *regulatory perspective*, i.e., the extant regulation on AI auditing
2. An *economic perspective*, which is related to the costs that the AI auditing entails
3. The *procedural/technical perspective* refers to how an AI audit should be performed
4. The *cultural perspective*, i.e., the expected change that AI auditing is presumed to make to the auditing profession
5. The *social perspective*, i.e., the accountability of and the audience for AI auditing

1. The regulatory perspective. From a regulatory perspective, AI's auditing should be required by law. Governments and regulatory agencies play a key role in the updating of the rules and in new technologies' assimilation. A regulatory perspective therefore implies that governments implement new regulations regarding the mandatory disclosure of algorithms and the handling of user data.

   Such regulation should offer a very clear definition of the AI auditing process as well as clarify the auditors' legal liability. In addition, a supervisory board should be established to control the process and penalize abuses. If this were not done, an informal and poorly structured regulation of AI assurance could lead to uncertainty. Ambiguous goals could also lead all audit firms to offer the same assurance model, which would allow audit-washing, and the false assurance that audits performed without clear third-party standards give.

   The EU Digital Services Act's Article 28, for instance, requires very large online platforms to submit to yearly external audits in order to be certified that they comply with systemic risk mitigation measures and reporting requirements, although it does not require auditors to actually provide an independent risk assessment.

   However, the EU released the first harmonized rules on AI in the world with its recent AI Act (9 December 2023), which is a global standard for AI regulation in other jurisdictions. As like traditional financial auditing, the AI Act regulation follows a risk-based approach: the higher the risk, the stricter the rules. Article 15 specifically states that "[h]igh-risk AI systems shall be designed and developed in such a way that they achieve, in the light of their intended purpose, an appropriate level of accuracy, robustness, and cybersecurity, and perform consistently in those respects throughout their lifecycle." Importantly, Article 43 (conformity assessment) requires high-risk AI systems where the provider has applied harmonized standards (Article 40) in order to opt for one of the following procedures:

(a) The conformity assessment procedure based on internal control

(b) The conformity assessment procedure based on assessment of the quality management system and assessment of the technical documentation, with the involvement of a notified body

Procedure (a) is only an option where the high-risk AI system is fully compliant with the requirements set out in the AI Act. When compliance is only partial or harmonized standards do not as yet exist, providers are obliged to follow procedure (b). While option (a) could be deemed a kind of internal auditing (Mökander et al., 2022), under option (b), the notified body is a third-party body that performs conformity assessment activities, including testing, certification, and inspection, which are compliant with a set of requirements, notably regarding independence, competence, and absence of conflicts of interests. The notified body issues conformity assessment certificates, which should not exceed 5 years. Finally, in case of an infringement of the provisions of the AI Act, a complaint could be presented to the relevant market surveillance authority (i.e., a national authority).

Consequently, the AI Act adopts an approach to high-risk AI systems that comprises a combination of self-regulation, voluntary adherence to standards, and government oversight (Goodman & Trehu, 2022). Regarding the latter, DEW is forbidden, and administrative fines are prescribed for the "supply of incorrect, incomplete or misleading information to notified bodies and national competent authorities in reply to a request" (Article 71).

2. The economic perspective. From the economic perspective, the decision whether to provide an AI conformity assessment based on internal control or involving a notified body could essentially be a cost/benefit decision based on the various providers of conformity's relative costs, although not all AI auditing benefits and the costs could be estimated in these terms. The cost of obtaining assurance by using internal auditors could be far less relative to that of an external auditor, although the issue of the firm's reputation should also be considered when demanding AI assurance from large audit firms.

   Since to complying with the requirements mentioned in the AI Act, providers and users of AI systems might need to appoint new roles to their organizations (Mökander et al., 2022), Article 55 of the EU AI Act outlines that it is especially important to consider SME providers' and AI systems users' economic interests. This applies specifically when notified bodies charge conformity assessment fees, by reducing the fees in proportion to SMEs size, market size, and other relevant indicators. Auditing processes, for example, might require an entity to divert its limited resources from its innovation activities, which might impair new entrants' and smaller firms' ability to compete (Goodman & Trehu, 2022). Consequently, the size of the company being audited plays a significant role from the economic perspective. However, the good fit in this regard could reduce auditors' opportunities to provide their smaller clients with a substantial (and more profitable) assurance, thereby increasing these entities' auditwashing risk. Moreover, the conformity assessment team must either have adequate competencies to be allowed to audit AI, or they need to hire an AI technical specialist to complete the process, which increases the auditing fee.

3. The technical/procedural perspective. This perspective examines possible changes in AI auditing's procedures and practice. In the AI era, new skills and greater competency are critically important for auditors. Larger firms, such as E&Y, have developed algorithmic auditing capabilities (Roberts et al., 2023). In line with the social perspective (described later), auditors need to widen their focus to satisfy the growing stakeholder expectations. For example, keeping human and relational capital in mind, an audit's objective might be to confirm compliance with human rights standards' requirements in terms of fairness, non-discrimination, and data protection (human capital-related AI auditing) and to guarantee stakeholders that the system is fair, accurate, and privacy protected (relational capital-related AI auditing).

   Algorithmic auditing could potentially take different forms and approaches, ranging from an impact self-assessment to a rigorous review conducted by independent entities with access to the relevant data. However, the conformity assessment that Article 43 of the EU AI Act requires, especially when a notified body is involved, implies that AI auditing does not mean formal compliance. For example, according to Article 9 (§ 6), "[t]esting procedures may include testing in real world conditions," while Article 11 (§ 1) states that "(t)he technical documentation shall be drawn up in such a way to demonstrate that the high-risk AI system complies with the requirements set out in this chapter and provide national competent authorities and notified bodies with all the necessary information in a clear and comprehensive form to assess the compliance of the AI system with those requirements."

   Further, in dynamic processes such as AI, AI auditing is iterative and constantly renews itself. AI auditing should examine an AI system's full life cycle. In this regard, Article 9 (§2) of the EU AI Act states that "[t]he risk management system shall be understood as a continuous iterative process planned and run throughout the entire lifecycle of a high-risk AI system, requiring regular systematic updating" and (§ 7) that "[t]he testing of the high-risk AI systems shall be performed, as appropriate, at any point in time throughout the development process, and, in any event, prior to the placing on the market or the putting into service." Similarly, providers need to establish post-market monitoring plans (Article 61) to document and analyze high-risk AI systems' performance throughout their lifetimes.

4. The cultural perspective. A cultural perspective entails significant changes, like a highly developed and professionally qualified auditor profile—gained by means of a technical/procedural experience's direct outcome—and the strong education of those who are involved in the AI implementation. The support of scholars, experts, and practitioners is essential for promoting and disseminating

AI knowledge in order to solve auditing issues. A cultural approach would specifically allow practitioners and auditors to monitor AI developments and audit applications. Academics and scholars should continue investigating and communicating AI-related auditing issues in order to prevent DEW and auditwashing. Telkamp and Anderson (2022) suggested that AI systems' auditors with diverse moral foundations should be better able to discuss and identify ethical issues. The AI auditing process should be interdisciplinary and multi-staged, since it is undertaken internally for entities developing and deploying AI systems and externally for independent auditors. For example, the EU IA Act requires deployers of high-risk AI systems to better protect rights by being obliged to conduct a fundamental rights impact assessment prior to allowing an AI system to be used.

Furthermore, auditing practice reveals a number of opportunities that auditors could use to encourage additional auditing and assurance services by fostering the AI Act requirements' voluntary application in those cases not subject to mandatory conformity assessments. Providers of non-high-risk AI systems could therefore prove their adherence to voluntary standards, such as codes of conduct (Article 69), that lie beyond existing regulations (Mökander et al., 2022). This demand for voluntary ethics-based auditing would allow organizations to validate their claims about their AI systems and could play a constructive role in their public relations (Mökander & Floridi, 2021). Under the influence of professional auditing networks, AI auditing practices would therefore diffuse rapidly across audit firms, especially if they are assigned relevant economic opportunities.

5. The social perspective. An algorithm audit should have the potential to provide meaningful public accountability as a potential way of providing positive social change (Bandy, 2021). Providing AI assurance is aimed at improving trust in AI and, ultimately, at supporting these systems' adoption (Freeman et al., 2022). Algorithmic audits are therefore deemed as a way to increase accountability and improve AI systems' governance through a legitimacy- and consensus-building strategy (Goodman & Trehu, 2022) that providers or end users of AI systems use to mitigate reputational risks (Mökander et al., 2022).

   Since AI auditing aims to ensure that stakeholders (e.g., regulators, the public, customers, investors, and civil rights groups) and society as a whole are protected against harm, stakeholder involvement is a necessary step to identify potential harm. From a social perspective, AI auditing should therefore include the various public groups whose interests and rights it is supposed to protect (Selinger et al., 2023), but which are often divergent.

   However, the public is not informed of how providers ensure compliance with the AI Act. A detailed description of auditing processes could also entail the proprietary costs and the loss of competitive advantages and could even reveal confidential information related to consumers. Consequently, different audit reports containing different levels of information and analyses should be produced, taking the different stakeholders' roles and responsibilities into consideration (Selinger et al., 2023).

Moreover, auditors' credibility will depend on their professionalism (i.e., whether they agree with the above technical and cultural perspectives), their degrees of access to data, and their independence (Goodman & Trehu, 2022).

Notwithstanding the EU's efforts with the release of the AI Act, which is aimed at combining ex ante conformity assessments with post-market monitoring, it is a good and robust way of reducing DEW, although the risk of adversarial behavior during conformity assessments remains. DEW, auditwashing, and symbolic conformity assessment risks might persist, due to the AI Act's ambitious goals, abstract requirements, broad AI definition, and its vague and imprecise language (Mökander et al., 2022).

2.8 Conclusions

This research's goal was to observe digital ethicswashing practices by investigating the reliability of disclosures specifically related to AI use's social aspects and to provide tools for detecting digital ethicswashing strategies.

The existing literature highlights gaps in the analysis of AI reporting's ethical use. Specifically, research that addresses AI's social profile is still scarce. We therefore endeavored to fill this gap by considering digitalization's ethical aspects when proxied by ESG topics' social dimension. We did so by developing an exploratory analysis and by assuming that a greater level of reporting unreliability tends to highlight a misleading approach's greater intensity and, therefore, that of digital ethicswashing strategies.

Our results show that firms realize DEW by mostly using vague and misleading claims associated with jargon and irrelevant claims. Low-frequency exaggerations and inaccurate claims do not necessarily indicate that they are irrelevant but rather that detecting certain kinds of claims is more difficult. The high frequency of vague and misleading claims specifically allows us identify LU cases. This evidence could mean that this kind of claim is easiest for firms to make and for researchers to detect.

The data we collected and organized to reveal DEW strategies' peculiarities could be finalized to create a dashboard that provides a systematic DEW vision. The above is our first contribution in this regard. This tool is a useful one for helping insiders and auditors. From the latter perspective, the dashboard allows DEW behavior to emerge, allowing third-party industry experts to mitigate audit companies' reporting and reduce public skepticism about the disclosed AI contents (Bernini et al., 2024). In the last section, we proposed approaches for AI's external auditing. Our second contribution therefore indicates the need for AI auditing tools to minimize DEW practices.

Notwithstanding the EU's efforts regarding the release of the AI Act (European Commission, 2019) and that of the recent Resolution of the European Parliament regarding the rules on AI (European Parliament, 2024), the risk of adversarial behavior during conformity assessments remains, as does the auditwashing risk and the symbolic conformity assessment one (Mökander et al., 2022). Consequently, the need to prevent and reduce DEW also suggests further regulatory pushes that should be derived from the institutional context and should specifically be focused on AI disclosure and on reporting's audit process.

Among this research's possible limitations, we highlight the results' low variability, which suggests the need to review and broaden the sample. In turn, possible future development emerged from this limitation. We specifically highlighted the possibility of conducting multiple longitudinal case studies observed over a longer period, which could identify changes related to companies' approaches toward AI's social aspect and resulting from new regulations.

Appendix

References

Adams, C. A. (2004). The ethical, social and environmental reporting-performance portrayal gap. *Accounting, Auditing Accountability Journal, 17*(5), 731–757.

Adams, C. A., & Abhayawansa, S. (2022). Connecting the COVID-19 pandemic, environmental, social and governance (ESG) investing and calls for 'harmonisation' of sustainability reporting. *Critical Perspective in Accounting, 82.*

Ali, B. J., & Anwar, G. (2021). Intellectual capital: A modern model to measure the value creation in a business. *International Journal of Engineering, Business and Management, 5*(2), 31–43.

Ballestar, M. T., García-Lazaro, A., Sainz, J., & Sanz, I. (2022). Why is your company not robotic? The technology and human capital needed by firms to become robotic. *Journal of Business Research, 142*, 328–343.

Bandy, J. (2021). Problematic machine behavior: A systematic literature review of algorithm audits. *Proceedings of the ACM on Human-Computer Interaction, 5*(CSCW1), 1–34.

Beattie, V., & Thomson, S. J. (2007). Lifting the lid on the use of content analysis to investigate intellectual capital disclosures. *Accounting Forum, 31*(2), 129–163.

Beattie, V., McInnes, W., & Fearnley, S. (2004). A methodology for analysing and evaluating narratives in annual reports: A comprehensive descriptive profile and metrics for disclosure quality attributes. *Accounting Forum, 28*(3), 205–236.

Bennedsen, M., & Nielsen, K. M. (2010). Incentive and entrenchment effects in European ownership. *Journal of Banking and Finance, 34*(9), 2212–2229.

Bernini, F., & La Rosa, F. (2024). Research in the greenwashing field: Concepts, theories, and potential impacts on economic and social value. *Journal of Management and Governance, 28*, 405–444.

Bernini, F., Ferretti, P., & Angelini, A. (2022). The digitalization-reputation link: A multiple case-study on Italian banking groups. *Meditari Accountancy Research, 30*(4), 1210–1240.

Bernini, F., Giuliani, M., & La Rosa, F. (2023). Measuring greenwashing: A systematic methodological literature review. *Business Ethics, the Environment and Responsibility, 00*, 1–19.

Bernini, F., Ferretti, P., Gonnella, C., & La Rosa, F. (2024). Measuring machinewashing under the corporate digital responsibility theory: A proposal for a methodological path. *Business Ethics, the Environment and Responsibility.*

Berrone, P., Fosfuri, A., & Gelabert, L. (2017). Does greenwashing pay of? Understanding the relationship between environmental actions and environmental legitimacy. *Journal of Business Ethics, 144*(2), 363–379.

Bonsón, E., & Bednárová, M. (2022). Artificial intelligence disclosures in sustainability reports: Towards an artificial intelligence reporting framework. In V. Kumar, J. Leng, V. Akberdina, &

E. Kuzmin (Eds.), *Digital Transformation in Industry* (Lecture Notes in Information Systems and Organisation) (Vol. 54). Springer.

Bonsón, E., Alejo, V., & Lavorato, D. (2021a). *Artificial intelligence disclosure in the annual reports of Spanish IBEX-35 companies (2018–2019) (b).*

Bonsón, E., Lavorato, D., Lamboglia, R., & Mancini, D. (2021b). Artificial intelligence activities and ethical approaches in leading listed companies in the European Union. *International Journal of Accounting Information Systems, 43*(a).

Bostrom, N., & Yudkowsky, E. (2014). The ethics of artificial intelligence. *The Cambridge handbook of artificial intelligence* (pp. 316–334). doi:https://doi.org/10.1017/Cbo9781139046855.

Brusseau, J. (2022). AI human impact: Toward a model for ethical investing in AI-intensive companies. *Journal of Sustainable Finance and Investment*, 1–28.

Cabrita, M. D. R. M. F., Ribeiro da Silva, M. L., Gomes Rodrigues, A. M., & Muñoz Dueñas, M. D. P. (2017). Competitiveness and disclosure of intellectual capital: An empirical research in Portuguese banks. *Journal of Intellectual Capital, 18*(3), 486–505.

Camilleri, M. A. (2023). Artificial intelligence governance: Ethical considerations and implications for social responsibility. *Expert Systems.*

Campbell, D., Ridhuan, M., & Rahman, A. (2010). A longitudinal examination of intellectual capital reporting in Marks & Spencer annual reports, 1978–2008. *The British Accounting Review, 42*(1), 56–70.

Cho, C., Fabrizi, M., Pilonato, S., & Ricceri, F. (2022). Not all bad news is harmful to a good reputation: Evidence from the most visible companies in the US. *Journal of Management and Governance.*

Clarkson, P., Li, Y., Richardson, G., & Vasvari, F. (2008). Revisiting the relation between environmental performance and environmental disclosure: An empirical analysis. *Accounting Organizations and Society, 33*(4–5), 303–327.

Deegan, C., & Unerman, J. (2011). Unregulated corporate reporting decisions: Considerations of systems-oriented theories. In *Financial accounting theory* (2nd European ed.). McGraw-Hill.

Deegan, C., Rankin, M., & Tobin, J. (2002). An examination of the corporate social and environmental disclosures of BHP from 1983–1997: A test of Legitimacy Theory. *Accounting, Auditing and Accountability Journal, 15*(3), 312–343.

Dempretic, S., Klein, C., & Zwergel, B. (2020). The influence of firm size on the ESG score: Corporate sustainability ratings under review. *Journal of Business Ethics, 167*(2), 333–360.

Easterby-Smith, M., Jaspersen, L. J., Thorpe, R., & Valizade, D. (2021). *Management and business research.* Sage.

Elliott, K., Price, R., Shaw, P., Spiliotopoulos, T., Ng, M., Coopamootoo, K., & van Moorsel, A. (2021). Towards an equitable digital society: Artificial intelligence (AI) and corporate digital responsibility (CDR). *Society, 58*(3), 179–188.

EU AI Act. (2022). European Parliament legislative resolution of 13 March 2024 on the proposal for a regulation of the European Parliament and of the Council on laying down harmonised rules on Artificial Intelligence (Artificial Intelligence Act) and amending certain Union Legislative Acts.

European Commission. (2019). *Ethics guidelines for trustworthy AI.* https://ec.europa.eu/digital-single-market/en/news/ethics-guidelines-trustworthy-ai/

European Parliament legislative resolution of 13 March 2024 on the proposal for a regulation of the European Parliament and of the Council on laying down harmonised rules on Artificial Intelligence (Artificial Intelligence Act) and amending certain Union Legislative Acts.

Felicetti, A. M., Corvello, V., & Ammirato, S. (2024). Digital innovation in entrepreneurial firms: A systematic literature review. *Review of Managerial Science, 18*, 315–362.

Freeman, R. E. (1994). The politics of stakeholder theory: Some future directions. *Business Ethics Quarterly, 4*(4), 409–421.

Freeman, L., Batarseh, F. A., Kuhn, D. R., Raunak, M. S., & Kacker, R. N. (2022). The path to a consensus on artificial intelligence assurance. *Computer*, 55(3), 82–86.

Ghitti, M., Gianfrate, G., & Palma, L. (2023). The agency of greenwashing. *Journal of Management and Governance*, 1–37.

Goddard, K., Roudsari, A., & Wyatt, J. C. (2012). Automation bias: A systematic review of frequency, effect mediators, and mitigators. *Journal of the American Medical Informatics Association, 19*(1), 121–127.
Goodman, E. P., & Trehu, J. (2022). Algorithmic auditing: Chasing AI accountability. *Santa Clara High Technology Law Journal, 39*, 289.
Guix, M., Ollé, C., & Font, X. (2022). Trustworthy or misleading communication of voluntary carbon offsets in the aviation industry. *Tourism Management, 88*, 104430.
Gunz, S., & Thorne, L. (2020). Thematic symposium: The impact of technology on ethics, professionalism and judgement in accounting. *Journal of Business Ethics, 167*, 153–155.
Haenlein, M., & Kaplan, A. (2020). Artificial intelligence and robotics: Shaking up the business world and society at large. *Journal of Business Research, 124*, 405–407.
Haenlein, M., Huang, M. H., & Kaplan, A. (2022). Guest editorial: Business ethics in the era of artificial intelligence. *Journal of Business Ethics*, 1–3.
Hagendorff, T. (2020). The ethics of AI ethics: An evaluation of guidelines. *Minds and Machines, 30*, 99–120.
Hahn, R., & Lülfs, R. (2014). Legitimizing negative aspects in GRI-oriented sustainability reporting: A qualitative analysis of corporate disclosure strategies. *Journal of Business Ethics, 123*(3), 401–420.
Herden, C. J., Alliu, E., Cakici, A., Cormier, T., Deguelle, C., Gambhir, S., et al. (2021). Corporate digital responsibility. *Sustainability Management Forum| NachhaltigkeitsManagementForum, 29*(1), 13–29.
Herse, S., Vitale, J., Tonkin, M., Ebrahimian, D., Ojha, S., Johnston, B., Judge, W., & Williams, MA (2018). Do you trust me, blindly? Factors influencing trust towards a robot recommender system. *2018 27th IEEE international symposium on robot and human interactive communication (RO-MAN)*, Nanjing (pp. 7–14).
Hossnofsky, V., & Junge, S. (2019). Does the market reward digitalization efforts? Evidence from securities analysts' investment recommendations. *Journal of Business Economics, 89*(8/9), 965–994.
Humphreys, A., & Jen-Hui Wang, R. (2018). Automated text analysis for consumer research. *Journal of Consumer Research, 44*(6), 1274–1306.
Jensen, M. C., & Meckling, W. H. (1976). Theory of the firm: Managerial behavior, agency costs and ownership structure. *Journal of Financial Economics, 3*(4), 305–360.
Kartajaya, H., Setiawan, I., & Kotler, P. (2021). *Marketing 5.0: Technology for humanity*. Wiley.
Khan, H. Z., Bose, S., Mollik, A. T., & Harun, H. (2021). "Green washing" or "authentic effort"? An empirical investigation of the quality of sustainability reporting by banks. *Accounting, Auditing and Accountability Journal, 34*(2), 338–369.
Koshiyama, A., Kazim, E., Treleaven, P. Rai, P., Szpruch, L., Pavey, G., Ahamat, G., Leutner, F., Goebel, R., & Knight, A. (2021). *Towards algorithm auditing: A survey on managing legal, ethical and technological risks of AI, ML and associated algorithms, working paper.*
Krippendorff, K. (1980). Validity in content analysis. In E. Mochmann (Ed.), *Computerstrategien für die kommunikationsanalyse* (pp. 69–112). Campus. http://repository.upenn.edu/asc_papers/291
Kumar, P., & Firoz, M. (2019). Accounting for certified emission reductions (CERs) in India: An analysis of the disclosure and reporting practices within the financial statements. *Meditari Accountancy Research, 28*(2), 365–389.
La Rosa, F., & Caserio, C. (2013). Are auditors interested in XBRL? A qualitative survey of big auditing firms in Italy. In *Accounting information systems for decision making* (pp. 13–45).
Laufer, W. S. (2003). Social accountability and corporate greenwashing. *Journal of Business Ethics, 43*(3), 253–261.
Li, W., Li, W., Seppänen, V., & Koivumäki, T. (2023). Effects of greenwashing on financial performance: Moderation through local environmental regulation and media coverage. *Business Strategy and the Environment, 32*(1), 820–841.

Mahoney, L. S., Thorne, L., Cecil, L., & LaGore, W. (2013). A research note on standalone corporate social responsibility reports: Signaling or greenwashing? *Critical Perspectives on Accounting, 24*, 350–359.

Mention, A. L. (2011). Exploring voluntary reporting of intellectual capital in the banking sector. *Journal of Management Control, 22*(3), 279–309.

Meske, C., Bunde, E., Schneider, J., & Gersch, M. (2022). Explainable artificial intelligence: Objectives, stakeholders, and future research opportunities. *Information Systems Management, 39*(1), 53–63.

Michelon, G., & Parbonetti, A. (2012). The effect of corporate governance on sustainability disclosure. *Journal of Management and Governance, 16*(3), 477–450.

Minkkinen, M., Niukkanen, A., & Mäntymäki, M. (2024). What about investors? ESG analyses as tools for ethics-based AI auditing. *AI & Society, 39*(1), 329–343.

Mökander, J., & Floridi, L. (2021). Ethics-based auditing to develop trustworthy AI. *Minds Mach, 31*, 323–327.

Mökander, J., Axente, M., Casolari, F., & Floridi, L. (2022). Conformity assessments and post-market monitoring: A guide to the role of auditing in the proposed European AI regulation. *Minds and Machines, 32*(2), 241–268.

Morley, J., Elhalal, A., Garcia, F., Kinsey, L., Mökander, J., & Floridi, L. (2021). Ethics as a service: A pragmatic operationalisation of AI ethics. *Minds and Machines, 31*(2), 239–256.

Munoko, I., Brown-Liburd, H. L., & Vasarhelyi, M. (2020). The ethical implications of using artificial intelligence in auditing. *Journal of Business Ethics, 167*, 209–234.

Okazaki, S., Plangger, K., Roulet, T., & Menéndez, H. D. (2020). Assessing stakeholder network engagement. *European Journal of Marketing, 55*(5), 1359–1384.

Oliver, C. (1991). Strategic responses to institutional processes. *Academy of Management Review, 16*(1), 145–179.

Pierli, G., Murmura, F., & Bravi, L. (2023). *Digital transformation and sustainability. A systematic literature review*.

Rahwan, I. (2018). Society-in-the-loop: Programming the algorithmic social contract. *Ethics and Information Technology, 20*(1), 5–14.

Refinitiv. (2022). *Environmental, social and governance scores from Refinitiv*. https://www.refinitiv.com/content/dam/marketing/en_us/documents/methodology/refinitiv-esg-scores-methodology.pdf

Roberts, H., Babuta, A., Morley, J., Thomas, C., Taddeo, M., & Floridi, L. (2023). Artificial intelligence regulation in the United Kingdom: A path to good governance and global leadership? *Internet Policy Review, 12*(2), 1–31.

Sætra, H. S. (2022). The AI ESG protocol: Evaluating and disclosing the environment, social, and governance implications of artificial intelligence capabilities, assets, and activities. *Sustainable Development, 31*(2), 1027–1037.

Sætra, H. S. (2023). The AI ESG protocol: Evaluating and disclosing the environment, social, and governance implications of artificial intelligence capabilities, assets, and activities. *Sustainable Development, 31*, 1027–1037.

Schneider, J., Handali, J., Vlachos, M., & Meske, C. (2020). Deceptive AI explanations: Creation and detection. *arxiv, 2001*, 07641.

Schultz, M. D., & Seele, P. (2023). Towards AI ethics' institutionalization: Knowledge bridges from business ethics to advance organizational AI ethics. *AI and Ethics, 3*, 99–111.

Schultz, M. D., Conti, L. G., & Seele, P. (2023). *Corporate legitimacy via digital ethicswashing? A systematic review on misleading AI communication*. Academy of Management.

Schultz, M. D., Conti, L. G., & Seele, P. (2024). *Digital ethicswashing: A systematic review and a process-perception-outcome framework*. AI Ethics.

Seele, P., & Gatti, L. (2017). Greenwashing revisited: In search of a typology and accusation-based definition incorporating legitimacy strategies. *Business Strategy and the Environment, 26*(2), 239–252.

Seele, P., & Schultz, M. D. (2022). From greenwashing to machinewashing: A model and future directions derived from reasoning by analogy. *Journal of Business Ethics, 178*, 1063–1089.

Selinger, E., Leong, B., & Cahn, A. (2023). AI audits: Who, when, how...or even if? (September 11, 2023). In *Collaborative intelligence: How humans and AI are transforming our world*. MIT Press (Forthcoming). Available at SSRN: https://ssrn.com/abstract=4568208

Shen, Y., & Zhang, X. (2024). The impact of artificial intelligence on employment: The role of virtual agglomeration. *Humanities and Social Sciences Communications, 11*, 122.

Si, S., Hall, J., Suddaby, R., Ahlstrom, D., & Wei, J. (2023). Technology, entrepreneurship, innovation and social change in digital economics. *Technovation, 119*.

Siani, G. (2022). *Rischi e Innovazione: l'approccio della Vigilanza*. Associazione Bancaria ItalianaConvegno "Supervision, Risks & Profitability". Milano, 21 giugno 2022.

Suchman, M. C. (1995). Managing legitimacy: Strategic and institutional approaches. *Academy of Management Review, 20*, 571–610.

Telkamp, J. B., & Anderson, M. H. (2022). The implications of diverse human moral foundations for assessing the ethicality of Artificial Intelligence. *Journal of Business Ethics, 178*(4), 961–976.

Vakkuri, V., & Abrahamsson, P. (2018). The key concept of ethics of artificial intelligence. A keywords based systematic mapping study. In *2018 IEEE international conference on engineering, technology and innovation (ICE/ITMC)* (pp. 1–6).

Van Maanen, G. (2022). *AI ethics, ethics washing, and the need to politicize data ethics*. Digital Society.

Venuesa, R., Azizpour, H., Leite, I., Balaam, M., Dignum, V., Domisch, S., Tegmark, M., & Nerini, F. F. (2020). The role of artificial intelligence in achieving the sustainable development goals. *Nature Communications, 11*(1), 1–10.

Verhoef, P. C., Broekhuizen, T., Bart, Y., Bhattacharya, A., Dong, J. Q., Fabian, N., & Haenlein, M. (2021). Digital transformation: A multidisciplinary reflection and research agenda. *Journal of Business Research, 122*, 889–901.

Viglia, G., Pera, R., & Bigné, E. (2018). The determinants of stakeholder engagement in digital platforms. *Journal of Business Research, 89*, 404–410.

Wade, M. (2020). *Corporate responsibility in the digital era*. https://sloanreview.mit.edu.

Walker, K., & Wan, F. (2012). The harm of symbolic actions and green-washing: Corporate actions and communications on environmental performance and their financial implications. *Journal of Business Ethics, 109*, 227–242.

Wang, S., & Esperança, J. P. (2023). Can digital transformation improve market and ESG performance? Evidence from Chinese SMEs. *Journal of Cleaner Production, 419*(20).

Weber, R.P. (1985). Basic Content Analysis, Sage Wimmer, New Delhi.

Wright, S. A., & Schultz, A. E. (2018). The rising tide of artificial intelligence and business automation: Developing an ethical framework. *Business Horizons, 61*(6), 823–832.

Xiao, L., Shen, X. L., Cheng, X., Mou, J., & Zarifis, A. (2020). Call for papers - The dark sides of AI. *Electronic Markets*. February 2022, *32*(1), 1–5.

Xu, X., Lu, Y., Vogel-Heuser, B., & Wang, L. (2021). Industry 4.0 and industry 5.0—inception, conception and perception. *Journal of Manufacturing Systems, 61*, 530–535.

Zharfpeykan, R. (2021). Representative account or greenwashing? Voluntary sustainability reports in Australia's mining/metals and financial services industries. *Business Strategy and the Environment, 30*, 2209–2223.

Chapter 3
Barriers and Drivers for the Integration of ESG into Risk Management and Performance Measurement Systems: A Field Study in the Italian Context

Lorenzo Leto, Diletta Vito, and Francesca Bernini

3.1 Introduction[1]

The importance of environmental, social, and governance (ESG) factors in stakeholders' assessment of company success is rising, primarily due to their impact on both financial metrics (e.g., risk assessment and financial performance) and non-financial aspects (e.g., corporate reputation and stakeholder legitimacy) (Lokuwaduge & Heenetigala, 2017). As a result, more companies are disclosing ESG information, driven by growing investor demand and evolving non-financial disclosure regulations (Cordazzo et al., 2020; Serafeim & Yoon, 2022).

However, prior research suggests that merely disclosing ESG information does not provide stakeholders with valuable insights into a company's ESG behavior (Cordazzo et al., 2020). Scholars and practitioners argue that investors are more interested in understanding how companies integrate ESG factors into their corporate practices than in relying solely on reports lacking financial materiality, consistency, and reliability (Gebhardt et al., 2023; McKinsey & Company, 2019). Consequently, integrating ESG into management systems is recognized as an effective way to create value for both companies and stakeholders (Ronalter et al., 2023). However, recent studies primarily focus on the benefits of such integration (Ronalter

[1] All the authors contributed to the design and implementation of the research, as well as the analysis of the results. Dr. Lorenzo Leto and Dr. Diletta Vito also contributed to the writing of the manuscript. Specifically, Dr. Lorenzo Leto wrote Sects. 3.2.2, 3.3, 3.4, and 3.5, and Dr. Diletta Vito wrote Sects. 3.1, 3.2.1, and 3.6.

L. Leto (✉) · D. Vito · F. Bernini
Department of Economics and Management, University of Pisa, Pisa, Italy
e-mail: lorenzo.leto@pologistica.unipi.it; diletta.vito@ec.unipi.it; francesca.bernini@unipi.it

F. Bernini (ed.), *Creating Value Through Sustainability*, SIDREA Series in Accounting and Business Administration,
https://doi.org/10.1007/978-3-031-74292-7_3

et al., 2023) and do not provide evidence of the empirical conduct of these practices. This study advances the research by investigating the process of integrating ESG factors into risk management (RM) and performance management systems (PMS) through a management accounting change framework.

There are several reasons for this research interest. Firstly, the literature generally argues that PMS should align with the company's adopted strategy and changes in the external environment (Bourne, 2005), as this facilitates the achievement of corporate objectives (Speziale & Klovienė, 2014). Previous studies have proposed PMS that effectively monitor environmental, social, and economic performance measures simultaneously (Searcy, 2012) and have highlighted how PMS can enhance sustainability-related performance management (Asiaei et al., 2021). However, evidence on the process of integrating ESG factors into PMS remains scarce. Exploring how companies execute this integration could help identify facilitators and obstacles, ensuring meaningful non-financial disclosure for stakeholders and contributing positively to the firm's sustainable growth and value.

Secondly, the literature indicates that stakeholders, especially institutional investors, view the integration of ESG risks into traditional risk management (RM) systems as crucial (Rau & Yu, 2023). However, scholars argue that current RM practices are not adequately addressing ESG challenges (Chairani & Siregar, 2021), mainly due to the difficulty in quantifying ESG risks monetarily and their perceived lower priority compared with other risks. This may result in diminished attention and resource allocation for effective ESG–RM integration. Examining how companies navigate this process can deepen our understanding of the internal or external factors that facilitate or hinder its success and how companies address these challenges.

The chapter is structured as follows: Sect. 3.2 analyzes recent literature on the integration of ESG considerations into company practices and presents the main proposals related to management accounting change, focusing on frameworks for analyzing change processes; Sect. 3.3 outlines the methodology employed; Sect. 3.4 presents the study's results; Sect. 3.5 discusses the findings; Sect. 3.6 concludes the discussion.

3.2 Literature Review

3.2.1 ESG, Risk Management, and Performance Measurement Systems

In recent years, increased scrutiny of corporate ESG performance by various stakeholders (Sheehan et al., 2023) has prompted the implementation of new requirements by national and supranational bodies. In the European context, the Corporate Sustainability Reporting Directive (CSRD), which entered into force at the beginning of 2023, has modernized and strengthened the rules concerning the social and environmental information that companies have to report. The CSRD ensures that investors and other stakeholders have access to the information they need to assess not only the impacts of companies on people and the environment but also financial risks and opportunities related to sustainability issues. These rules apply on four different dates, depending on the status of the undertaking.[2]

Consequently, companies must deal with changes in social values and regulatory frameworks that mandate proactive actions (Dhanesh, 2020).

In this context, an emerging body of literature is focusing on how companies respond to the new ESG requirements, primarily by examining subtopics such as disclosure (Tsang et al., 2023) and organizational and/or accounting changes (Leto & Vito, 2024).

Regarding ESG disclosure, most research focuses on exploring the motivations and consequences associated with both voluntary and mandated ESG information disclosure. In this regard, Chung et al. (2023) highlight two major theories: the regulatory theory, which applies when ESG disclosure is mandatory and aims to prevent accounting failures and safeguard investors (von Alberti-Alhtaybat et al., 2012), and the manager incentives theory, typically associated with voluntary ESG disclosure, where managers disclose ESG information to reduce information asymmetry between their company and stakeholders and attract external capital. Both theories are based on a cost–benefit analysis, weighing the costs of disclosing information against the potential benefits that such disclosure might generate (Cooke, 1992; Scott, 2015). With specific reference to voluntary disclosure, managers are willing to disclose ESG information when the perceived benefits outweigh the total costs of disclosure (Wang et al., 2023). The benefits can be seen as positive externalities that emerge from the relationship between a company and various stakeholders—such as shareholders, managers, employees, and society at large (Tsang et al., 2023)—and contribute to improved financial performance (Radhakrishnan et al., 2018) and greater firm value (Yu et al., 2018). Broadening the scope to non-financial disclosure, other theories have been advanced by researchers, particularly in the context of voluntary disclosure (Tsang et al., 2023). Legitimacy theory (Busco et al., 2019; Cho & Patten, 2007) suggests that non-financial disclosures can legitimize companies, especially if they are underperforming, by compensating for their poor performance. Social movement theory (Islam & Van Staden, 2018) views non-financial disclosure as an outcome of social pressures that compel firms to conform to disclosure practices. Agency theory (Ness & Mirza, 1991) considers non-financial disclosure through the lens of the self-interest of managers who may use ESG to manipulate their firms' reputations by presenting themselves as better ESG performers than they are. The resource-based view (Qiu et al., 2016) connects non-financial disclosure to competitive advantage by suggesting it can improve reputation. The theory of self-regulation (Zhang et al., 2021) interprets non-financial

[2] The CSRD mandates that companies currently preparing non-financial statements under the Non-Financial Reporting Directive (Directive 2014/95/EU) for the financial year 2024 must publish their first report under the new rules in 2025. Other large companies will have to publish their first report in 2026, referring to the financial year 2025. Listed SMEs and non-EU companies listed on EU markets will publish their first report in 2027 for the financial year 2026, with a possible derogation to opt out until 2028. Finally, non-EU companies that generate over EUR 150 million on the EU market must publish their first report in 2029, referring to the financial year 2028.

disclosure as an attempt to avoid stringent future governmental disclosure regulations. Institutional theory considers non-financial disclosure as a way to optimize benefits within a specific environmental context (de Villiers & Alexander, 2014). Finally, the affect-as-information theory (Elliott et al., 2014; Guiral et al., 2020) suggests that non-financial disclosure may influence investor decision-making. This wide range of theories reflects a multifaceted understanding of the motivations and implications behind companies' decisions to disclose non-financial information and highlights the maturity of non-financial disclosure literature.

A second emerging strand of literature examines how companies adapt to new ESG requirements through organizational and/or accounting changes. A study by Vito et al. (2024) on Italian companies engaging in voluntary ESG disclosure reveals organizational adjustments such as establishing new ESG units or integrating specialized personnel. In terms of accounting changes, recent studies underscore the need to adapt traditional management control systems in order to incorporate ESG considerations (Fiandrino & Tonelli, 2021; Leto & Vito, 2024) or, more broadly, social and environmental aspects (Durden, 2008).

Management control systems are sets of procedures aimed at achieving stakeholder satisfaction regarding specific demands (Castellano, 2011). They are implemented to systematically handle stakeholders' needs in both internal and external organizational contexts (Rebelo et al., 2016) and are designed for the continuous improvement of operations and procedures (Robson et al., 2007). According to Gond et al. (2012), traditional management control systems are oriented toward achieving organizations' business and economic goals, which may limit their capacity to address environmental and social issues, along with their inter-relationships with financial issues. However, as companies today are key contributors to socially responsible behavior, the way managers use a management control system can be instrumental in transforming company practices to align with ESG requirements (Gond et al., 2012). Consequently, management control systems that encompass sustainability and environmental aspects have emerged to support organizational non-financial objectives (Gond et al., 2012; Lueg & Radlach, 2016; Johnstone, 2019). These systems are management accounting tools that connect organizational strategy with operations in a specific context by providing information and direction, as well as monitoring and motivating firms to continually develop sustainable practices and procedures for enhanced future sustainability performance (Johnstone, 2019).

A lot of literature analyzes the benefits associated with integrating ESG factors into management control systems. Evidence suggests that integrating ESG factors into these systems has reduced emissions (e.g., Russo, 2009), improved control of environmental accidents (e.g., Bravi et al., 2020), facilitated environmental management practices (e.g., Wong et al., 2020), enhanced staff motivation (e.g., Abad et al., 2014), fostered better partnerships with stakeholders (e.g., Rebelo et al., 2014), and improved organizational culture (e.g., Simon et al., 2012).

In the realm of management control systems, RM and PMS are crucial parts (Allegrini & D'Onza, 2011).

RM involves the decisions, policies, procedures, and tools used by corporate actors to identify, assess, and manage organizational risks (D'Onza, 2008). Its primary goal is to preserve corporate value, thereby supporting sustainable development and maintaining competitiveness (Hopkin, 2018). RM should encompass various risks, including those related to ESG factors. However, current RM systems, like enterprise risk management (ERM), often fail to address ESG risks due to their non-monetary nature and unpredictability. To bridge this gap, some authors propose sustainability risk management (SRM) as an evolved form of ERM that incorporates ESG aspects (Abdul Aziz et al., 2016). Nevertheless, evidence on the process of introducing ESG risk into RM systems is still limited.

PMS has also been influenced by the evolving social value and regulatory landscape related to ESG aspects. Designed to detect, monitor, and assess a company's performance, PMS has adapted to meet various information needs. Since the early 2000s, scholars have proposed changes in PMS to enable more effective monitoring of ESG performance alongside economic performance, reflecting the increasing global focus on sustainability issues (Searcy, 2012). One notable example is the sustainability balanced scorecard (SBSC), which evolved from the well-known balanced scorecard (BSC) to incorporate and measure ESG factors (Kaplan & Norton, 1996; Figge et al., 2002). Scholars emphasize the suitability of SBSC for identifying indicators to measure ESG factors and highlight how these tools can enhance sustainable growth and firm value by improving performance management (Asiaei et al., 2021; Wijethilake et al., 2018). However, also in this case, there are limited studies examining how companies adjust these systems with an ESG orientation, as much of the research focuses on proposing theoretical alternative systems to measure sustainability aspects (e.g., Searcy, 2012). In this regard, the literature recognizes that understanding whether companies integrate the ESG aspect into their management control systems—by designing new control systems or retooling existing management controls (Johnstone, 2019; Ghosh et al., 2019)—deepens knowledge on the implementation and effectiveness of ESG practices within organizations. Empirical evidence of this issue remains limited.

3.2.2 Management Accounting Change Frameworks

Research in the field of management accounting change (MAC) often involves developing frameworks to examine and interpret the process of organizational change (e.g., Brignall & Modell, 2000; Burns & Scapens, 2000; Arroyo, 2012; Alsharari et al., 2015) and identifying and analyzing the factors influencing its realization (e.g., Kasurinen, 2002; Giannetti et al., 2021; Pigatto et al., 2023; Alsharari, 2024).

Scholars in this area have repeatedly highlighted the complexity of studying change-related phenomena and have not yet reached a consensus on the precise nature of organizational and management accounting change (Burns & Vaivio, 2001; Macchia, 2019). This is because it is difficult to precisely define the boundaries of this phenomenon: it can entail changes in a firm's management control, accounting systems, and their use, but it can also include shifts in organizational culture and operational routines (Busco et al., 2007). In addition, in terms of the management accounting systems considered, MAC studies have focused on both advanced performance measurement and management tools (Vaivio, 1999; Franco-Santos et al., 2012), such as the balanced scorecard, and more traditional systems, such as budgeting and activity-based costing (Argyris & Kaplan, 1994). More recently, MAC studies have also examined the implementation of management accounting systems for measuring and managing sustainability aspects (Riccaboni & Leone, 2010; Arroyo, 2012; Järvenpää & Länsiluoto, 2016).

In the field of MAC, there is considerable diversity in the approaches and theories used to analyze the process of change, although some have been more widely adopted than others. A significant body of research in this area relies on the application of sociological theories (Alsharari et al., 2015; Alsharari, 2019). This is largely due to the widespread adoption of certain theoretical frameworks such as those proposed by Burns and Scapens (2000) and Brignall and Modell (2000), which are grounded in institutional and neo-institutional theories (e.g., Veblen, 1898, 1919; DiMaggio & Powell, 1983; DiMaggio, 1988). These frameworks have laid the groundwork for many subsequent qualitative studies aimed at explaining the dynamics related to the MAC process (Siti-Nabiha & Scapens, 2005; Arroyo, 2012; Macchia, 2019). Among the other theories that still belong to the field of sociology but can serve as alternatives to institutional theory for the analysis of MAC processes, Giddens's (1984) structuration theory is particularly significant (Makrygiannakis & Jack, 2016). Structuration theory has been occasionally integrated with institutional theories to analyze change phenomena (Dillard et al., 2004; Hassan, 2005; Alsharari & Abougamos, 2017), but it has also been used several times as an independent analytical framework (Englund & Gerdin, 2008; Coad et al., 2016).

Analyses based on sociological theories have often focused on the role of external factors and forces, such as pressure from governments and regulators (Alsharari et al., 2015), the influence of a parent company over its subsidiaries (Lukka, 2007), or the impact of the diffusion of certain tools among organizations operating in the same context (Jensen & Berg, 2012). However, there is also a significant amount of research that, despite the use of sociological theories, has mostly focused on the internal dynamics of organizations. This includes elements such as group interaction and power distribution, which can shape the process of change and the adoption of new management accounting tools and practices (Burns & Scapens, 2000; Dillard et al., 2004; Carlucci et al., 2015).

Concerning MAC frameworks based on institutional theories, the one by Burns and Scapens (2000) remains one of the most cited works. Their framework, rooted in old institutional economics (Veblen, 1898, 1919), has laid the foundation for many empirical studies. It has been subject to numerous expansions (e.g., Alsharari et al., 2015; Bogt & Scapens, 2019) and criticisms (Lounsbury, 2008). Not coincidentally, subsequent revisions of their work have specifically addressed some of these criticisms to improve the framework and address its limitations (Alsharari et al., 2015). The focus of Burns and Scapens's (2000) MAC framework is on the internal dynamics of an individual organization rather than external factors. It considers the interactions between different groups within the organization and internal institutions. However, this approach has shown limitations in addressing the influence of the external environment on the change process (Alsharari et al., 2015) and has been criticized for overlooking the issue of power distribution, which is considered essential in explaining the dynamics of success or failure in implementing certain changes (Dillard et al., 2004).

An alternative to the framework of Burns and Scapens (2000) is that proposed by Brignall and Modell (2000). Their framework is specifically designed to study the implementation of advanced performance measurement systems, composed of financial and non-financial indicators, in public companies. In particular, it examines how the socio-political dynamics and operational contexts of public sector organizations influence the adoption of performance measurement tools, highlighting the role of three main stakeholder groups: funding bodies, internal professional service providers, and service purchasers. This framework is based on new institutional sociology (DiMaggio & Powell, 1983; DiMaggio, 1988) and focuses primarily on the operating environment and the external institutions while leaving the interactions between groups of individuals within the company, which was the focus of Burns and Scapens's (2000) framework, in the background.

Finally, although old institutional economics and new institutional sociology have often been treated as opposing theories, there have also been some approaches that have attempted to integrate and view them as complementary in an attempt to overcome the limitations of both theories (Arroyo, 2012; Alsharari et al., 2015). For example, Alsharari et al. (2015) developed a hybrid framework by combining old institutional economics and new institutional sociology to simultaneously examine the change dynamics both within and outside firms.

Among the studies dealing with the phenomenon of management accounting change, there are also frameworks not based on sociological or institutional frameworks, focusing instead on identifying and categorizing the effects of individual factors that facilitate or hinder the implementation of management accounting tools. One notable example is Kasurinen's (2002) framework, which built upon and expanded the frameworks previously proposed by Innes and Mitchell (1990) and Cobb et al. (1995). From analyzing a case study on the implementation of a balanced scorecard, Kasurinen identified and categorized several factors that could either facilitate or hinder the initiative's success. The author developed different categories to explain how certain factors affect the MAC phenomenon by distinguishing between elements that drive and impede change while also assessing their intensity and magnitude. This framework will be examined in more detail in the next section, as it is chosen to analyze the phenomenon of ESG integration.

3.3 Research Design and Methodology

3.3.1 The Theoretical Framework

This chapter presents the theoretical framework by Kasurinen (2002) since it was employed to analyze results collected in the field study. The choice to use this framework was made for several reasons. Firstly, it has already been successfully applied in previous studies to examine elements that favored or inhibited the implementation of new management accounting systems (Farneti, 2009; Munir et al., 2013), demonstrating its validity for purposes similar to those of the current study. Secondly, the topic we focus on in our research is still relatively new and evolving. Although there are multiple frameworks for analyzing the phenomenon of change, as seen in the literature review, these are usually more suited for case study analysis, possibly in a longitudinal context (Macchia, 2019, 2021). With its more static approach, Kasurinen's (2002) framework seems well suited for exploratory field studies in emerging contexts, whereas frameworks based on institutional theories (e.g., Brignall and Modell, 2000; Burns and Scapens, 2000) seem more challenging to apply. The suitability of this framework for analyzing this context is also supported by the fact that its original version, proposed by Innes and Mitchell (1990), was developed through a field study and adopted a static approach similar to the one used in this study.

Finally, given the unique aspects of management control tools for managing sustainability (Gond et al., 2012) and the novelty of the phenomenon under analysis, it is beneficial to use this framework to identify and preliminarily classify factors that may hinder or facilitate ESG integration, as well as their impact on the implementation process. For all these reasons, we considered Kasurinen's (2002) framework the most appropriate for use in this study, despite the growing variety of frameworks developed in the field of management accounting change.

Figure 3.1 provides a visual representation of Kasurinen's (2002) framework and its constituent components.

To begin with, *motivators* are elements that generally influence and facilitate change. They do not induce the adoption of a specific type of organizational transformation but promote in individuals the development of a sense of urgency concerning the introduction of new solutions in business practice. Examples might include increased market competition, technological developments, and changes in the operating environment. These factors do not specifically promote a particular kind of change but potentially favor the implementation of various types of change as they create the perception that the current status quo might not be sustainable in the long term.

Facilitators are factors that are not sufficient on their own to produce change. Yet, they facilitate change in management accounting systems and, because of this, often prove essential for their successful adoption. In some instances, they might relate to the presence or acquisition of specific expertise and abilities, such as in accounting or IT, or to the variety and quantity of financial resources available.

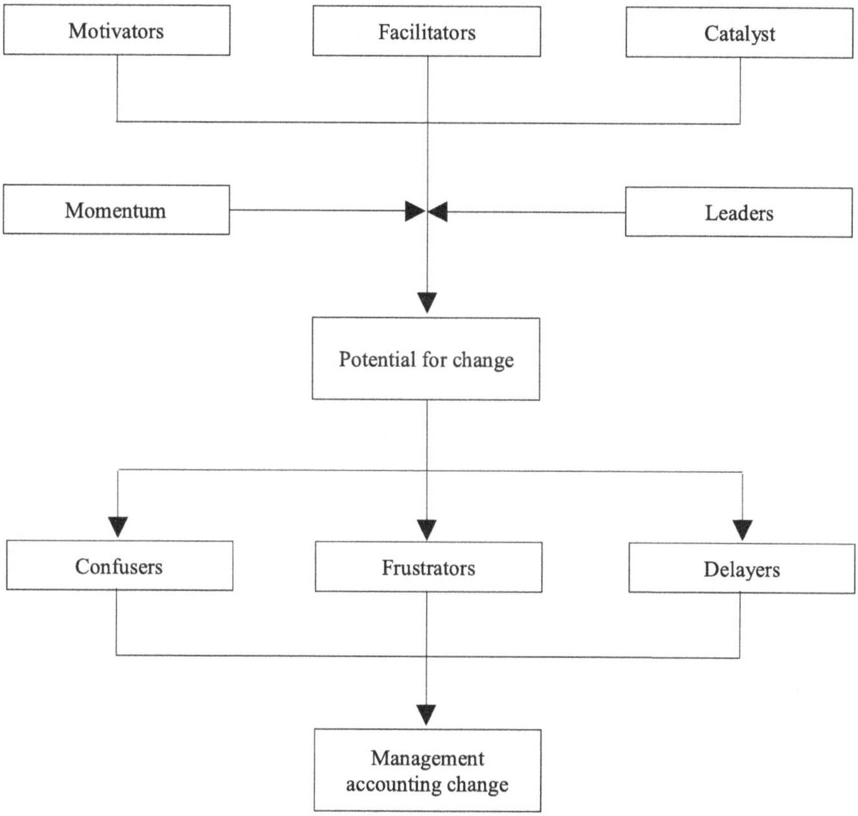

Source: Kasurinen (2002)

Fig. 3.1 Management accounting change framework. Source: Kasurinen (2002)

Catalysts are factors directly related to a specific type of change, and their occurrence directly influences the timing and steps that constitute its realization (Innes & Mitchell, 1990). Some examples might include major regulatory changes, the introduction of new substitute products, and the arrival of a new controller or CFO who actively promotes the dissemination and adoption of certain performance measurement tools.

Leaders act as key initiators in the early stages of change initiatives and remain key supporters throughout the project (Cobb et al., 1995). In other words, the role of these individuals is crucial not only during the initial stages of implementation but also after the process has been completed. If there is a loss of commitment from leadership or if new, more pressing issues arise, the process of change could be interrupted, or a gradual abandonment of the tool could be observed even after it has been formally introduced (Bourne et al., 2002; Franco & Bourne, 2003; Bourne, 2005).

Momentum represents the impetus toward the completion of the change process, arising from the sense of progression and the gradual realization of an outcome that the members of the organization perceive as valuable.

In exploring the elements that hinder change efforts in management control systems, Kasurinen's (2002) framework extends the work of Cobb et al. (1995). This extension involves categorizing the barriers to change into three distinct groups, each defined by their specific negative impact on the implementation process.

Firstly, there are *confusers*, which are factors that can bring the change process to a sudden, temporary, or permanent halt. They might involve, for example, the departure of one of its main sponsors or leaders or misunderstandings and disagreements regarding the implications and goals of the change.

Frustrators are hindering elements that tend to directly suppress the change attempt. This category might include an organizational culture that does not favor change and innovation, as well as management resistance to change.

Finally, *delayers* are temporary and technical barriers that can significantly slow down the change process during both the design and the implementation phases. Such barriers might include the lack of a reliable information system and the absence of a well-developed strategy.

3.3.2 Companies Selection, Data Collection, and Analysis

Our work adopts the field study approach to explore the dynamics and factors influencing the integration of ESG metrics in RM and PMS. We chose this approach as it allows for an in-depth analysis of new and dynamic elements in a real-world context, providing a valuable balance between the wide depth typical of case studies and the broad scope found in survey-based methods (Lillis & Mundy, 2005; Merchant and Stede, 2006). Moreover, this approach is particularly appropriate for this research because the aim is not to provide conclusive explanations but rather to shed some light on a new area of inquiry by highlighting certain issues while necessarily minimizing the focus on others (Granlund Malmi, 2002). In other words, this study sets the stage for more detailed and in-depth future investigations.

For data collection, we mainly relied on semi-structured interviews with individuals directly engaged in incorporating ESG metrics into their companies' RM and PMS. The selection of interviewees was deliberate and not random (Lillis & Mundy, 2005), as we specifically chose to interview those responsible for integrating these metrics into their company's systems. This decision was made because we believed these individuals, by sharing their experiences and the challenges they faced, could help us identify the factors that hindered or facilitated the implementation process. We began by identifying companies that had started or partially completed this process. After identifying and reaching out to these firms, we specifically requested interviews with individuals involved and responsible for the initiative. In addition, we selected companies for our study that were voluntarily integrating ESG factors at the time of our research but are required to comply with CSRD requirements within the next 2 or 3 years. These are large companies that have not yet prepared the non-financial statement under prior EU regulations or listed SMEs. It is also important to underscore that the companies involved in the study operate in different industries and vary in size. The choice to include subjects from such diverse entities was made to account for the specific challenges or enablers that these aspects might create in integrating ESG factors. We believe that by exploring these differences, our study might uncover some sector- and size-related hindering and facilitating factors, providing a richer and broader understanding of the phenomenon under analysis.

We conducted a total of 12 interviews in 4 companies over 6 months. The interviewees held positions such as CEO, CFO, controller, risk manager, and sustainability director. For the sake of clarity, the latter usually had a different set of roles and responsibilities. In one case, the sustainability expert was part of the external relations department. In two cases, the experts belonged to a specialized sustainability management department. In another case, the individual was an external consultant brought onto the Board of Directors to provide expertise and guidance.

The interview guidelines were developed with the support of the MAC literature and the literature related to integrating the element of sustainability into RM and PMS. Even though a specific analytical framework had not been selected at the time of conducting the interviews, the questions were designed to explore the dynamics that facilitated, initiated, hindered, or obstructed the integration process. We also aimed to understand, through our questions, the role played by individuals, factors, and events in the dynamics of success or failure of this type of change. The interviews were conducted entirely online with the support of Microsoft Teams or Google Meet and lasted, on average, around 1 h.

After conducting the interviews, we applied Kasurinen's (2002) framework, presented in Sect. 3.3.1, to code the data. Specifically, we first tried to identify the factors that appeared to have a positive or negative impact on the implementation process. Subsequently, we aimed to understand the nature and magnitude of each factor's impact. Based on this assessment, we classified each factor into one of the categories provided in the theoretical framework.

Table 3.1 summarizes the information about the companies involved in the study.

Table 3.1 Company descriptions

		Company A	Company B	Company C	Company D
Companies general information	*Ownership structure*	Listed company	Joint venture	Private company	Listed company
	Major shareholders	Founder family	Founder family	Founder families	Founder family
	Dimension (number of employees)	200	1500	7000	80
	Industry	Light mechanical	Consumer goods	Tissue papers	Technical gas production
	Interviewees	Sustainability director, investor relations officer, and risk manager	CFO, communication department, and controller	Sustainability director, CSR department, and controller	CEO, CFO, and marketing department
	Level of ESG Integration	Included in strategy planning but not in RM and PMS yet	Partial implementation in both RM and PMS	Partial implementation in both RM and PMS	Included in strategy planning but not in RM and PMS yet

Source: Authors' elaboration

3.4 Results

The companies involved in the study are at different stages of implementing ESG aspects in their management systems. However, a common trait found in all of these companies is that the decision to introduce ESG within the RM and PMS is mainly linked to external forces. In particular, compliance with evolving regulatory requirements for sustainability reporting, as outlined in the CSRD, appears to be the most significant driver, shared by Companies A, B, and C.

To begin with, Company C, despite its long-standing dedication to environmental sustainability, recognized the need to consider also the other ESG aspects in its RM and PMS in order to be prepared when the new regulations come into effect. Its sustainability expert stated that the "new ESG-oriented adjustments that the company is currently undertaking voluntarily in its practices and structures will serve to address future regulatory reporting standards."

Company C's commitment to sustainability is demonstrated by more than 15 years of membership in several international programs, such as WWF Climate Savers. This early involvement has facilitated the inclusion of the environmental sustainability element in the company's RM and PMS, as well as in its strategic planning processes. To improve the management of sustainability-related issues, Company C initially established a sustainability office within its communications department, which later evolved into a dedicated sustainability management department. The existence of an RM system and a PMS that addressed environmental sustainability before the inclusion of ESG factors significantly facilitated the integration initiative. This was because certain elements were already included in the company's strategy and systems. Moreover, the company already had considerable expertise in environmental matters and fostered an organizational culture that considers sustainability a core value. In Company C, the "employees have developed environmental awareness through the training they have received through the years." Specifically, "a significant amount of training is devoted to environmental issues but also health and safety." In addition, the employees' interest in this topic "is also motivated by the fact that their compensation is linked to environmental performance." Finally, in Company C, top management has been promoting this orientation for many years, thus encouraging the company's ongoing focus and adaptability to developments in sustainability issues. Therefore, the integration of ESG elements represents a somewhat natural progression of the company's historical commitments. The company has never had "investors other than the owners," and, consequently, "the impetus for this early focus on sustainability comes from the two owning families themselves." Finally, two other significant elements that have facilitated this transition in Company C are the support of consultants in updating the RM and PMS and access to European funding intended for initiatives related to sustainable development. The former played an important role in redefining risk appetite and identifying new performance indicators, while the latter provided the necessary financial resources for the transition. Although Company A has not yet completed the adoption of ESG factors, it appears to be well on its way to doing so, as it is gradually and overall smoothly integrating them into its management systems.

Focusing on Company B, its primary driver for ESG integration is still related to the need to comply with regulatory changes, as it will need to adapt to the CSRD in 2025. However, a significant key driver emerged from the engagement with the market and customer base. The company realized through market research that "today's and tomorrow's consumers will not buy a product just because they're used to or loyal to it." The management of Company B believes the "ability to thrive and retain loyal customers depends on how well our brand manages to stay relevant to people, and therefore, how well it can integrate the cultural and mindset changes of our time." In particular, the company's general manager was the first to advocate for this type of integration, having recognized the changes on the market. This individual was a strong proponent from the beginning and continues to be heavily involved in the initiative. This commitment is based on the belief that integrating ESG factors into the RM system and PMS will help the company achieve long-term benefits in terms of enhanced value and reputation. The CFO of Company B also stated that the "CEO sees outputs connected to RM and PMS, such as the materiality analysis, as a source of data that can help develop the sustainability strategy." The role of external consultants was also essential, with the controller noting that the company "chose to act based on the consultants' recommendations (...) to identify the most relevant ESG issues for the key stakeholders." The company has also appointed two experts to the Board of Directors to manage and promote the sustainability aspect at both corporate and technical levels: a sustainability expert and a technology and innovation expert.

As noted by the marketing manager of Company B, "the journey toward sustainability and the integration of ESG metrics has been gradual but systemic." Yet, one element that is currently hindering the redefinition of the strategy and the RM and PMS is the disparity in market expectations. The company, which operates in both the US and European markets, is struggling to balance the different expectations of these markets by addressing the sustainability issues important to each. As a result, Company B needs to adopt different ESG-oriented approaches tailored to each market, leading to increased complexity and integration costs.

Company A is also required to comply with new sustainability legislation over the next 3 years. However, the decision to integrate ESG into management systems was also driven by shifts in the financial markets and the initiative of the investor relations officer, which raised awareness of the urgency of promoting such a change. As explained by the company's risk manager: "The topic of sustainability came up several years ago on the initiative of the investor relations officer. He outlined a new situation in the financial markets, namely one in which the attention of institutional investors on ESG issues and the actions taken by companies in this area was becoming paramount (…). Our first real impulse toward ESG issues was exactly that." The investor relations officer, who is also the company's CEO, remains the most important supporter of this integration initiative to date.

In this case, the institutional investors themselves, who hold a significant amount of capital, specifically requested more detailed disclosure of the company's initiatives to improve its sustainability performance. As explained by the investor relations officer: "A key factor motivating our early interest in ESG issues, ahead of regulatory or rule-based requirements, is investor demand for updates on our sustainability efforts." Furthermore, the customers, who are among the company's most significant stakeholders, have also become more interested in sustainability issues, providing an additional external driver for the company to better manage its ESG performance. As explained by the investor relations officer, "The first push came from institutional investors, then from our clients. Probably because our clients, in turn, felt the same pressure as we did in the financial markets."

Although Company A has not yet integrated ESG factors into its management systems, it is trying to gradually raise awareness of sustainability issues within the company. As the risk manager claims, one of the company's goals is "to spread the ESG culture throughout the organization and, thus, to foster a widespread awareness of the relevance of the topic." According to this individual, doing so can help foster "greater participation in activities related to ESG issues, from the implementation phase of the sustainability plan to the reporting and development phase of the sustainability report."

To facilitate this cultural change, the company has engaged external experts in ESG, who provide new insights to the company's management. Moreover, Company A has appointed a permanent sustainability expert to its Board of Directors "who helped outline a less utilitarian and more integrated view of ESG issues." The Board now includes members "with proven experience in the ESG field, and we continue to rely on the support of external consultants." The new sustainability expert at

Company A explained that the "awareness of these [sustainability] issues was also supported through board induction sessions, which covered both the regulatory and reporting part and the formation of the ESG plan and policy." Despite ongoing efforts, the company faces delays partly due to challenges in compiling required sustainability reports. These challenges include identifying the necessary information and determining the scope of the reporting statement. For these reasons, the company deemed it necessary to seek further assistance from external consultants. According to the investor relations officer: "In the area of ESG, understanding what the mandatory and optional steps are when publishing a document as a listed company can be challenging. For example, one difficulty is understanding the difference between the sustainability report and the non-financial statement." In addition, the company recognizes the need to spend at least "two to three years to familiarize with the subject matter and adequately educate all various functions about the goal and what they need to do."

Finally, another issue is the difficulty in identifying the most appropriate performance indicators. One of the main reasons is that Company A has an underdeveloped information system. As the company's CEO explained: "Right now, there is no automation in the system that allows me to directly calculate KPIs. For some KPIs, you have to find the data, extract it, and calculate the KPI separately." Another challenge involves monitoring suppliers' ESG performance. The CEO elaborated: "You first need to understand how feasible this monitoring is, delve into the supply chain, conduct due diligence, and then get a good understanding of how the suppliers can manage these aspects. Only after this can you try to identify some KPIs." Because of these difficulties, management has not yet developed a reward system linked to sustainability performance, although this may be a transitional situation.

Unlike the companies mentioned so far, Company D does not need to develop external sustainability reporting in the near future because it operates in a non-polluting sector. However, the company has always prioritized sustainability issues as it operates in a "green" sector like hydrogen gas production. Here, investor influence is present but less pronounced. As stated by the CEO of Company D: "Some investors have pointed out the ESG aspect to us, but there has not been a strong push. (…) It's really in our DNA to do that. (…) We've always tried to develop machines that pollute as little as possible. (…) We produce hydrogen, so we're clearly green."

The CEO also explained that his company has always tried to promote an organizational culture oriented toward sustainability and "in line with the most appropriate principles for preserving the environment and reducing pollution."

As the company is experiencing solid growth, the CEO has decided to increase its focus on ESG monitoring. In fact, the acquisition of new resources has enabled the company to hire a new consultant, such as a sustainability expert, to begin integrating this aspect into the management systems. As the marketing manager explained, "for the company to continue this growth, it is necessary to take into account the emerging expectations of present and future investors. For this reason, we needed to develop a greater focus on monitoring ESG elements, as they appear to be gaining relevance." At the same time, a new CFO was brought in to integrate ESG elements and improve the company's existing management control systems. The CEO of Company D "felt it was necessary to introduce this position because the growth makes it imperative to better monitor overall performance and incorporate ESG indicators into a more structured system. Some aspects, such as safety and environmental impact, are already quite well monitored, and we're certified for this, but we feel that, with the current growth of the company, there's a need for more stringent monitoring."

In any case, Company D is still in the very early stages of this implementation, and new difficulties and opportunities may arise along the way.

3.5 Discussion

While none of the examined companies have fully integrated ESG aspects into their RM and PMS, certain factors are beginning to emerge as enablers or hinderers of change.

Therefore, to better understand their impact on the change process, we now employ Kasurinen's (2002) framework to analyze the results.

To begin with, an initial driver of ESG adoption appears to be changes at the regulatory level, specifically the upcoming CSRD. Companies A, B, and C are not yet required by law to provide reporting concerning ESG performance. However, all three companies perceive the need to proactively prepare for the enactment of this regulation and to integrate this new element into their RM and PMS. The impending regulatory change seems to act as a *catalyst*, pushing companies in one direction (Innes & Mitchell, 1990): integrating ESG issues into their management systems. This observation is consistent with prior MAC literature, as the anticipation of new regulation appears to be a widely recognized driver and enabler of change (Kasurinen, 2002; Bouten & Hoozée, 2013; Munir et al., 2013).

A further driver observed across all companies concerns the evolving expectations of investors and customers (Oyewo et al., 2019). In the case of Company D, the push from investors was somewhat reduced, as it already operates in a sector perceived as environmentally friendly. Despite this, the influence of these groups remained evident. The growing interest in ESG among stakeholders seems to serve as another MAC *catalyst*, pushing companies toward this specific kind of change (Contrafatto & Burns, 2013).

Beyond these two main drivers of change, however, some additional elements seem to have facilitated or supported the integration under study. The existence of an organizational culture already focused on sustainability measurement and management (De Waal, 2003; Sgrò et al., 2020), which is remarkably evident in

Companies C and D and, to a lesser extent, Company B, seems to have served as a *motivator*. These companies are naturally inclined to stay updated with innovations and new developments in sustainability (Sroufe, 2017). This cultural orientation has supported the implementation of a MAC (Yazdifar et al., 2008) that could improve ESG performance and commitment.

Among the factors that have acted as *facilitators*, a significant role was played by the presence of existing knowledge (De Waal, 2003; Bourne et al., 2003; Cavalluzzo & Ittner, 2004) in the area of sustainability, as observed in Companies B, C, and D. In Company A, where knowledge was limited, a significant *delayer* (Sgrò et al., 2020; Kasurinen, 2002) related to the challenge of understanding the information required for ESG reporting was encountered. This, in turn, temporarily impacted the company's capability to identify the elements to monitor through its management systems (Wouters & Wilderom, 2008; Andon et al., 2007). In any case, knowledge in this area was partly limited in all the companies analyzed, given the need to resort to consultants, who proved to be an essential *facilitator* of this transition. The prior presence of information and management systems (Wouters & Sportel, 2005) specifically designed for managing and monitoring sustainability seems to be a *facilitator* as well, as observed in Company C. By contrast, the lack of an adequate information system to monitor ESG elements proved to be another *delayer*, as in the case of Company A. In Company A, the challenge of identifying appropriate performance indicators is compounded by the difficulty of monitoring the performance of suppliers located in different regions and subject to different regulatory frameworks (Hofmann et al., 2018; Brandenburg et al., 2024). This issue tends to act more as a *frustrator* than a *delayer*, as the company has not yet found a viable method to effectively monitor their actions.

A *facilitator* present in Companies A, B, and C is the permanent introduction of ESG experts on the board and in specific departments (Munir et al., 2013). These experts provide technical support and help spread the values of sustainability.

The presence of resources dedicated to this type of activity is another *facilitator* (Sgrò et al., 2020) as it allows the companies to develop an adequate information system and obtain the support of external consultants.

The importance of individuals who have established themselves as permanent *leaders* and supporters of the change (Kasurinen, 2002; Franco & Bourne, 2003; Taylor & Taylor, 2013; Beusch et al., 2022), such as the CEOs of Companies A, C, and D, as well as the general manager of Company B, is also evident. These leaders seem to have seen benefits from the beginning and throughout the implementation, which helped create and maintain *momentum*.

Finally, one hindering factor identified only in Company B concerns the challenge of meeting the different expectations of various stakeholders (Contrafatto & Burns, 2013). This issue has acted as a *confuser* for the company, complicating the process of defining clear goals and implications for the change.

Table 3.2 presents a summary of the identified hindering and enabling factors.

Table 3.2 Description of hindering and enabling factors in the ESG and RM–PMS integration process

Factor	Description	Factors identified in the study
Enablers of change		
Motivators	Promotes change in a general way Stimulates the development of a sense of urgency for the introduction of new solutions and approaches	Proactive, sustainability-oriented culture
Facilitators	Incentivizes and facilitates change in management accounting systems	Knowledge related to ESG issues Resources allocated for the initiative Permanent inclusion of ESG experts on the Board of Directors and in specialized sustainability functions Support from external consultants
Catalysts	Directly promotes a specific change	Change in regulations Evolving expectations of investors and customers
Leaders	Serve as catalysts for change	CEO General manager
Momentum	Provides impetus for completing the change	Perceived advantages and benefits
Barriers to change		
Confusers	Cause a sudden interruption of the change process	Challenge of meeting stakeholder expectations
Frustrators	Actively suppress the attempt to change	Difficulty in monitoring the performance and actions of suppliers
Delayers	Temporarily hinder and slow down the change process	Lack of knowledge related to ESG issues Lack of adequate information system

Source: Authors' elaboration

3.6 Conclusion

This chapter examined the integration process of ESG factors into RM and PMS through the lens of a management accounting change framework. Our results suggest that in an evolving scenario, where stakeholders' expectations and the regulatory landscape are changing, companies recognize the need to adjust their processes to sustain growth. The pre-existence of an ESG-oriented organizational culture enables companies to effectively capture the shift in stakeholder expectations and motivates them to integrate ESG factors into their processes and systems. However, some factors make this process more difficult (e.g., lack of knowledge related to ESG issues and inadequate information systems). In this light, our findings suggest that, even though awareness among companies is increasing, their implementation of ESG-oriented management control systems is still in the early stages.

This study contributes to both literature and practice. By analyzing how companies undertake ESG implementation within their management systems, our study complements literature on the benefits of such implementation (e.g., Rebelo et al., 2014; Russo, 2009; Simon et al., 2012) and offers insights into the enablers of and barriers to the process. Furthermore, the adoption of Kausurinen's (2002) framework enhances our understanding of why companies decide to engage in ESG disclosure. This investigation adds to the literature on the antecedents and consequences of voluntary disclosure (Rezaee & Tuo, 2017) by highlighting the crucial role of shifting stakeholder expectations and the regulatory landscape as catalysts for non-financial disclosure. Moreover, this study contributes to the literature on management accounting change (e.g., Burns & Scapens, 2000; Brignall & Modell, 2000; Arroyo, 2012; Alsharari et al., 2015) by drawing attention to the usefulness of its related frameworks in analyzing scenarios such as the introduction of ESG into a company's management systems. Finally, this study also offers practical insights into the enablers of and barriers to the ESG integration process that may be beneficial for organizations choosing to engage in this process.

This study has limitations that may pave the way for future research. Firstly, it focuses solely on companies currently undergoing the ESG implementation process, excluding those that have already completed it. This limitation restricts the study's ability to identify hindering and enabling factors encountered during the process. Moreover, the relatively small number of companies included in the study, and the incomplete status of the implementation in some cases may potentially weaken the identification of both barriers and enablers. For example, some companies may be aware of the benefits obtained by an organization that voluntarily conducted and concluded the ESG implementation process and, consequently, emulate their practices to gain similar benefits (Othman et al., 2011). Future research could expand the analysis by including companies that have completed the implementation process, thus providing a more comprehensive understanding of the challenges and successes. The limited number of companies in the sample might also constrain the diversity of experiences and perspectives. Their specific contexts, industry landscapes, and governance structures might hinder the generalizability of these insights to other organizations. Including a more extensive range of cases across various industries and regions could offer a broader understanding of the barriers and drivers involved in integrating ESG into management systems. Finally, this study focuses on companies for which the adoption of ESG requirements is expected to become mandatory in the near future. While the study provides valuable insights into the proactive measures these companies are taking in anticipation of regulatory shifts, it might overlook factors that act as enablers, catalysts, delayers, or barriers in companies that have voluntarily integrated ESG into their RM systems and PMS without impending regulatory requirements. Further research could investigate this aspect and offer a more detailed understanding of the topic.

References

Abad, J., Dalmau, I., & Vilajosana, J. (2014). Taxonomic proposal for integration levels of management systems based on empirical evidence and derived corporate benefits. *Journal of Cleaner Production, 78*, 164–173.

Abdul Aziz, N. A., Manab, N., & Othman, S. (2016). Sustainability risk management (SRM): An extension of enterprise risk management (erm) concept. *International Journal of Management and Sustainability, 5*, 1–10.

Allegrini, M., & D'Onza, G. (2011). Corporate governance, risk management e responsabilità sociale fra presente e futuro dell'attività di internal auditing. *Management Control*, 2011/1.
Alsharari, N. M. (2019). Management accounting and organizational change: Alternative perspectives. *International Journal of Organizational Analysis, 27*(4), 1124–1147.
Alsharari, N. M. (2024). The interplay of strategic management accounting, business strategy and organizational change: As influenced by a configurational theory. *Journal of Accounting and Organizational Change, 20*(1), 153–176.
Alsharari, N. M., & Abougamos, H. (2017). The processes of accounting changes as emerging from public and fiscal reforms: An interpretive study. *Asian Review of Accounting, 25*(1), 2–33.
Alsharari, N. M., Dixon, R., & Youssef, M. A. E.-A. (2015). Management accounting change: Critical review and a new contextual framework. *Journal of Accounting and Organizational Change, 11*(4), 476–502.
Andon, P., Baxter, J., & Chua, W. F. (2007). Accounting change as relational drifting: A field study of experiments with performance measurement. *Management Accounting Research, 18*, 273–308.
Argyris, C., & Kaplan, R. S. (1994). Implementing new knowledge: The case of activity-based costing. *Accounting Horizons, 8*(3), 83–105.
Arroyo, P. (2012). Management accounting change and sustainability: An institutional approach. *Journal of Accounting and Organizational Change, 8*(3), 286–309.
Asiaei, K., Bontis, N., Barani, O., & Jusoh, R. (2021). Corporate social responsibility and sustainability performance measurement systems: Implications for organizational performance. *Journal of Management Control, 32*(1), 85–126.
Beusch, P., Frisk, J. E., Rosén, M., & Dilla, W. (2022). Management control for sustainability: Towards integrated systems. *Management Accounting Research, 54*, 100777.
Bogt, H. J., & Scapens, R. W. (2019). Institutions, situated rationality and agency in management accounting: A research note extending the Burns and Scapens framework. *Accounting, Auditing and Accountability Journal, 32*(6), 1801–1825.
Bourne, M. (2005). Researching performance measurement system implementation: The dynamics of success and failure. *Production Planning and Control, 16*(2), 101–113.
Bourne, M., Neely, A., Platts, K., & Mills, J. (2002). The success and failure of performance measurement initiatives – Perceptions of participating managers. *International Journal of Operations and Production Management, 22*(11), 1288–1310.
Bourne, M., Neely, A., Mills, J., & Platts, K. (2003). Why some performance measurement initiatives fail: Lessons from the change management literature. *International Journal of Business Performance Management, 5*(2–3), 245–269.
Bouten, L., & Hoozée, S. (2013). On the interplay between environmental reporting and management accounting change. *Management Accounting Research, 24*(4), 333–348.
Brandenburg, M., Warasthe, R., & Seuring, S. (2024). Impact pathways: Improving supply chain sustainability by due diligence acts? Insights from a German case. *International Journal of Operations & Production Management, 44*(4), 859–874.
Bravi, L., Santos, G., Pagano, A., & Murmura, F. (2020). Environmental management system according to ISO 14001:2015 as a driver to sustainable development. *Corporate Social Responsibility and Environmental Management, 27*(6), 2599–2614.
Brignall, S., & Modell, S. (2000). An institutional perspective on performance measurement and management in the new public service. *Management Accounting Research, 11*(3), 281–306.
Burns, J., & Scapens, R. W. (2000). Conceptualizing management accounting change: An institutional framework. *Management Accounting Research, 11*, 3–25.
Burns, J., & Vaivio, J. (2001). Management accounting change. *Management Accounting Research, 12*(4), 389–402.
Busco, C., Quattrone, P., & Riccaboni, A. (2007). Management accounting issues in interpreting its nature and change. *Management Accounting Research, 18*(2), 125–149.

Busco, C., Malafronte, I., Pereira, J., & Starita, M. G. (2019). The determinants of companies' levels of integration: Does one size fit all? *The British Accounting Review, 51*(3), 277–298. https://doi.org/10.1016/j.bar.2019.01.002

Carlucci, D., Schiuma, G., & Sole, F. (2015). The adoption and implementation of performance measurement process in Italian public organisations: The influence of political, cultural and rational factors. *Production Planning and Control, 26*(5), 363–376.

Castellano, N. (2011). Modelli e misure di performance aziendale: Analisi della letteratura e spunti di ricerca. *Management Control*, 2011/1.

Cavalluzzo, K. S., & Ittner, C. D. (2004). Implementing performance measurement innovations: Evidence from government. *Accounting, Organizations and Society, 29*(3–4), 243–267.

Chairani, C., & Siregar, S. (2021). The effect of enterprise risk management on financial performance and firm value: The role of environmental, social and governance performance. *Meditari Accountancy Research, 29*, 647–670.

Cho, C. H., & Patten, D. M. (2007). The role of environmental disclosures as tools of legitimacy: A research note. *Accounting, Organizations and Society, 32*(7), 639–647. https://doi.org/10.1016/j.aos.2006.09.009

Chung, R., Bayne, L., & Birt, J. L. (2023). Determinants of ESG disclosure among listed firms under voluntary and mandatory ESG disclosure regimes in Hong Kong. *Journal of Applied Accounting Research*, ahead-of-print(ahead-of-print). https://doi.org/10.1108/JAAR-07-2022-0179

Coad, A., Jack, L., & Kholeif, A. (2016). Strong structuration theory in accounting research. *Accounting, Auditing & Accountability Journal, 29*(7), 1138–1144.

Cobb, I., Helliar, C., & Innes, J. (1995). Management accounting change in a bank. *Management Accounting Research, 6*, 155–175.

Contrafatto, M., & Burns, J. (2013). Social and environmental accounting, organisational change and management accounting: A processual view. *Management Accounting Research, 24*(4), 349–365.

Cooke, T. E. (1992). The impact of size, stock market listing and industry type on disclosure in the annual reports of Japanese listed corporations. *Accounting and Business Research, 22*(87), 229–237.

Cordazzo, M., Bini, L., & Marzo, G. (2020). Does the EU Directive on non-financial information influence the value relevance of ESG disclosure? Italian evidence: Business Strategy & the Environment (John Wiley & Sons, Inc). *Business Strategy and the Environment, 29*(8), 3470–3483.

Dillard, J. F., Rigsby, J. T., & Goodman, C. (2004). The making and remaking of organization context: Duality and the institutionalization process. *Accounting, Auditing & Accountability Journal, 17*(4), 506–542. https://doi.org/10.1108/09513570410554542

D'Onza, G. (2008). *Il sistema di controllo interno nella prospettiva del risk management*. Giuffrè Editore.

De Waal, A. (2003). *Behavioral factors important for the successful implementation and use of performance management systems. Management Decision, 41*(8), 688–697.

de Villiers, C., & Alexander, D. (2014). The institutionalisation of corporate social responsibility reporting. *The British Accounting Review, 46*(2), 198–212. https://doi.org/10.1016/j.bar.2014.03.001

Dhanesh, G. S. (2020). Who cares about organizational purpose and corporate social responsibility, and how can organizations adapt? A hypermodern perspective. *Business Horizons, 63*(4), 585–594.

DiMaggio, P. J. (1988). *Interest and agency in institutional theory, institutional patterns and organizations* (pp. 3–21). Cambridge University Press.

DiMaggio, P. J., & Powell, W. W. (1983). The iron cage revisited: Institutional isomorphism and collective rationality in organizational fields. *American Sociological Review*, 147–160.

Durden, C. (2008). Towards a socially responsible management control system. *Accounting, Auditing and Accountability Journal, 21*(5), 671–694. https://doi.org/10.1108/09513570810872969

Elliott, W. B., Jackson, K. E., Peecher, M. E., & White, B. J. (2014). The unintended effect of corporate social responsibility performance on investors' estimates of fundamental value. *The Accounting Review, 89*(1), 275–302. https://doi.org/10.2308/accr-50577

Englund, H., & Gerdin, J. (2008). Structuration theory and mediating concepts: Pitfalls and implications for management accounting research. *Critical Perspectives on Accounting, 19*(8), 1122–1134.

Farneti, F. (2009). Balanced scorecard implementation in an Italian local government organization. *Public Money and Management, 29*(3), 313–320.

Fiandrino, S., & Tonelli, A. (2021). A text-mining analysis on the review of the non-financial reporting directive: Bringing value creation for stakeholders into accounting. *Sustainability, 13*(2), 18.

Figge, F., Hahn, T., Schaltegger, S., & Wagner, M. (2002). The sustainability balanced scorecard – Linking sustainability management to business strategy. *Business Strategy and the Environment, 11*(5), 269–284.

Franco, M., & Bourne, M. (2003). Factors that play a role in managing through measures. *Management Decision, 41*, 698–710.

Franco-Santos, M., Lucianetti, L., & Bourne, M. (2012). Contemporary performance measurement systems: A review of their consequences and a framework for research. *Management Accounting Research, 23*(2), 79–119.

Gebhardt, M., Thun, T. W., Seefloth, M., & Zülch, H. (2023). Managing sustainability—Does the integration of environmental, social and governance key performance indicators in the internal management systems contribute to companies' environmental, social and governance performance? *Business Strategy and the Environment, 32*(4), 2175–2192.

Ghosh, B., Herzig, C., & Mangena, M. (2019). Controlling for sustainability strategies: Findings from research and directions for the future. *Journal of Management Control, 30*(1), 5–24. https://doi.org/10.1007/s00187-019-00279-8

Giannetti, R., Cinquini, L., Miolo Vitali, P., & Mitchell, F. (2021). Management accounting change as a learning process: A longitudinal analysis. *Qualitative Research in Accounting and Management, 18*(4–5), 484–515.

Giddens, A. (1984). *The Constitution of Society. Outline of the Theory of Structuration*. University of California Press.

Gond, J.-P., Grubnic, S., Herzig, C., & Moon, J. (2012). Configuring management control systems: Theorizing the integration of strategy and sustainability. *Management Accounting Research, 23*(3), 205–223. https://doi.org/10.1016/j.mar.2012.06.003

Granlund, M., & Malmi, T. (2002). Moderate impact of ERPS on management accounting: A lag or permanent outcome? *Management accounting research, 13*(3), 299–321.

Guiral, A., Moon, D., Tan, H.-T., & Yu, Y. (2020). What drives investor response to CSR performance reports? *Contemporary Accounting Research, 37*(1), 101–130. https://doi.org/10.1111/1911-3846.12521

Hassan, M. K. (2005). Management accounting and organizational change: An institutional perspective. *Journal of Accounting and Organizational Change, 1*(2), 125–140.

Hofmann, H., Schleper, M. C., & Blome, C. (2018). Conflict minerals and supply chain due diligence: An exploratory study of multi-tier supply chains. *Journal of Business Ethics, 147*, 115–141.

Hopkin, P. (2018). *Fundamentals of risk management: Understanding, evaluating and implementing effective risk management*. Kogan Page Publishers.

Innes, J., & Mitchell, F. (1990). The process of change in management accounting: Some field study evidence. *Management Accounting Research, 1*(1), 3–19.

Islam, M. A., & van Staden, C. J. (2018). Social movement NGOs and the comprehensiveness of conflict mineral disclosures: Evidence from global companies. *Accounting, Organizations and Society, 65*, 1–19. https://doi.org/10.1016/j.aos.2017.11.002

Järvenpää, M., & Länsiluoto, A. (2016). Collective identity, institutional logic and environmental management accounting change. *Journal of Accounting and Organizational Change, 12*(2), 152–176.

Jensen, J. C., & Berg, N. (2012). Determinants of traditional sustainability reporting versus integrated reporting. An institutionalist approach. *Business Strategy and the Environment, 21*(5), 299–316.

Johnstone, L. (2019). Theorising and conceptualising the sustainability control system for effective sustainability management. *Journal of Management Control, 30*(1), 25–64. Scopus. https://doi.org/10.1007/s00187-019-00277-w

Kaplan, R. S., & Norton, D. P. (1996). Linking the balanced scorecard to strategy. *California Management Review, 39*(1), 53–79.

Kasurinen, T. (2002). Exploring management accounting change: The case of a balanced scorecard implementation. *Management Accounting Research, 13*, 323–343.

Leto, L., & Vito, D. (2024). Il contributo dei sistemi di RM e PM alla sostenibilità integrata: Il caso B&C Speakers. *Management Control*, 2023/3.

Lokuwaduge, C. S. D. S., & Heenetigala, K. (2017). Integrating environmental, social and governance (ESG) disclosure for a sustainable development: An Australian study. *Business Strategy and the Environment, 26*(4), 438–450. https://doi.org/10.1002/bse.1927

Lillis, A. M., & Mundy, J. (2005). Cross-sectional field studies in management accounting research—closing the gaps between surveys and case studies. *Journal of management accounting research, 17*(1), 119-141.

Lounsbury, M. (2008). Institutional rationality and practice variation: New directions in the institutional analysis of practice. *Accounting, Organizations and Society, 33*(4–5), 349–361.

Lueg, R., & Radlach, R. (2016). Managing sustainable development with management control systems: A literature review. *European Management Journal, 34*(2), 158–171. https://doi.org/10.1016/j.emj.2015.11.005

Lukka, K. (2007). Management accounting change and stability: Loosely coupled rules and routines in action. *Management Accounting Research, 18*(1), 76–100.

Macchia, S. (2019). A review on management accounting change. What's next? *Economia Aziendale Online, 10*(1), 107–134.

Macchia, S. (2021). Are we ready to change? : A case study of Management Accounting Change (MAC) in an Italian co-operative. *Management Control, Special Issue 1*, 141–164.

Makrygiannakis, G., & Jack, L. (2016). Understanding management accounting change using strong structuration frameworks. *Accounting, Auditing and Accountability Journal, 29*(7), 1234–1258.

McKinsey & Company. (2019). *More than values: The value-based sustainability reporting that investors want.* Available at: https://www.mckinsey.de/~/media/McKinsey/Business%20Functions/Sustainability/Our%20Insights/More%20than%20values%20The%20value%20based%20sustainability%20reporting%20that%20investors%20want/More%20than%20values-VF.pdf

Merchant, K. A., & Stede, W. A. V. D. (2006). Field-based research in accounting: Accomplishments and prospects. *Behavioral Research in Accounting, 18*(1), 117-134.

Munir, R., Baird, K., & Perera, S. (2013). Performance measurement system change in an emerging economy bank. *Accounting, Auditing and Accountability Journal, 26*(2), 196–233.

Ness, K. E., & Mirza, A. M. (1991). Corporate social disclosure: A note on a test of agency theory. *The British Accounting Review, 23*(3), 211–217. https://doi.org/10.1016/0890-8389(91)90081-C

Othman, S., Darus, F., & Arshad, R. (2011). The influence of coercive isomorphism on corporate social responsibility reporting and reputation. *Social Responsibility Journal, 7*(1), 119–135. https://doi.org/10.1108/17471111111114585

Oyewo, B., Ajibolade, S., & Obazee, A. (2019). The influence of stakeholders on management accounting practice. *Journal of Sustainable Finance and Investment, 9*(4), 295–324.

Pigatto, G., Cinquini, L., Tenucci, A., & Dumay, J. (2023). Serendipity and management accounting change. *Meditari Accountancy Research, 31*(7), 88–115.

Qiu, Y., Shaukat, A., & Tharyan, R. (2016). Environmental and social disclosures: Link with corporate financial performance. *The British Accounting Review, 48*(1), 102–116. https://doi.org/10.1016/j.bar.2014.10.007

Radhakrishnan, S., Tsang, A., & Liu, R. (2018). A corporate social responsibility framework for accounting research. *The International Journal of Accounting, 53*(4), 274–294.

Rau, P. R., & Yu, T. (2023). A survey on ESG: Investors, institutions and firms. *China Finance Review International, 14*(1), 3–33.

Rebelo, M., Santos, G., & Silva, R. (2014). Conception of a flexible integrator and lean model for integrated management systems. *Total Quality Management and Business Excellence, 25*, 683–701. https://doi.org/10.1080/14783363.2013.835616

Rebelo, M. F., Santos, G., & Silva, R. (2016). Integration of management systems: Towards a sustained success and development of organizations. *Journal of Cleaner Production, 127*, 96–111.

Rezaee, Z., & Tuo, L. (2017). Voluntary disclosure of non-financial information and its association with sustainability performance. *Advances in Accounting, 39*, 47–59.

Riccaboni, A., & Leone, E. L. (2010). Implementing strategies through management control systems: The case of sustainability. *International Journal of Productivity and Performance Management, 59*(2), 130–144.

Robson, L. S., Clarke, J. A., Cullen, K., Bielecky, A., Severin, C., Bigelow, P. L., Irvin, E., Culyer, A., & Mahood, Q. (2007). The effectiveness of occupational health and safety management system interventions: A systematic review. *Safety Science, 45*(3), 329–353.

Ronalter, L. M., Bernardo, M., & Romaní, J. M. (2023). Quality and environmental management systems as business tools to enhance ESG performance: A cross-regional empirical study. *Environment, Development and Sustainability, 25*(9), 9067–9109.

Russo, M. V. (2009). Explaining the impact of ISO 14001 on emission performance: A dynamic capabilities perspective on process and learning. *Business Strategy and the Environment, 18*(5), 307–319.

Scott, W. R. (2015). *Financial accounting theory* (7th ed.). Pearson.

Searcy, C. (2012). Corporate sustainability performance measurement systems: A review and research agenda. *Journal of Business Ethics, 107*.

Serafeim, G., & Yoon, A. S. (2022). Understanding the business relevance of ESG issues. *Journal of Financial Reporting, 7*(2), 207–212.

Sgrò, F., Palazzi, F., Ciambotti, M., & Gelsomini, M. (2020). The design, implementation and use of intellectual capital measurements: A case study. *Management Control, Suppl. 1*, 19–38.

Sheehan, N. T., Vaidyanathan, G., Fox, K. A., & Klassen, M. (2023). Making the invisible, visible: Overcoming barriers to ESG performance with an ESG mindset. *Business Horizons, 66*(2), 265–276.

Simon, A., Karapetrovic, S., & Casadesús, M. (2012). Difficulties and benefits of integrated management systems. *Industrial Management and Data Systems, 112*(5), 828–846.

Siti-Nabiha, A. K., & Scapens, R. (2005). Stability and change: An institutionalist study of management accounting change. *Accounting, Auditing and Accountability Journal, 18*(1), 44–73.

Speziale, M.-T., & Klovienė, L. (2014). The relationship between performance measurement and sustainability reporting: A literature review. *Procedia - Social and Behavioral Sciences, 156*, 633–638.

Sroufe, R. (2017). Integration and organizational change towards sustainability. *Journal of Cleaner Production, 162*, 315–329.

Taylor, A., & Taylor, M. (2013). Antecedents of effective performance measurement system implementation: An empirical study of UK manufacturing firms. *International Journal of Production Research, 51*(18), 1–14.

Tsang, A., Frost, T., & Cao, H. (2023). Environmental, Social, and Governance (ESG) disclosure: A literature review. *The British Accounting Review, 55*(1), 101149.

Vaivio, J. (1999). Exploring a "non-financial" management accounting change. *Management Accounting Research, 10*(4), 409–437.

Veblen, T. (1898). Why is economics not an evolutionary science? *Quarterly Journal of Economics*, 12, 373–397. Reprinted in Veblen, T. (1919). *The place of science in modern civilisation and other essays* (pp. 56–81). Huebsch.

Veblen, T. (1919). *The place of science in modern civilization and other essays*. Huebsch.

Vito, D., Leto, L., Bernini, F., & D'Onza, G. (2024). Double materiality in corporate sustainability: Insights from Italian companies. In: Castellano, N., De Luca, F., D'Onza, G., Maffei M., Melis A. *Environmental, Social, Governance (ESG): Risk, Performance, Monitoring*. Springer.

von Alberti-Alhtaybat, L., Hutaibat, K., & Al-Htaybat, K. (2012). Mapping corporate disclosure theories. *Journal of Financial Reporting and Accounting, 10*(1), 73–94. https://doi.org/10.1108/19852511211237453

Wang, N., Pan, H., Feng, Y., & Du, S. (2023). How do ESG practices create value for businesses? Research review and prospects. *Sustainability Accounting, Management and Policy Journal.*

Wijethilake, C., Munir, R., & Appuhami, R. (2018). Environmental innovation strategy and organizational performance: Enabling and controlling uses of management control systems. *Journal of Business Ethics, 151*(4), 1139–1160.

Wong, C. W. Y., Wong, C. Y., & Boon-itt, S. (2020). Environmental management systems, practices and outcomes: Differences in resource allocation between small and large firms. *International Journal of Production Economics, 228*, 107734.

Wouters, M., & Sportel, M. (2005). The role of existing measures in developing and implementing performance measurement systems. *International Journal of Operation and Production Management, 25*(11), 1062–1082.

Wouters, M., & Wilderom, C. (2008). Developing performance-measurement systems as enabling formalization: A longitudinal field study of a logistics department. *Accounting, Organisations and Society, 33*(4–5), 488–516.

Yazdifar, H., Zaman, M., Tsamenyi, M., & Askarany, D. (2008). Management accounting change in a subsidiary organisation. *Critical Perspectives on Accounting, 19*(3), 404–430.

Yu, E. P., Guo, C. Q., & Luu, B. V. (2018). Environmental, social and governance transparency and firm value. *Business Strategy and the Environment, 27*(7), 987–1004.

Zhang, L., Tang, Q., & Huang, R. H. (2021). Mind the gap: Is water disclosure a missing component of corporate social responsibility? *The British Accounting Review, 53*(1), 100940. https://doi.org/10.1016/j.bar.2020.100940

Chapter 4
ESG and the Reformed Italian Constitution: Toward a Constitutionally Oriented Reading of Corporate Sustainability

Pietro Milazzo

4.1 Introduction

A connection between constitutional law and corporate ESG criteria may sound far-fetched. The fundamental pattern of the political order and attaining the values and organizational choices of enterprises and entrepreneurs may appear quite far apart.

This is however not the case, as the political and social development direction taken in the constitution affects political life as well as economic and social models. There is a connection with ancient roots, involving complex relationships between the state's general structure and principles on the one hand and entrepreneurial autonomy on the other hand.

As is well known, the part of the constitution about (formal) economic relations resulted from a political compromise in the constituent assembly that promotes substantially different economic and social models. These range from socialism that retained a Marxist imprint to more classic liberalism to a social view of the economy supported by a majority of the Democrazia Cristiana (Christian Democrats). Consequently, they did not permit the adoption of a clear economic doctrine and established a complex and ambiguous constitutional regulatory context (Iannella, 2023).

Against this backdrop, eminent Italian scholars (Cassese, 2007)—not without criticism (Luciani, 2002)—proposed the idea of an economic constitution. This entailed that general constitutional laws, constitutional legislation concerning economic relations, as well as principles that did not form part of the formal constitution had to be considered to analyze the relationship between the state and the economy accurately. This also applied to the administrative profiles that control the

P. Milazzo (✉)
Department of Law, University of Pisa, Pisa, Italy
e-mail: pietro.milazzo@unipi.it

F. Bernini (ed.), *Creating Value Through Sustainability*, SIDREA Series in Accounting and Business Administration,
https://doi.org/10.1007/978-3-031-74292-7_4

relationship between the constitution, the law, and practice. In other words, it is a constitution in the material sense that develops in tandem with the formal constitution.

The ambiguity and complexity of the general economic model are already clear in the original text of Article 41, which contains three principles. The first, with overall relevance, states that "private economic enterprise is free," linking the constitutional system to a market economy. The second, stating that "it may not be carried out against the common good or in a way that may harm public security, liberty, or human dignity," introduces limitations to private economic enterprise aimed at the protection of other constitutional interests assessed as prevailing over the free exercise of private initiative. According to the third, "the law determines appropriate planning and controls so that public and private economic enterprises may be directed and coordinated toward social ends."

From this provision, and from its various degrees of implication and balance (Cassetti, 2021) between freedom of enterprise and social constraints as well as political-economic planning, a debate has arisen about the functionalization (or the possible degree thereof) of enterprises in the framework of purposes a political decision-maker identified (Niro, 2006).

The thesis of total or predominant enterprise functionalization has however not been adopted by constitutional case law, as it appears to subject individuals' private economic initiative legislative directives that may not be questioned, while no one can be forced, even by law, to start any economic activity against their will. The constitutional court has always held that freedom of enterprise "translates into the possibility of directing one's activities in the economic field freely, according to one's own convenience" and that limitations on private economic enterprise cannot be "such as to render its exercise impossible or extremely difficult" (Corte cost., 21/5/1970, n. 78).

From a different perspective, it has been questioned whether Article 41 imposes an authoritarian or centralized economic model or whether its limitations exclude any form of economic planning, while leaving broad discretion to the legislator. The prevailing view is the latter, also because Article 41 refers to programs instead of plans. This identifies programming as the constitutionally favorite tool for public economic regulation, even though the only example of general—not just sectoral—economic planning, attempted by Law 867/1957, is generally considered a failure.

Among the limitations and constraints on entrepreneurial autonomy envisaged by Article 41's original text, there were no direct references to environmental values and sustainability. The latter is a concept which, with its current multifaceted implications, was not recognized at the time the constitution came into force. Nevertheless, in constitutional case law, the reference to the safety limitation—to be understood as protecting the safety of workers but also that of the wider community—is often read jointly with health protection and does not seem to be alien to a broad concept of "environment" as the context in which fundamental human needs are manifested. As an example, rulings on the Ilva of Taranto case where the court, among other things, held that "promptly removing factors that risk the health, safety, and life of workers constitutes the minimum and indispensable condition for productive activity to be carried out in harmony with constitutional principles, which always attend to the basic needs of the person first" (Corte cost., 28/3/2018, n. 58).

On the other hand, the constitutional reference to social utility as a limitation to enterprise freedom is configured as a safety-valve principle (Luciani, 1983) and irreducibly multifaceted, legislatively defined on a case-by-case basis (Rossano, 1963, Baldassarre, 1971). It was included in the constitution to enable the legislator to limit enterprise freedom based on general interest (Olivetti, 2022). According to the main interpretative approach of the constitutional court, interests that "ultimately or immediately pertain to the national community and not exclusively to single categories of workers" can be considered as social. It therefore seems that social utility represents a broader notion compared to simple public interest, as it concerns the utility of "society as a whole and not of its parts, expressions, or fractions." Social utility does not necessarily coincide with the interests of de facto disadvantaged social categories, but it is the synthesis of societal interests, not those of single groups.

The constitutional court has linked this multifaceted notion of social utility to the protection of various interests not expressly mentioned in Article 41, including environmental protection, for example "the maximum limit of pollutant emissions (…) can never exceed the absolute and indispensable threshold represented by the tolerability for the protection of human health and the environment in which people live: protection entrusted to the fundamental principle of Article 32 of the constitution, to which Article 41, second paragraph, refers" (Corte cost. 16/3/1990, n. 127; Corte cost. 11/7/2018, n. 150).

Similarly, "it is established in constitutional case law that the social utility limit, to which private economic enterprise is subject by virtue of Article 41, cannot be said to exclude legislative interventions that are not unreasonably (Article 3) aimed at protecting the environment" (Corte cost., 14/6/2001, n. 190).

Before 2022's reform, the constitution already made reference to the environment as a principle and value. The word "environment" was included in the text of the reformed constitution of 2001, which gave the state legislative competence in environmental protection matters (Salerno, 2023). In addition, the environmental issue had already permeated constitutional law by means of constitutional case law, which recognized it as a constitutional value by referring to the interpretation of the provisions around landscape protection (Article 9) and the right to health (Article 32) as well as other parameters, including Article 41 (Grassi, 2023). Consequently, at least since the mid-1980s, genuine constitutional environmental case law has been developing and consolidating (Cecchetti, 2022).

In the context of this case law, both before and after the 2001 constitutional reform, the constitutional court has shaped the environment as an asset of primary and absolute value (Corte cost., 27/6/1986, n. 151; Corte cost., 30/12/1987, n. 641, inter alia). It is seen as a sort of constitutional supervalue that can affect subjective rights arising from other sources of constitutional rank (Dell'Anno, 2009).

On the eve of 2022's constitutional reform—with particular reference to Articles 9 and 41—it emerged that certain aspects related to what is now perceived as companies' external sustainability (meaning the complex concept of the environment) already represented a scenario that private economic enterprise and its constitutional boundaries had to confront.

4.2 The Reformed Articles 9 and 41: The Intergenerational Dimension as a Paradigm of the Action of Public Powers

In 2022, the Italian constitution underwent a significant revision. It was established that the republic "safeguards the environment, biodiversity, and ecosystems, also in the interest of future generations" (Article 9) and that private economic enterprise cannot be carried out in a manner that may harm health and the environment. In addition, the law determines appropriate programs and checks to ensure that public and private economic enterprise is directed at and coordinated for social and environmental purposes (Article 41).

Among the extensive commentary on the reforms (Cecchetti, 2021; Benvenuti, 2023, Santini, 2021), it emerged that the fundamental aspect of the new provisions did not lie in the "constitutionalization" of the environment (which, as mentioned above, already had broad protection before and after its citation in the 2001 constitutional reform concerning the distribution of power between the state and regions). It was rather the reference to the intergenerational dimension (Bifulco, 2008; Porena, 2018) and the prevalence of the sustainability of human activities in relation to the environment itself, not entirely new to previous constitutional case law (Arconzo, 2021). This reference implies the long-term, or even the extremely long-term, commitment of the republic (in its various articulations) to protecting the environment and therefore the projection of its initiatives into a future for which, however distant, it is necessary to assume immediate and precise responsibilities.

This interpretation of the new Article 9 and its intergenerational dimension is confirmed by the simultaneous amendment of Article 41. By including environmental value in the possible limitations to private economic enterprise (setting the environment apart from the general perimeter of social utility) and adding environmental goals to those for which binding programs can be imposed to companies, the constitutional legislator of 2022 identified an area of particular significance for achieving the purposes of the new Article 9 (Jona, 2023). This is the area of economic activity and private economic enterprise, perceived as a critical context to fulfill the recently constitutionalized intergenerational perspective—a context where the issue of sustainability is particularly relevant (Buzzacchi, 2023).

A remaining problem concerns the tools through which the constitutional reform will impact private economic enterprise. The constitutional legislator chose to shape the environment not as an individually enforceable right but as a value toward which public authorities have a duty of activation. This duty can be expressed in negative terms (a limitation on private economic initiative) as well as in positive terms (the content of the program provided for by Article 41).

This perspective may not be new, but thanks to an explicit constitutional reference, it now has a clearer description, aiming to resolve the conflict between individual or entrepreneurial pursuit of maximizing profit and shareholderism and the contribution of enterprises to the fulfillment of solidaristic and clear environmental principles outlined in the first part of the constitution. This is a perspective of further accountability for the company that complements public authorities' accountability (expressed in terms of duty) in pursuing these objectives.

4.3 ESG Criteria: The New Boundaries of Private Autonomy and the Test of Sustainability

The new boundaries of private economic enterprise, as redefined by the 2022 constitutional reform, were set in a context that was not indifferent to "contaminated" mediation between the pure logic of corporate profit and the pursuit of different values and objectives, by balancing the interests of shareholders with those of stakeholders. This is the level of corporate social responsibility (CSR) from an ESG (environmental, social, and governance) point of view, aiming to overcome a short-term perspective to satisfy the long-term expectations of companies and stakeholders in order to create a socially shared and responsible value (Conte, 2022).

In recent years, the increasing attention paid to the social function of modern corporate enterprises has culminated in a series of initiatives aimed at stimulating discussions about the opportunity to mitigate the traditional paradigm of profitability, which has always represented the parameter of such phenomena. Several significant external issues (social and especially environmental) have emerged that fuelled criticism about the shareholder primacy model, according to which it is exclusively the interests of shareholders that affect enterprise management decisions. Based on Milton Friedman's famous maxim that "the social responsibility of business is to increase profit," this model is criticized because of a tendency toward short termism, which is often incompatible with a company's sustainable existence. This shareholderist approach—characterized, for example, by an increasing propensity of companies to adopt policies aimed at maximizing shareholder profit—tends to overlook the development of negative externalities toward subjects external to the company and is perceived as no longer being socially acceptable.

This led to reflections on the opportunity to adopt management policies capable of balancing shareholder interests with those of parties outside the enterprise ownership structure, but that nevertheless find themselves in the position to bear (to varying degrees) the consequences of business activities (the stakeholders). Managing a company with a constant focus on satisfying short-term interests is generally considered incompatible with stakeholder protection as well as with the company's own long-term interests. Short-term profit maximization can indeed depress investments in research and development, with obvious negative consequences for the future projection of the company's activities and profitability.

This approach positioned the topic of enterprises' social responsibility at the core of the debate, and it is now not only common but quite ordinary to witness companies of all sizes acknowledging their social responsibility. This is the case even when the objectives are clearly incompatible with ESG values and a profession of social responsibility therefore is a façade (greenwashing or socialwashing) or consists of a mere application of the well-known principle that accountability to everyone means accountability to no one.

At first, the consideration of ESG values in a CSR framework was essentially voluntary, guided by international provisions that often fell in the realm of soft law. An enterprise's strategic choices and convenience determined the choice, also at a competitive level, aimed at maintaining or improving its reputational profile. ESG values were frequently used as marketing strategies, aimed at increasing profit by exploiting the commercial appeal and image return of adhering to values such as legality, a business's environmental sustainability, and human rights awareness.

The integration of ESG criteria in the CSR context—although initially on a voluntary or utilitarian (or even opportunistic) base—progressively had an ever more complex legal framework (Fimmanò, 2023). This is because the notion of sustainable development with its general social implications expanded and the centrality of the enterprise and its conduct in pursuing this form of development was fully understood. Since the Green Paper "Promoting a European framework for corporate social responsibility" of 2001 (COM (2001) 366 final) and the communication "A renewed EU strategy (2011–14) for corporate social responsibility" (COM(2011) 681 final), the European Commission has established a framework for CSR as "a concept whereby companies integrate social and environmental concerns in their business operations and in their interaction with their stakeholders on a voluntary basis."

More recently, international regulatory pressure—even though often in the shape of soft law or non-binding commitments—increased significantly. At the most general and global level, there is the "Transforming our world: the 2030 agenda for sustainable development," signed in 2015 by the governments of 193 UN member countries as an action plan for people, the planet, and prosperity that includes 17 sustainable development goals with 169 targets. The Paris Agreement on climate change of 2016 (ratified by the European Union in the same year), followed by the Katowice package of 2018 (COP24), is also relevant.

As examples, in this context the European Union adopted:

(i) Regulation (EU) 2019/2088 of 27 November 2019 on sustainability-related disclosures in the financial services sector, where it is provided that all financial market participants shall publish information about their policies on the integration of sustainability risks in their investment decision-making process and where they consider principal adverse impacts of investment decisions on sustainability factors, a statement on due diligence policies with respect to those impacts, taking due account of their size, the nature and scale of their activities, and the types of financial products they make available, or where they do not consider adverse impacts of investment decisions on sustainability

factors, clear reasons for why they do not do so, including, where relevant, information as to whether and when they intend to consider such adverse impacts
(ii) Regulation (EU) 2020/852 of 18 June 2020 on the establishment of a framework to facilitate sustainable investment that establishes the criteria for determining whether an economic activity qualifies as environmentally sustainable for the purpose of establishing the degree to which an investment is environmentally sustainable
(iii) Directive (EU) 2017/828 of 17 May 2017 on the encouragement of long-term shareholder engagement, in which mechanisms for the remuneration of directors were envisaged to incentivize long-term interests and a company's sustainability
(iv) Directive (EU) 2022/2464 of 14 December 2022 (in the framework of the European Green Deal), on corporate sustainability reporting, in which sustainability reporting obligations are confirmed and strengthened (information necessary to understand the undertaking's impacts on sustainability matters and information necessary to understand how sustainability matters affect the undertaking's development, performance, and position)

The European Union has also adopted some disciplines related to the topic being here discussed, but with reference to individual sectors or areas, by way of example, EU Batteries Regulation, EU Deforestation Regulation (EUDR), EU Conflict Minerals Regulation, EU Packaging and Packaging Waste Regulation (EU PPWR).

At the time of writing, the final stage of the complex approval process for a general regulation was underway. This regulation aims to address the risk of inappropriate short-termism policies by means of rules on directors' due diligence (Enriques, 2021; Corvese, 2023). This applies only to companies of a significant size in terms of employees and turnover or to those involved in sectors that are particularly critical for potential negative externalities (Tombari, 2021; Rosini, 2022).

According to the text of the Corporate Sustainability Due Diligence Directive (CSDDD) the European Parliament approved on 24 April 2024, the aim is to ensure that companies that are active in the internal market contribute to sustainable development and the sustainable transition of economies and societies through identifying and, where necessary, prioritizing, preventing, mitigating, bringing to an end, minimizing, and offering remediation of human rights and environmental impacts. The CSDDD lays down rules on (a) obligations for companies regarding actual and potential human rights adverse impacts and environmental adverse impacts, with respect to their own operations, those of their subsidiaries, and those carried out by their business partners; (b) liability for violations of the obligations in point (a); and (c) an obligation for companies to adopt and put into effect a transition plan for climate change mitigation which aims to ensure, through best efforts, compatibility of their business model and strategy with transitioning to a sustainable economy and limiting global warming to 1.5 °C, in line with the Paris Agreement.

In this scenario, according to the CSDDD, member states shall ensure that companies conduct risk-based human rights and environmental due diligence through the following actions: (a) integrate due diligence into their policies and risk management systems; (b) identify and assess actual or potential adverse impacts and, where necessary, prioritize them; (c) prevent and mitigate potential adverse impacts, bring actual adverse impacts to an end, and minimize their extent; (d) provide remediation for actual adverse impacts; (e) carry out meaningful engagement; (f) establish and maintain a notification mechanism and a complaints procedure; (g) monitor the effectiveness of their due diligence policy and measures; and (h) publicly communicate about due diligence.

A crucial point of the CSDDD establishes that each member state shall designate one or more authorities to supervise compliance with the obligations in national law provision. This is so that such an authority shall have adequate powers and resources to carry out the tasks assigned to it under the directive, including the power to require companies to provide information and carry out investigations related to compliance with the directive's obligations. The supervisory authority may start an investigation on its own initiative or as a result of substantiated concerns communicated to it, where it considers that it has sufficient information indicating a possible breach by a company of the obligations in the national law provisions adopted in accordance with the directive.

If a supervisory authority identifies a failure to comply with the provisions, it shall grant the company concerned an appropriate period to take remedial action, if such action is possible. Remedial action shall not preclude the imposition of penalties or the triggering of civil liability. The supervisory authority shall have at least the power to (a) order the company to (i) cease infringements of the national law provisions by performing an action or ceasing conduct, (ii) refrain from any repetition of the relevant conduct, and (iii), where appropriate, provide remediation proportionate to the infringement and necessary to bring it to an end; (b) impose penalties; and (c) adopt interim measures in the event of an imminent risk of severe and irreparable harm.

The system of principles and rules, particularly of EU origin, may not effectively guarantee, with binding effect, a responsible behavior on the part of economic players or the introduction of specific commitments and duties. As observed, this network of provisions with varying levels of binding force is likely to promote a dialog among enterprises. This could facilitate the spontaneous observance of correct behaviors and the adoption of ethical codes that would become real sources of mutual responsibility regardless of mandatory external regulations.

The system of international and especially European regulations can however not be read solely as a kind of public nudge regarding enterprises' activities. These provisions have recently assumed more binding characteristics and a perspective oriented to setting real limitations and prescriptions for enterprises. They place companies in a complex regulatory scenario and grant them a significant role in it, such as that related to the Paris Agreement, the European Green Deal, and other transitions that characterize recent perspectives of European legislation.

4.4 ESG and the Italian Constitution: Neo-Functionalizing Private Autonomy or Affirming the Principle of Solidarity?

Two approaches emerge that can be read in a single historical-political and normative perspective. On the one hand, ESG values in a CSR framework have developed significantly, both voluntarily and in the context of promoting tools aimed at strengthening their role and function. Especially at the EU level, these tools take into account social, environmental, and governance objectives that are politically determined and correspond to enterprises' performance targets that are considered politically desirable and technically achievable. On the other hand, the 2022 constitutional reform in Italy transformed the environment from a value without distinct features into a fundamental principle inserted in the first part of the constitutional text with a particular intergenerational meaning. In addition, it explicitly inserted the environment in the dynamic balance that governs the mechanisms of Article 41 and helps to outline the constitutional perimeter of economic enterprise in the context of general freedom, limits of general interest, and political planning conceived as criteria that guide wealth production.

Evident connections and inferences between the two approaches have emerged. The new Article 41 is affected by the doctrine and political developments regarding the notion of sustainable development, while the intergenerational dimension of the general environment principle of Article 9 alludes to a horizon of sustainability.

From a constitutional perspective, it can be inferred that a joint reading of the new Articles 9 and 41 outlines a type of responsible enterprise, also from an environmental point of view (Buzzacchi, 2023). This would be an enterprise that can overcome the private interests of entrepreneurs and shareholders and can produce wealth that is not only vested in its own structure but also distributed externally in the general interest. An aspect that is worth further investigation is whether this general goal may be pursued by public authorities only through soft tools, so that the will of the company remains spontaneous, by catalyzing and enhancing CSR-oriented initiatives that already exist in the company dynamics, or if the constitutional reform requires a more robust public intervention with stricter constraints. Such constraints will force enterprises and their competitive dynamics to effectively reach the desired purpose as far as environment, health, and all the meanings of social utility under paragraph 2 and social purposes under paragraph 3 of Article 41 are concerned.

A preference for the second option (a substantial and binding public intervention) lends itself to criticism. Functionalizing economic enterprise to pursue objectives selected by politics and that are external to the company may turn the company itself into an instrument for political goals. This is a perspective that is difficult to accept in a market economy and in a context that affirms the freedom of economic initiative. The key appears to be a balance between freedom of economic enterprise and values/principles that may abstractly limit it in order to safeguard other objectives (e.g., socially, environmentally, and politically desirable objectives). But how could this balance be attained? Could those values—considered as belonging to the ESG category and being at the core of the constitution, such as in the new Article 9—bend under the weight of economic freedom, conceived as a self-referential principle and not as a fundamental one, and also not as one that protects further interests?

Analyzing how the constitutional court conducts this type of balancing or verifies the balancing carried out by the legislator, at least recently, the risk of functionalizing enterprise activity appears to be diminished (in addition to being weakened by exposure to principles of European Union origin). In its most recent case law, particularly (but not exclusively) concerning the Ilva case in Taranto, the constitutional court reshaped the relationship between constitutional principles in secular terms, by claiming that in balancing there are no "tyrant values" whose protection prevails over other values and principles. For example, in the judgment of 9 May 2013, no. 85, the constitutional court stated, "All fundamental rights protected by the constitution are in a relationship of mutual integration and it is therefore not possible to identify one of them as having absolute precedence over the others. The protection must always be systemic and not fragmented into a series of inconsistent provisions that are potentially in conflict with each other. If this were not the case, there would be an unlimited expansion of one of those values, which would become a tyrant value against other constitutionally recognized and protected values which together constitute expression of individual dignity."

Consequently, even though the constitutional court has often defined environment and health as primary values, this does not imply a rigid hierarchy among fundamental rights. According to the court, the Italian constitution, similar to other contemporary democratic and pluralist constitutions, "requires a continuous and mutual balancing between fundamental principles and rights, without claims of absoluteness for any of them." The qualification of the environment and health as primary values therefore means that they cannot be sacrificed for other interests, even if constitutionally protected, but not that they are placed at the top of an absolute hierarchical order. The point of equilibrium, precisely because it is dynamic and not predetermined, has to be assessed—by the legislator in formulating laws and by a constitutional judge in a review process—according to criteria of proportionality and reasonableness, so that their essential core is not sacrificed (Grifoni, 2022).

According to the court, those principles—observed through the lens of economic enterprise freedom—imply that limitations to said freedom have to comply with the parameters of reasonableness and proportionality. The identification of these limitations cannot be arbitrary, nor can it pursue measures that are manifestly incongruous or excessive, "to condition entrepreneurial choices to such a high degree as to substantially lead to the functionalization of economic activity, [...] sacrificing its fundamental options or restricting the scope and object of these organizational choices within rigid boundaries" (Corte cost., 9/5/2022, n. 113). There must be a "fair balance between the general interest of the community and interference with the individual right to the enjoyment of goods" (Corte cost., 23/5/2023, n. 101). In this case, it seems highly implausible that a paradoxical effect could occur, leading to externally imposed ESG values (borrowing the term from enterprise experience) to the extent of directing the general purpose of the company to the pursuit of those values.

A reconstruction of this kind should also alleviate the concern about the undesirable consequence of a high level of functionalization of companies to social/environmental values. This refers to managerial irresponsibility resulting from the indefinite expansion of the recipients of the decisions and of the subjects to whom the decisions are inspired, from simple shareholders to various categories of stakeholders.

A different way of looking at the new constitutional context could be the principle of solidarity. As observed, the fulfillment of the inalienable duties of political, economic, and social solidarity—a fundamental element of the pluralistic state—has been modestly valued in constitutional case law. It has however shown great expansive potential before ordinary judges, who have applied the principle of solidarity in diverse contexts (although with significant uncertainty due to the difficulty of expressing the concrete scope of the principle and its challenging applicability to contractual relationships between private parties where individual interest is traditionally pursued structurally).

Applying the principle of solidarity (in a "horizontal" sense) in case law ensures that private autonomy is exercised in accordance with constitutional precepts, meaning that it is not the domain of individual selfish arbitrariness but rather a tool to realize interests and functions worthy of protection and socially useful according to Article 41. The principle of solidarity guarantees that private autonomy is exercised in a proportional and reasonable manner with respect to individual interests. The duty arising from solidarity can therefore be defined as an external limitation to exercising individual rights and freedoms (including enterprise freedom), imposing on everyone, as members of society, the burden of a common weight.

May "everyone" also be understood to include enterprises? Are enterprises also recipients of the duty of solidarity? For this purpose, the interpretation of corporate citizenship becomes relevant. This stance mirrors the idea that companies have duties analogous to those of citizens (Denozza, 2022). If a company can be considered a social formation through which the individual, "by sharing their needs and representing their demands, contributes to the definition of specific interests and the formation of precise instances of the community" (Ricci, 2010), it should not be able to evade the duty to contribute in solidarity to the collective well-being, safeguarding common goods, and promoting the general interest. This is especially true in the context of the reformed Article 41, which emphasized and enhanced the social and environmental limitations around private economic enterprise. Consequently, there would be a private economic enterprise where management rules are accompanied by a precept that mandates running the business in accordance with the purposes established by the entrepreneur "in compliance with the principle of constitutional solidarity" (Cerrato, 2022). This constitutional substratum would oblige directors to orient their actions according to the principles of proportionality, reasonableness, and balancing their interests and those of the individuals who may be affected by their initiatives (including a future intergenerational perspective).

From this perspective, ESG (environmental, social, and governance) principles should not simply be "transplanted" into the company's corporate purpose but should instead constitute a benchmark for complying with the principle of constitutional solidarity. This view seems fascinating and convincing, although it currently faces the issue that judges have in practice never applied the principle of solidarity to enterprise management practices. Furthermore, any potential judgment on adherence to the principle of solidarity would likely rely on parameters that are not particularly robust.

In the context of this analysis, the affirmation of ESG values may be approached in a less ambitious manner by conceding that the possible intent of the reform was (also) to provide a direct constitutional foundation—and a specific reception in Italy—to the latest international regulatory and programmatic approaches (Paris Agreement, European Green Deal, Green Transition, circular economy, Green and Blue Economy, etc.). In these contexts, ESG values tend to be somewhat codified, externally imposed, and therefore removed from their original voluntary basis, which are sometimes ambiguous in their aims and always inconsistent in their outcomes.

If this is the possible premise, the inclusion of the environment and environmental objectives in Article 41 should not be seen only as a new limitation or a further space where programming and directing economic initiative but rather—positively—as the point of connection between the constitutional framework of private economic enterprise and a new conception of the environment. The environment appears to be not only the object of protection but also a driver of sustainable economic and institutional development, especially concerning future generations. In this scenario, private economic enterprise and the environment may find points of contact (rather than conflict) in a horizon of mutual enhancement.

ESG values constitute a tool that is fully compatible with the new constitutional framework and that is useful for the promotion of its full expression. The numerous European interventions—even though they face limitations due to the choices made and the perimeters of application—constitute an interesting field of research, where a model for applying ESG values is being experimented with. As that model is translated to the Italian context and viewed through the lens of the new Article 42—as interpreted by the relevant constitutional case law—it anticipates a constitutionally oriented reading and therefore the application of corporate social responsibility.

References

Arconzo, G. (2021). La tutela dei beni ambientali nella prospettiva intergenerazionale: il rilievo costituzionale dello sviluppo sostenibile alla luce della riforma degli articoli 9 e 41 della Costituzione. *Diritto dell'economia, 157–185.*

Baldassarre, A. (1971). *Iniziativa economica privata. Enciclopedia del diritto* (Vol. XXI, pp. 582–621). Giuffré.

Benvenuti, M. (2023). La revisione dell'articolo 41, commi 2 e 3, della costituzione, i suoi destinatari e i suoi interpreti. *Rivista AIC, 2*, 59–83.
Bifulco, R. (2008). *Diritto e generazioni future. Problemi giuridici della responsabilità intergenerazionale*. Franco Angeli.
Buzzacchi, C. (2023). Attività economiche e ambiente nel prisma (o mantra?) della «sostenibilità». *Rivista AIC, 4*, 207–226.
Cassese, S. (2007). *La nuova costituzione economica*. Laterza.
Cassetti, L. (2021). Salute e ambiente come limiti "prioritari" alla libertà di iniziativa economica? *Federalismi, 16*, 1–7.
Cecchetti, M. (2021). La riforma degli articoli 9 e 41 Cost.: un'occasione mancata per il futuro delle politiche ambientali? *Quaderni costituzionali*, 351–354
Cecchetti, M. (2022). Virtù e limiti della modifica degli articoli 9 e 41 della Costituzione. *Corti supreme e salute, 1*, 127–154.
Cerrato, S. A. (2022). Appunti per una «via italiana» all'ESG. L'impresa «costituzionalmente solidale» (anche alla luce dei «nuovi» artt. 9 e 41, comma 3, Cost.). *Analisi giuridica dell'economia, 1*, 63–114.
Conte, F. (2022). La finanza sostenibile: limiti e profili evolutivi. *Federalismi, 33*, 1–26.
Corvese, G. C. (2023). La proposta di direttiva sulla Corporate Sustainability Due Diligence e i suoi (presumibili) effetti sul diritto societario italiano. *Orizzonti del diritto commerciale*, 1, 1–29.
Dell'Anno, P. (2009). La tutela dell'ambiente come "materia" e come valore costituzionale di solidarietà e di elevata protezione. *Ambiente e sviluppo*, 285–298.
Denozza, F. (2022). Due concetti di stakeholderism. *Orizzonti del diritto commerciale*, 1, 37–68.
Enriques, L. (2021). The European Parliament draft directive on corporate due diligence and accountability: Stakeholder-oriented governance on steroids. *Rivista delle società*, 319–324.
Fimmanò, F. (2023). Art. 41 della Costituzione e valori ESG: esiste davvero una responsabilità sociale dell'impresa? *Orizzonti del Diritto Commerciale, 1*, 1–32.
Grassi, S. (2023). La cultura dell'ambiente nell'evoluzione costituzionale. *Rivista AIC, 3*, 1–39.
Grifoni, D. (2022). Il concetto di "utilità ambientale" nell'art. 41 cost. Riflessioni a seguito della legge costituzionale n. 1/2022. *AmbienteDiritto, 3*, 1–18.
Iannella, M. (2023). *Costituzione e nuova economia pubblica*. Ed. Scientifica.
Jona, E. (2023). La libertà di iniziativa economica e la protezione dell'ambiente e della salute. *Federlismi, 2*, 104–119.
Luciani, M. (1983). *La produzione economica privata nel sistema costituzionale*. Cedam.
Luciani, M. (2002). Brevi cenni sulla cosiddetta "costituzione economica" europea e sul suo rapporto con la Costituzione italiana. In S. Panunzio & E. Sciso (Eds.), *Le riforme istituzionali e la partecipazione dell'Italia all'Unione europea* (pp. 47–55). Giuffré.
Niro, R. (2006). Articolo 41. In A. Celotto, M. Olivetti, & R. Bifulco (Eds.), *Commentario della Costituzione* (Vol. I, pp. 844–852). Utet.
Olivetti, M. (2022). *Gli altri diritti fondamentali*. Giappichelli.
Porena, D. (2018). *Il principio di sostenibilità. Contributo allo studio di un programma costituzionale di solidarietà intergenerazionale*. Giappichelli.
Ricci, P. (2010). L'articolo 41 della Costituzione italiana e la responsabilità sociale d'impresa. *Rivista italiana di ragioneria e economia aziendale* (pp. 142–150).
Rosini, M. (2022). From CSR to HRDD: An overview of approaches, initiatives and measures adopted by the European Union. *International Community Law Review* (pp. 57–78).
Rossano, C. (1963). Riserva di legge ex art. 41 Cost. e accordi economici collettivi. *Rassegna di diritto pubblico*, 670–681.
Salerno, G. (2023). Ambiente e articolazione costituzionale delle competenze tra Stato e Regioni. *Rivista AIC, 3*, 1–17.
Santini, G. (2021). Costituzione e ambiente: la riforma degli artt. 9 e 41 Cost. *Forum di Quaderni Costituzionali - Rassegna*, 460–481.
Tombari, U. (2021). La Proposta di Direttiva sulla Corporate Due Diligence e sulla Corporate Accountability: prove (incerte) di un "capitalismo sostenibile". *Rivista delle società*, 375–380.

Chapter 5
Administrative Controls for Sustainability: A Case Study of an Italian Bank

Paola Ferretti and Pierluigi Martino

5.1 Introduction

This chapter investigates the role played by administrative controls in banks' commitment to sustainability.

Sustainability has become a key focus in today's financial landscape. A growing number of stakeholders are paying attention to environmental, social, and governance (ESG) issues and urging banks to proactively engage in sustainability-driven activities (Avrampou et al., 2019; La Torre & Chiappini, 2018; Houston & Shan, 2022; Bruno & Lagasio, 2021; La Torre et al., 2021). Notably, there is significant pressure from policymakers and regulators focused on promoting sustainable economic growth, which requires banks to promptly address sustainability challenges. In the context of the European Union (EU), for instance, regulators have outlined a specific trajectory to align the banking sector with sustainable growth (EC, 2018; EBA, 2019, 2020). Given its key role in the provision of financial resources to the economy, banks are called upon to promote the transition toward sustainable economic growth. This particularly involves supporting business initiatives that combine economic-financial objectives with ESG goals, as well as promoting sustainable investments in the allocation of customer savings. Moreover, it is worth noting the recent establishment of the UN-backed Net-Zero Banking Alliance (NZBA) in 2021 in Glasgow, which comprises a coalition of banks representing over 40% of global banking assets and committed to achieving net-zero emissions by 2050.[1]

[1] NZBA members pledge not only to achieve net zero in their operations but also to educate their clients and align their loan and investment portfolios with net-zero objectives. However, they are

P. Ferretti · P. Martino (✉)
Department of Economics and Management, University of Pisa, Pisa, Italy
e-mail: paola.ferretti@unipi.it; pierluigi.martino@unipi.it

F. Bernini (ed.), *Creating Value Through Sustainability*, SIDREA Series in Accounting and Business Administration,
https://doi.org/10.1007/978-3-031-74292-7_5

Hence, integrating ESG factors into banking activities is becoming increasingly imperative. Regulatory and supervisory authorities are requiring banks to incorporate ESG components into their strategic plans, internal control frameworks, and decision-making processes (EBA, 2019, 2022; ECB, 2020). To this end, sustainability should be integrated into banks' business strategy (e.g., Procopio et al., 2020; Galletta et al., 2021). This integration requires the development and diffusion of a sustainability culture, starting with the banks' strategic supervisory and management bodies and extending to the functions engaged in lending policies and the provision of financial services to customers, including risk management (Ferretti & Martino, 2023). To this end, establishing adequate administrative controls (Malmi & Brown, 2008) is crucial to guide and facilitate the transition toward business models that fully integrate ESG issues. It is widely acknowledged in the literature that administrative controls are crucial for implementing significant behavioral changes, including in the realm of sustainability (Coulson, 2009; Birindelli et al., 2018; Christensen et al., 2018; Dicuonzo et al., 2022). However, despite extensive discussion of ESG issues in banking literature (e.g., Birindelli et al., 2015; Broccardo et al., 2016; Galletta et al., 2021), there is limited research on how banks incorporate ESG factors into their operations (Galletta et al., 2022; Ferretti et al., 2024; La Torre et al., 2024).

We seek to fill this gap by exploring how banks integrate ESG factors within their administrative controls to enhance their commitment to sustainability. Our goal is to point out the mechanisms through which banks can effectively align their operations with ESG objectives. For our analysis, we employed a single-case study methodology on an Italian bank. We organized the empirical data by using the definition of administrative controls proposed by Malmi and Brown (2008), which includes three control mechanisms: (1) organizational structures, (2) governance structures, and (3) policies and procedures.

The structure of this chapter is as follows. The next section examines banking practices in the context of sustainable finance, while Sect. 5.3 explores the role of administrative controls in fostering banks' commitment to sustainability. Section 5.4 describes the methodology employed in our study. Section 5.5 presents the analysis results, and Sect. 5.6 discusses these findings and offers concluding remarks.

5.2 Banking Practices and Sustainable Finance

The transition to a model of sustainable economy constitutes a priority at global scale. In this context, the EU has not only embraced this essential transition but also been at the forefront of various initiatives to ensure its successful implementation.

---

not required to immediately stop lending to fossil fuel companies or curtail investment bank financing to such enterprises. Instead, they are committed to gradually transitioning their loan and investment portfolios to net zero over time. For more details, see https://www.unepfi.org/net-zero-banking

Among the various initiatives undertaken in this area, the EU has spearheaded efforts to develop a financial system that inherently facilitates the financing of the transition to a sustainable economy. Since 2018, the European Commission (EC) has been developing a comprehensive policy agenda on sustainable finance, which involves integrating ESG considerations into investment decisions within the financial sector. Such an approach is indispensable for channeling investments more effectively into long-term, sustainable economic activities and projects.

On this journey toward sustainability, the banking sector is called upon to play a leading role in financing the transition to a greener and more sustainable economy (Wu & Shen, 2013; Bose et al., 2018; Ahmed et al., 2018; EC, 2018; EBA, 2019; 2020; La Torre et al., 2021; Chen et al., 2022). The strategic position of banks is linked to their specific activities, which include screening, monitoring, enforcing, and potentially considering ESG factors in funding provision and investment activities (Cosma et al., 2020). In other words, banks are pivotal in facilitating the reallocation of financial resources needed to support the shift toward more sustainable economic systems. This entails supporting the financing of business initiatives that merge economic-financial objectives with ESG goals and promoting sustainable investments in the management of customer savings (Miralles-Quirós et al., 2019; Umar et al., 2021). In this respect, EU banking regulators have defined a precise ESG pathway to further align the banking industry with sustainability (EBA, 2019, 2020). Particularly, through the "Action Plan on Sustainable Finance" (2019), the EBA has defined a process for regulating the integration of ESG factors into banks' strategies, business models, and risk management by 2025. This plan includes, above all, a prudential discipline and sustainability disclosure criteria. Furthermore, in 2022, the EBA issued a detailed roadmap that specifies the goals and timelines for executing mandates and responsibilities in the domain of sustainable finance and ESG risks (EBA, 2022). This roadmap delineates the UE approach to integrating ESG risk considerations into the banking framework and supporting the transition to a more sustainable economy.

In light of these developments, a growing number of banks have recently strengthened their commitment to sustainability by incorporating ESG factors into their assessments of customer lending and creditworthiness (Ehlers et al., 2022; D'Apolito et al., 2024). These banks are also innovating by offering products and services designed to support ESG investments and launching initiatives that align with ESG objectives (e.g., Birindelli et al., 2015; Broccardo et al., 2016; Li et al., 2018; Avrampou et al., 2019). It is also noteworthy to mention the Principles for Responsible Banking, signed by 130 international banks. These principles aim to ensure that banks' offerings and business strategies not only meet the needs and expectations of their clients and investors but also reflect broader societal values and goals, particularly aligning with the Paris Agreement on climate change and the United Nations Sustainable Development Goals.[2]

---

[2]The Sustainable Development Goals (SDGs) were introduced by the 2030 Agenda, a project endorsed on 25 September 2015 by 193 UN countries. These countries have committed to achieving 17 SDGs and 169 targets within 15 years, aiming for completion by 2030.

However, although banks have made efforts to incorporate ESG issues into their business, existing literature (EBA, 2021; Ehlers et al., 2022; Nguyen et al., 2022; Ferretti et al., 2024) reveals that challenges remain, especially in incorporating ESG factors into banks' decision-making processes and core business functions, where the integration process is still in its early stages. This points to the need for banks to intensify their efforts to achieve a comprehensive integration of ESG factors into their operations, which is crucial for genuine sustainability engagement (e.g., Procopio et al., 2020; Galletta et al., 2021; Ferretti et al., 2024). Specifically, banks are required to integrate ESG considerations into their strategic plans, internal control frameworks, and decision-making processes (EBA, 2019). This involves creating and disseminating a sustainability culture that encompasses the bank's supervisory and management bodies, covering departments responsible for the operational management of credit processes, finance, and customer services, as well as the risk management function (Ferretti & Martino, 2023). To this end, establishing adequate administrative controls (Malmi & Brown, 2008) is crucial to guide and facilitate the transition toward business models that fully integrate ESG issues. As we discuss in the next section, administrative controls in terms of governance arrangements, organizational structures, and policies and procedures are key for implementing significant behavioral changes and, consequently, for enhancing banks' commitment to sustainability (Christensen et al., 2018; Cosma et al., 2022; Dicuonzo et al., 2022).

5.3 Administrative Controls for Sustainability

In this study, we use the definition of administrative controls as proposed by Malmi and Brown (2008), which includes three control mechanisms: (1) organization design and structure, (2) governance structures, and (3) policies and procedures. According to Malmi and Brown (2008), these mechanisms are essential for promoting and facilitating substantive behavioral changes within an organization (Christensen et al., 2018). Accordingly, they are also crucial for fostering a sustainability-oriented culture within the organization (Ditillo & Lisi, 2014; Lueg & Radlach, 2016; Ferretti et al., 2024).

The first mechanism, *organizational design and structure*, involves shaping interactions and relationships among units and employees to encourage certain outcomes (Malmi & Brown, 2008). In the context of sustainability, this approach can be instrumental in directing banking activities toward ESG goals. The consideration of ESG issues directly influences the functions of various business lines and internal control mechanisms (EBA, 2021), which have to align their operations with ESG goals. Establishing clear and formal structures becomes paramount to facilitate coordination among the different organizational units dealing with ESG matters. Such structures are key to enhancing communication and collaboration, accelerating the dissemination of information and ideas across different business lines and control functions, and effectively orchestrating sustainability activities (Ditillo & Lisi, 2014; Soderstrom & Weber, 2020; Mio et al., 2022).

Governance structures refer to formal lines of authority and accountability, including systems that ensure coordination of activities across various functions and organizational units both vertically and horizontally (Malmi & Brown, 2008). This includes the structure and composition of the board of directors, management, and project teams. The literature identifies banks' internal governance arrangements as critical for the successful implementation of ESG considerations and the management of ESG risks (Birindelli & Palea, 2022; Cosma et al., 2022; Dicuonzo et al., 2022; Murè, 2022). Firstly, integrating ESG issues into banks' business operations requires active involvement from the board of directors. As the body responsible for approving and controlling the bank's strategic objectives achievement, the board must also endorse strategic guidelines and policies related to sustainability. In this respect, several studies (e.g., Birindelli et al., 2018; Velte & Stawinoga, 2020; Cosma et al., 2022) highlight the importance of establishing a committee dedicated to sustainability issues as an important governance tool. This committee can help the board by ensuring the effective integration of ESG concerns into corporate strategies. According to these studies, an ESG-specific committee can be essential in advising the board on ESG matters, evaluating ESG performance, ensuring compliance with sustainability risk regulations, managing the reporting of ESG information, providing regular updates to the board on sustainability issues, and overseeing related public disclosures. In addition to the board of directors, the commitment of top management is vital for effectively integrating ESG issues within an organization (Velte & Stawinoga, 2020). Responsible for the organizational strategies and decisions, top management plays a vital role in articulating a vision for ESG goals and formulating, executing, and overseeing the bank's sustainability strategy (Wijethilake & Lama, 2019; Rahman et al., 2023). Moreover, top management raises awareness and reinforces the priority of ESG goals across the organization, thus ensuring that various business functions are actively committed to achieving them. In this vein, the introduction of dedicated leadership positions can reflect and influence an organization's strategic focus on sustainability and ESG objectives. Some studies (e.g., Zorn 2004; Strand, 2014; Fu et al., 2020) show that new positions within the top management team that are specifically dedicated to ESG issues, such as a Chief Sustainability Officer, serve both an internal and external signaling function about the strategic or symbolic importance the corporation places on these issues at any given time.

The last administrative control mechanism is *policies and procedures*, which include action controls—behavioral constraints, pre-action reviews, and action accountability—as defined by Merchant and Van der Stede (2007). As Ditillo and Lisi (2014) note, integrating specific ESG considerations within company policies and procedures is a crucial step toward fully embracing sustainability principles. Implementing these policies can promote sustainability-oriented behaviors within organizations, ensuring that ESG issues are appropriately identified and managed and contributing to the thorough monitoring of sustainability-related activities. This is particularly relevant for banks, which need to integrate ESG issues into their risk policies and procedures and overall risk management systems (Coulson, 2009; Weber, 2012; Dicuonzo et al., 2022). This process entails revising the Risk Appetite Framework to include ESG factors, from setting risk measurement and tolerance levels to managing optimal capital allocation and monitoring risks. Specifically, in credit risk management, assessing ESG-related factors becomes an integral part of the process, leading to changes in credit analysis models and default risk methodologies. In this context, it is useful to mention the EBA principles on granting and monitoring credit, which mandate banks to integrate ESG factors and associated risks into their credit risk appetite and risk management policies, as well as their credit risk policies and procedures, adopting a holistic approach (EBA, 2020).

Hence, the literature suggests that administrative controls are central to ensuring a holistic approach to the incorporation of ESG factors into the banks' business strategy, processes, and risk management. This view is supported by the 2021 EBA recommendations (EBA, 2021), which urge banks to weave ESG considerations into their governance structures. Notably, these recommendations emphasize the need to establish clear procedures and responsibilities for business lines, internal control functions, relevant committees, and the management body to ensure the effective implementation of ESG considerations and the management of ESG risks. Based on these considerations, we explore the extent to which banks integrate ESG factors into their administrative controls to strengthen their sustainability commitment.

5.4 Methodology

For our investigation, we adopted a qualitative approach, using an exploratory case study that focuses on an Italian bank (Creswell et al., 2007). This method is particularly suitable when the focus is on a contemporary and complex phenomenon within real-life contexts (Yin, 2013), which aligns with our research topic. Furthermore, the case study methodology allows researchers to employ various data collection methods, thereby enabling a more in-depth and comprehensive understanding of the phenomenon under investigation (Easton, 2010; Yin, 2014). Therefore, we contend that the case study is particularly valuable for conducting an extensive analysis of how banks are integrating ESG factors in their administrative controls to enhance their commitment to sustainability.

We conducted our investigation by collecting and examining analytical data on sustainability and administrative controls within an Italian banking group. This bank qualifies as a "significant entity" and, thus, falls under the direct supervision of the European Central Bank, according to the criteria established by the Single Supervisory Mechanism (e.g., Ielasi et al., 2023; Mango et al., 2023; La Torre et al., 2024).

The selected bank is notable, listed, and ranks among the largest Italian banking groups in terms of total assets. Since we aimed to explore how banks implement administrative controls for sustainability, we verified the selected bank's active involvement in sustainable issues. To this end, we carefully checked various information sources, particularly websites and press releases about the bank and its sustainable activities. Moreover, we verified whether the selected bank is listed on sustainable indices.

5.4.1 Data Collection and Analysis

Our data collection consisted of semi-structured interviews and secondary data analysis. Initially, we selected qualitative-based interviews as the main data collection method for this study. Semi-structured interviews allow for dealing with phenomena for which established knowledge is scarce, and they facilitate flexible data collection by allowing respondents to introduce emerging aspects not initially included in the interview's framework (Griffith et al., 2015; Bell et al., 2018). As part of this process, a semi-structured questionnaire with open-ended questions guided the collection of all empirical data (Eriksson & Kovalainen, 2015). Based on the framework of administrative controls defined by Malmi and Brown (2008), the interview agenda aimed to examine whether and how the selected bank integrates ESG considerations into its organizational structures, governance arrangements, and policies and procedures.

The interviews were carried out via online calls in June 2023 and involved participants selected for their expertise with the phenomena under investigation (Creswell & Poth, 2016). As reported in Table 5.1, we conducted two interviews with top managers responsible for key administrative control functions.

Each interview, averaging 68 min, was transcribed immediately afterward to prevent the loss of information, with the transcripts repeatedly cross-referenced with the original recordings to ensure accuracy and reliability. We then returned the case study reports to the informants for verification to deal with data validity (Yin, 2003). After the first round of interviews, we re-contacted each informant in order to confirm the overall results of the interview, consolidate all the information collected, cross-check relevant data, and clarify relevant issues. The feedback from the interviewees is crucial in order to prevent observer bias and ensure the accuracy of the data collection.

Finally, the data from the interviews was triangulated and integrated with information from various reports (i.e., corporate governance reports and sustainability

Table 5.1 Interview summary

Respondent	Role	Time duration (in minutes)
Respondent A	Senior director—Internal controls and capital adequacy	74
Respondent B	Risk management (ESG)	62

reports) and the bank's website. This dual approach of collecting data through interviews and external sources allowed us to validate our findings (Yin, 2003).

To analyze and summarize the data collected from our sources, we used manual content analysis procedures. Specifically, we conducted a detailed examination of the individual case study to discern how the selected bank incorporates ESG considerations into its administrative controls, in line with the framework set by Malmi and Brown (2008).

5.5 Results

The selected bank is a listed and large banking group operating across retail, corporate, and wealth management sectors, with a notable commitment to ESG. In addition to being part of the bank's mission and vision, ESG is also a key pillar of its latest strategic plan, with several long-term objectives focused on ESG topics.

Over the years, the bank has aligned with all the major UN sustainability initiatives relevant to the financial sector, which are part of achieving the SDG objectives. The bank's commitment to ESG goals is reflected in various initiatives, including offering credit lines tailored to companies (e.g., circular economy and sustainability loans), training initiatives for corporate customers on ESG issues, and sustainable investment products. Finally, as a testament to its strong ESG commitment, it should be noted that the bank is included in several sustainability indices and rankings (e.g., Dow Jones Sustainability Indices, MSCI ESG Indexes), determined by specialist rating agencies that evaluate companies not only for their financial performance but also for their results in ESG areas.

From the interviews, it became clear that the bank has extensively integrated ESG factors within its administrative controls to effectively support its commitment to sustainability. Below, we detail how it has implemented these controls, as defined by Malmi and Brown (2008).

5.5.1 Organizational Structures

As an initial step in implementing administrative controls for sustainability, the selected bank established two dedicated organizational units focused solely on ESG issues.

Firstly, in 2020, an "ESG control" unit was set up to assist the executive committee in identifying and prioritizing ESG initiatives based on their strategic relevance. This unit is tasked with supporting the executive committee in strategically addressing ESG issues and overseeing the operational coordination necessary for implementing these initiatives. To this end, the unit also relies on the expertise of 17 sustainability managers who are specifically appointed in each area and division of the bank to ensure comprehensive and integrated supervision of ESG initiatives within their respective structures and contribute to the strategic positioning of the group on these matters. As one interviewee (Respondent A) underscored, the "ESG control" unit functions as both a proactive and an operational entity within the bank. It actively gathers inputs from internal sources (e.g., business units) and significant input from sustainability managers, as well as from external stakeholders including regulators, peer banks, and non-governmental organizations. Its primary goal is to synthesize these diverse inputs to formulate a strategic direction that aligns with the group's level of ambition and ensure all initiatives within the bank are effectively channeled toward this established strategic trajectory.

Secondly, within the governance area of the Chief Financial Officer, an additional "ESG" unit was established to oversee the definition, approval, and update of guidelines in the realms of sustainability, accordingly with the bank's strategic plan. This organizational unit, in coordination with the "ESG control" unit, assists the executive committee in proposing guidelines and sustainability-related policies. It is also responsible for updating the ethical code and monitoring its implementation, as well as managing ESG and sustainability reporting (e.g., the Consolidated Non-Financial Statement (CNFS)). Furthermore, the "ESG" unit oversees relations with the financial community regarding ESG and sustainability issues and manages stakeholder engagement activities related to these topics. This involves, for instance, actively participating in dialogues with investors, regulatory bodies, and other financial institutions to ensure that the bank's ESG strategies and achievements are transparently communicated and aligned with industry best practices. For example, an examination of the bank's 2022 non-financial disclosure report reveals that the unit promoted specific initiatives throughout the year, including addressing numerous assessments from specialized companies and investors, as well as responding to various engagement requests and questionnaires focused on ESG topics. In collaboration with investor relations, there was also a commitment to numerous meetings with investors and analysts.

The creation of the two units mentioned above enabled the bank to adopt a more coordinated and strategic approach to sustainability. Indeed, this integrated organizational structure is crucial in ensuring that ESG initiatives are effectively implemented across all areas and divisions of the bank.

5.5.2 *Governance Structures*

At the governance level, strategic guidelines and sustainability-related policies were traditionally approved by the board of directors supported by the Risks Committee. Given the growing focus on sustainability issues over the years, as demonstrated by the inclusion of specific ESG goals within the bank's strategic plans, the bank has significantly strengthened its governance in the realm of sustainability.

In 2022, the Risks Committee has been strengthened in terms of ESG responsibilities, and as a consequence it has been renamed the "Risk and Sustainability" Committee. Specifically, the Risk and Sustainability Committee works for the board of directors by assessing and investigating the ESG issues and approving sustainability-related guidelines and policies. In this way it contributes to more efficient risk monitoring. Among other responsibilities, it also supports the board in approving updates to the code of ethics and the CNFS, in particular, by analyzing the most relevant ESG issues and any other significant reports in this area submitted to the board. For example, the analysis of the 2022 non-financial disclosure report reveals that several meetings were held throughout the year specifically focused on ESG issues (e.g., the analysis of the report on the implementation and governance of the ethical code, the discussion of the ECB Climate Stress Test outcomes, and the incorporation of sustainability features in internal regulations on investment services). Hence, as also emerged during the interviews, the structural changes concerning the risk committee ensured that ESG considerations were consistently represented in board discussions and decisions. This integration ensures that ESG concerns are not treated as peripheral issues but are integral to the bank's strategic planning and risk management framework.

At the executive level, it is worth mentioning the role of the Steering Committee, chaired by the Managing Director and Chief Executive Officer (CEO) and including their first reporting lines, the heads of governance areas and divisions. This committee collaborates in identifying potentially relevant ESG issues for the definition and updating of material issues, as well as in defining strategic guidelines and sustainability policies. In addition, it reviews the CNFS before submission to the board. The comprehensive engagement of management in ESG matters was deemed essential to thoroughly embedding ESG principles within all business operations and decision-making processes. This is because the involvement of management has reinforced the priority of ESG goals, resulting in a substantial commitment from all employees and managers within the bank to achieving these objectives.

The implementation of the abovementioned governance mechanisms for sustainability, involving both management and the board of directors, represents a fundamental shift in how the bank perceives and integrates ESG issues into its business model. As one of the respondents (Respondent A) mentioned, these governance mechanisms have been key to effectively embedding the ESG theme into the core decision-making processes at the highest levels of management and oversight. This has been instrumental in fully integrating the ESG theme into every business process, thereby raising the level of responsibility and accountability for ESG topics throughout the bank.

5.5.3 Policies and Procedures

The selected bank has incorporated ESG considerations into its existing policies and procedures aimed at governing the socio-environmental implications arising from its activities over the years. This integration was deemed necessary to transfer sustainability principles into actionable rules for managing customer relationships.

The integration of ESG factors within a bank's policies and procedures has involved different organizational areas. However, it is worth mentioning the integration of ESG factors within the overall risk management framework, particularly the Risk Appetite Framework (RAF), which focuses also on ESG and climate change risks. Notably, the RAF translates strategic guidelines into specific controls, setting annual limits, key risk indicators, and specific measures for containing ESG risks, in particular in the business areas most vulnerable. The development of RAF controls in the ESG area also considers the findings of the most relevant risk assessment processes (i.e., stress tests and scenario analysis). As Respondent B pointed out, the integration of ESG factors into the bank's RAF represents a significant advancement in risk management, marking a shift from traditional financial risk assessments to a more comprehensive approach that includes ESG risks. This structured approach enables the bank to proactively identify and mitigate potential ESG risks, particularly in sectors that are most vulnerable to ESG-related issues.

Within the RAF, special emphasis is placed on the Credit Risk Appetite Framework, which incorporates specific environmental risk/resilience aspects. These include the energy class and environmental certifications related to loans and other factors related to the ESG profile of the counterparties, particularly their ESG scores. These factors related to ESG risk exposure affect the pricing for customer financing transactions, especially for corporate customers. Moreover, the bank has defined some exclusion criteria to avoid the financing of activities and/or projects with significant environmental and social negative impacts. To this end, in 2022, the bank updated its ESG risk guidelines, which, among other things, define a list of ESG and/or reputational risks, general criteria to limit and exclude loans, as well as criteria applicable to individual sensitive sectors through the implementation of specific rules. For example, according to the internal regulations on ESG risks, the bank commits not to finance companies and projects that harm specific protected areas, such as the UNESCO World Heritage Sites.[3]

The process of integrating ESG factors within policies and procedures also extends to asset management activities and the client advisory process. Over the years, the bank has incorporated ESG factors into the analysis of the investments and the decision-making process and selection criteria for issuers. This involves evaluating potential investments not only based on financial returns but also on ESG performance. Finally, the bank has progressively improved the control of financial assets in terms of ESG performance and extended its offer of sustainable financial products.

The holistic integration of ESG factors into both credit risk assessment and investment analysis is a fundamental evolution in the bank's operational approach. By embedding ESG considerations into these key banking processes, the bank effectively aligns its core lending and investment practices with broader

[3] List of sites officially recognized by the United Nations Educational, Scientific, and Cultural Organization (UNESCO).

sustainability goals. This represents a crucial step in effectively translating the ESG strategy into concrete actions.

5.6 Conclusion

In this study, we explored whether and how administrative controls for sustainability are used to support banks' commitment to ESG goals. Our investigation, conducted at a significant Italian banking group, reveals that the bank has consistently integrated ESG considerations into its administrative controls over the years, as defined by Malmi and Brown (2008).

The bank established two distinct organizational units with a specific focus on ESG issues. These units have enabled a more coordinated and strategic approach to sustainability, ensuring that ESG initiatives are not only aligned with the bank's overall business objectives but also effectively implemented throughout the bank's areas and divisions. In line with prior research (Ditillo & Lisi, 2014; Soderstrom & Weber, 2020; Mio et al., 2022), our results highlight the importance of organizational structures in enhancing coordination among various units tasked with ESG matters. Notably, these structures have a crucial role in aligning the efforts of these units, thus facilitating the effective orchestration of sustainability activities. This enables a more unified and comprehensive approach to executing ESG strategies, ensuring their integration across the entire organization.

At the governance level, the bank introduced two pivotal mechanisms that involve both the board of directors and the management. Firstly, the bank built a sustainability management structure tasked with providing oversight and strategic direction in defining and implementing the ESG strategy. This structure ensures that sustainability is a central consideration in all strategic decisions. Secondly, the bank has significantly strengthened and increased the scope of responsibilities and activities of the existing Risks Committee in ESG-related matters. This is designed to help the board of directors in the oversight of the sustainability strategy, ensuring that ESG considerations are embedded at the highest level in the bank's decision-making processes. In this regard, our findings reveal that these governance mechanisms collectively enhance the ESG responsibility within the bank. Specifically, they aim to improve the effectiveness and full integration of ESG initiatives within the bank's overarching corporate strategy and operational processes. This marks a substantial strategic shift, elevating ESG considerations from simple compliance to essential elements of the bank's strategic and operational framework. These findings align with prior studies, which emphasize the importance of establishing dedicated ESG committees and managerial positions as key governance mechanisms to bolster a firm's focus on and commitment to sustainability-related issues (e.g., Mallin & Michelon, 2011; Birindelli et al., 2018; Hussain et al., 2018; Velte & Stawinoga, 2020).

Over the years, the bank has progressively embedded ESG considerations in its existing policies and procedures to manage the socio-environmental impacts arising from its operations. This integration has primarily concerned the risk management framework, influencing the bank's daily business, especially in the areas of lending and finance. For instance, the bank has incorporated ESG factors into its credit risk assessment processes. This involves evaluating the risk profiles of companies or sectors by using ESG criteria, which then informs key lending decisions, such as loan pricing. Moreover, this integration extends to the bank's asset management activities, where ESG factors are now integral to investment analysis and decision-making processes. This holistic integration is a pivotal step in effectively translating the ESG strategy into concrete actions, as it aligns the bank's core lending and investment practices with broader sustainability goals. In this respect, the literature points out the need for banks to incorporate ESG factors into their policies and procedures, particularly those of risk management, to ensure the successful implementation of ESG considerations and management of ESG risks (Weber, 2012; EBA, 2020; Dicuonzo et al., 2022; Ferretti et al., 2024). This is crucial to ensuring the widespread adoption of sustainability principles within organizations, transforming them into management practices (Ditillo & Lisi, 2014).

Hence, our findings indicate that administrative controls are key to implementing significant behavioral changes in the realm of sustainability (Malmi & Brown, 2008; Christensen et al., 2018), thereby fostering banks' commitment to ESG goals. Specifically, these controls enable the bank to systematically plan, execute, and oversee sustainability policies and strategies, ensuring their effective implementation.

5.6.1 Contributions, Limitations, and Future Research

This study has both theoretical and practical implications. Firstly, it builds on previous research in the field of sustainability in banking, particularly concerning the role of administrative controls (e.g., Weber, 2012; Birindelli et al., 2018; Galletta et al., 2022; Dicuonzo et al., 2022). Notably, while existing literature has explored the relationship between certain administrative controls (especially the board) and ESG outcomes such as ESG performance or disclosure, limited attention has been given to how banks implement these controls to foster their sustainability commitment. Our investigation, conducted at one of the largest Italian banking groups, sheds light on how banks incorporate ESG factors into their administrative controls to strengthen their ESG goals commitment, thereby addressing an important gap in the literature. Furthermore, by adopting a comprehensive definition of administrative controls that includes governance structures, organizational structures, and policies and procedures, we expand prior research that has predominantly focused on corporate governance mechanisms, such as the board of directors. Specifically, we illustrate how these combined control mechanisms enable the bank to formulate, execute, and oversee sustainability policies and strategies. Therefore, our exploratory study shows how banks engaged in sustainability can realize administrative controls to effectively help their ESG goals commitment.

Finally, our findings provide practical insights that can be instrumental for banks aiming to strengthen their sustainability endeavors. Our in-depth examination of the bank's approach to implementing administrative controls for sustainability allows us to delineate best practices for banks on the integration of ESG factors into their business strategies, internal governance arrangements, and risk management frameworks, as mandated by supervisory authorities (e.g., EBA, 2019, 2020). This is particularly important in the context of ESG sanctions, which can have a significant impact on banks by causing reputational damage and financial penalties. Given the role of supervisory authorities in prudential supervision and their heightened focus on ESG issues, these sanctions are especially critical for large, listed banking groups, which are subject to rigorous oversight and higher compliance expectations (Murè et al., 2021; Mango et al., 2023). Therefore, implementing adequate administrative controls for sustainability is essential to mitigate these risks and enhance operational resilience.

Our study presents some limitations that could be faced in future research. One limitation relates to the use of a single-case study methodology, which does not allow for the generalization of the results. Furthermore, the single-case study may not capture the diversity and complexity of different organizational practices and contexts, thus limiting the findings' applicability to other settings. Future research could, therefore, involve larger samples of banks from different institutional settings to promote a better understanding of how banks integrate ESG factors within their administrative controls to foster their commitment to sustainability. Finally, as existing studies focus only on corporate governance mechanisms (e.g., sustainability committee), future research could investigate how the combination of different administrative controls (e.g., governance, organizational structures, and policy and procedures) relates to ESG performance and risk management.

References

Ahmed, S. U., Ahmed, S. P., & Hasan, I. (2018). Why banks should consider ESG risk factors in bank lending? *Banks and Bank Systems, 13*(3), 71–80.

Avrampou, A., Skouloudis, A., Iliopoulos, G., & Khan, N. (2019). Advancing the sustainable development goals: Evidence from leading European banks. *Sustainable Development, 27*(4), 743–757.

Bell, S. T., Fisher, D. M., Brown, S. G., & Mann, K. E. (2018). An approach for conducting actionable research with extreme teams. *Journal of Management, 44*(7), 2740–2765. https://doi.org/10.1177/0149206316653805

Birindelli, G., & Palea, V. (2022). To green or not to green? How CSR mechanisms at the governance level affect the likelihood of banks pursuing green product strategies. *Corporate Governance: The International Journal of Business in Society, 23*(1), 219–242.

Birindelli, G., Ferretti, P., Intonti, M., & Iannuzzi, A. P. (2015). On the drivers of corporate social responsibility in banks: Evidence from an ethical rating model. *Journal of Management and Governance, 19*, 303–340.

Birindelli, G., Dell'Atti, S., Iannuzzi, A. P., & Savioli, M. (2018). Composition and activity of the board of directors: Impact on ESG performance in the banking system. *Sustainability, 10*(12), 4699.
Bose, S., Khan, H. Z., Rashid, A., & Islam, S. (2018). What drives green banking disclosure? An institutional and corporate governance perspective. *Asia Pacific Journal of Management, 35*, 501–527.
Broccardo, E., Costa, E., & Mazzuca, M. (2016). Corporate social responsibility and financial performance in Italian co-operative banks. In *Routledge handbook of social and sustainable finance* (pp. 280–295). Routledge.
Bruno, M., & Lagasio, V. (2021). An overview of the European policies on ESG in the banking sector. *Sustainability, 13*(22), 12641.
Chen, Z., Mirza, N., Huang, L., & Umar, M. (2022). Green banking—can financial institutions support green recovery? *Economic Analysis and Policy, 75*, 389–395.
Christensen, L., Rikhardsson, P., Rohde, C., & Batt, C. E. (2018). Changes to administrative controls in banks after the financial crisis. *Qualitative Research in Accounting and Management, 15*(2), 161–180.
Cosma, S., Venturelli, A., Schwizer, P., & Boscia, V. (2020). Sustainable development and European banks: A non-financial disclosure analysis. *Sustainability, 12*(15), 6146.
Cosma, S., Principale, S., & Venturelli, A. (2022). Sustainable governance and climate-change disclosure in European banking: The role of the corporate social responsibility committee. *Corporate Governance: The International Journal of Business in Society, 22*(6), 1345–1369.
Coulson, A. B. (2009). How should banks govern the environment? Challenging the construction of action versus veto. *Business Strategy and the Environment, 18*(3), 149–161.
Creswell, J. W., & Poth, C. N. (2016). *Qualitative inquiry and research design: Choosing among five approaches*. Sage.
Creswell, J. W., Hanson, W. E., Clark Plano, V. L., & Morales, A. (2007). Qualitative research designs: Selection and implementation. *The Counseling Psychologist, 35*(2), 236–264.
D'Apolito, E., Galletta, S., Iannuzzi, A. P., & Labini, S. S. (2024). Sustainability and bank credit access: New evidence from Italian SMEs. *Research in International Business and Finance, 69*, 102242.
Dicuonzo, G., Donofrio, F., Iannuzzi, A. P., & Dell'Atti, V. (2022). The integration of sustainability in corporate governance systems: An innovative framework applied to the European systematically important banks. *International Journal of Disclosure and Governance, 19*(3), 249–263.
Ditillo, A., & Lisi, I. E. (2014). Towards a more comprehensive framework for sustainability control systems research. In *Accounting for the environment: More talk and little progress* (Vol. 5, pp. 23–47). Emerald Group Publishing Limited.
Easton, G. (2010). Critical realism in case study research. *Industrial Marketing Management, 39*(1), 118–128.
Ehlers, T., Packer, F., & de Greiff, K. (2022). The pricing of carbon risk in syndicated loans: Which risks are priced and why? *Journal of Banking and Finance, 136*, 106180.
Eriksson, P., & Kovalainen, A. (2015). *Qualitative methods in business research: A practical guide to social research*. Sage.
European Banking Authority - EBA (2022). *The EBA roadmap on sustainable finance*. Available at: https://www.eba.europa.eu/sites/default/files/document_library/Publications/Reports/2022/ESG%20roadmap/1045378/EBA%20Roadmap%20on%20Sustainable%20Finance.pdf
European Banking Authority – EBA. (2019). *EBA action plan on sustainable finance*. Available at: https://www.eba.europa.eu/sites/default/documents/files/document_library/EBA%20Action%20plan%20on%20sustainable%20finance.pdf
European Banking Authority – EBA. (2020). *Final report guidelines on loan origination and monitoring*. Available at: https://www.eba.europa.eu/sites/default/documents/files/document_library/Publications/Guidelines/2020/Guidelines%20on%20loan%20origination%20and%20monitoring/884283/EBA%20GL%202020%2006%20Final%20Report%20on%20GL%20on%20loan%20origination%20and%20monitoring.pdf

European Banking Authority – EBA. (2021). *Report on management and supervision of ESG risks for credit institutions and investment firms*. Available at: https://www.eba.europa.eu/sites/default/documents/files/document_library/Publications/Reports/2021/1015656/EBA%20Report%20on%20ESG%20risks%20management%20and%20supervision.pdf

European Central Bank - ECB (2020). *Guide on climate-related and environmental risks Supervisory expectations relating to risk management and disclosure*. Available at: https://www.bankingsupervision.europa.eu/legalframework/publiccons/pdf/climate-related_risks/ssm.202005_draft_guide_on_climate-related_and_environmental_risks.en.pdf

European Commission – EC. (2018). *Action plan: Financing sustainable growth*. Available at: https://eur-lex.europa.eu/legal-content/EN/TXT/HTML/?uri=CELEX:52018DC0097&from=EN

Ferretti, P., & Martino, P. (2023). An introduction to sustainable finance. In *Banking and financial markets: New risks and challenges from Fintech and sustainable finance* (pp. 95–114). Springer International Publishing.

Ferretti, P., Gonnella, C., & Martino, P. (2024). Integrating sustainability in management control systems: An exploratory study on Italian banks. *Meditari Accountancy Research, 32*(7), 1–34.

Fu, R., Tang, Y., & Chen, G. (2020). Chief sustainability officers and corporate social (Ir) responsibility. *Strategic Management Journal, 41*(4), 656–680.

Galletta, S., Mazzù, S., & Naciti, V. (2021). Banks' business strategy and environmental effectiveness: The monitoring role of the board of directors and the managerial incentives. *Business Strategy and the Environment, 30*(5), 2656–2670.

Galletta, S., Mazzù, S., & Naciti, V. (2022). A bibliometric analysis of ESG performance in the banking industry: From the current status to future directions. *Research in International Business and Finance, 62*, 101684.

Griffith, E. E., Hammersley, J. S., & Kadous, K. (2015). Audits of complex estimates as verification of management numbers: How institutional pressures shape practice. *Contemporary Accounting Research, 32*(3), 833–863. https://doi.org/10.1111/1911-3846.12104

Houston, J. F., & Shan, H. (2022). Corporate ESG profiles and banking relationships. *The Review of Financial Studies, 35*(7), 3373–3417.

Hussain, N., Rigoni, U., & Orij, R. P. (2018). Corporate governance and sustainability performance: Analysis of triple bottom line performance. *Journal of Business Ethics, 149*, 411–432.

Ielasi, F., Bellucci, M., Biggeri, M., & Ferrone, L. (2023). Measuring banks' sustainability performances: The BESGI score. *Environmental Impact Assessment Review, 102*, 107216.

La Torre, M., & Chiappini, H. (Eds.). (2018). *Socially responsible investments: The crossroads between institutional and retail investors*. Springer.

La Torre, M., Leo, S., & Panetta, I. C. (2021). Banks and environmental, social and governance drivers: Follow the market or the authorities? *Corporate Social Responsibility and Environmental Management, 28*(6), 1620–1634.

La Torre, M., Bittucci, L., Paccione, C., & Palma, A. (2024). Evaluating the sustainability profile of banks: A comprehensive benchmarking analysis in the Italian context. *Business Strategy and the Environment*.

Li, Z., Liao, G., Wang, Z., & Huang, Z. (2018). Green loan and subsidy for promoting clean production innovation. *Journal of Cleaner Production, 187*, 421–431.

Lueg, R., & Radlach, R. (2016). Managing sustainable development with management control systems: A literature review. *European Management Journal, 34*(2), 158–171.

Mallin, C. A., & Michelon, G. (2011). Board reputation attributes and corporate social performance: An empirical investigation of the US best corporate citizens. *Accounting and Business Research, 41*(2), 119–144.

Malmi, T., & Brown, D. A. (2008). Management control systems as a package—Opportunities, challenges and research directions. *Management Accounting Research, 19*(4), 287–300.

Mango, F., Murè, P., Cardi, M., Paccione, C., & Bittucci, L. (2023). Supervisory sanctions, ESG practices, and banks' reputation: A market performance analysis of sanctioned banks. *Corporate Ownership and Control, 20*.

Merchant, K. A., & Van der Stede, W. A. (2007). *Management control systems: Performance measurement, evaluation and incentives*. Pearson Education.
Mio, C., Costantini, A., & Panfilo, S. (2022). Performance measurement tools for sustainable business: A systematic literature review on the sustainability balanced scorecard use. *Corporate Social Responsibility and Environmental Management, 29*(2), 367–384.
Miralles-Quirós, M. M., Miralles-Quirós, J. L., & Redondo-Hernández, J. (2019). The impact of environmental, social, and governance performance on stock prices: Evidence from the banking industry. *Corporate Social Responsibility and Environmental Management, 26*(6), 1446–1456.
Murè, P. (2022). La compliance in banca: tra le soluzioni Regtech e l'integrazione dei fattori ESG. *La compliance in banca*, 1–310.
Murè, P., Spallone, M., Mango, F., Marzioni, S., & Bittucci, L. (2021). ESG and reputation: The case of sanctioned Italian banks. *Corporate Social Responsibility and Environmental Management, 28*(1), 265–277.
Nguyen, D. D., Ongena, S., Qi, S., & Sila, V. (2022). Climate change risk and the cost of mortgage credit. *Review of Finance, 26*(6), 1509–1549.
Procopio, G., Trotta, A., Strano, E., & Iannuzzi, A. P. (2020). Green banking in Italy: Current and future challenges. *Contemporary issues in sustainable finance: Creating an efficient market through innovative policies and instruments* (pp. 205–258).
Rahman, H. U., Zahid, M., & Al-Faryan, M. A. S. (2023). ESG and firm performance: The rarely explored moderation of sustainability strategy and top management commitment. *Journal of Cleaner Production, 404*, 136859.
Soderstrom, S. B., & Weber, K. (2020). Organizational structure from interaction: Evidence from corporate sustainability efforts. *Administrative Science Quarterly, 65*(1), 226–271.
Strand, R. (2014). Strategic leadership of corporate sustainability. *Journal of Business Ethics, 123*, 687–706.
Umar, M., Ji, X., Mirza, N., & Naqvi, B. (2021). Carbon neutrality, bank lending, and credit risk: Evidence from the Eurozone. *Journal of Environmental Management, 296*, 113156.
Velte, P., & Stawinoga, M. (2020). Do chief sustainability officers and CSR committees influence CSR-related outcomes? A structured literature review based on empirical-quantitative research findings. *Journal of Management Control, 31*(4), 333–377.
Weber, O. (2012). Environmental credit risk management in banks and financial service institutions. *Business Strategy and the Environment, 21*(4), 248–263.
Wijethilake, C., & Lama, T. (2019). Sustainability core values and sustainability risk management: Moderating effects of top management commitment and stakeholder pressure. *Business Strategy and the Environment, 28*(1), 143–154.
Wu, M. W., & Shen, C. H. (2013). Corporate social responsibility in the banking industry: Motives and financial performance. *Journal of Banking & Finance, 37*(9), 3529–3547.
Yin, R. K. (2003). Designing case studies. *Qualitative research methods, 5*(14), 359–386.
Yin, R. K. (2013). Validity and generalization in future case study evaluations. *Evaluation, 19*(3), 321–332.
Yin, R. K. (2014). *Case study research: Design and methods* (5th ed.). Sage.
Zorn, D. M. (2004). Here a chief, there a chief: The rise of the CFO in the American firm. *American Sociological Review, 69*(3), 345–364.

Chapter 6
Integrating HRM and ESG Literature: From Triple to Quadruple Bottom Line

Silvia Barghini, Mariacristina Bonti, and Sara Sassetti

6.1 Introduction

The topic of corporate sustainability gets significant attention nowadays, and the role of human resource management (HRM) has become essential to successful companywide sustainable initiatives. The link between sustainable development and HRM is prominent in recent literature (Abualigah et al., 2023; Anlesinya & Susomrith, 2020; Dwivedi et al., 2023; Mukhuty et al., 2022; Podgorodnichenko et al., 2020; Santana & Lopez-Cabrales, 2019). HRM practices are often linked to sustainability, business ethics, and workplace justice and frequently fall under the terms of sustainable HRM. It is well recognized that HRM can play a critical role in enhancing corporate sustainability through policies and practices that benefit its people and society in general. It is generally agreed that all these initiatives must be documented and reported to gain visibility and credibility.

There has recently been a significant focus on the UN's Sustainable Development Goals (SDGs) and the aspects of the environment, society, and governance (ESG) that establish the standards for documenting and disclosing the relevant practices corporate enterprises implement. The SDGs and the ESG criteria are important for organizations to implement and report their sustainable initiatives, proving their sustainability commitment to their stakeholders (Papalexandris, 2022).

The SDGs follow the Millennium Development Goals (MDGs) and are 17 goals formulated around sustainable development to be achieved in environmental, social, and economic contexts (Obrecht et al., 2021; Pizzi et al., 2020).

In 2004, James Gifford, head of sustainable and impact advisory at Credit Suisse, coined the term "ESG." This abbreviation refers to the three main factors that are

S. Barghini · M. Bonti (✉) · S. Sassetti
Department of Economics and Management, University of Pisa, Pisa, Italy
e-mail: silvia.barghini@phd.unipi.it; mariacristina.bonti@unipi.it; sara.sassetti@unipi.it

F. Bernini (ed.), *Creating Value Through Sustainability*, SIDREA Series in Accounting and Business Administration,
https://doi.org/10.1007/978-3-031-74292-7_6

redefining how people think about investments around the world: environment, society, and governance. ESGs are therefore criteria that stakeholders adopted to assess business performance in environmental, social, and governance terms. Nowadays, the mobility of financial resources depends mostly on whether and how organizations implement and communicate their ESG strategy. In this regard, there are two relevant European regulations: the Sustainable Finance Disclosure Regulation (SFDR, 2021) and the Corporate Sustainability Reporting Directive (CSRD, 2022/2464).

The former aims to prevent greenwashing and improve the transparency of sustainability declarations by financial market participants. The latter introduces detailed transparency requirements for businesses regarding environmental impact, human rights protection, and compliance with social standards, by amending the Non-Financial Reporting Directive (NFRD, 2014/95).

According to the CSRD, the environmental factors a company should report on are those related to energy policies, the use of natural resources, waste treatment, and greenhouse gas emissions. Reporting social factors means communicating working conditions, the relationship with social partners (e.g., employees, suppliers, customers, and communities), and how an organization undertakes to respect human rights and the principles of equality, diversity, and inclusion. Regarding governance factors, the CSRD requires them to provide information about their governance bodies (e.g., administrative and control protocols), organizational structure, corporate ethics and culture, financial transparency, and risk management.

According to institutional theory (DiMaggio & Powell, 1983; Lewis et al., 2019; Meyer & Rowan, 1977), each organization is regulated by the environment in which it operates. The business practices and actions adhere to societal values and norms of the institutional context to remain competitive. An organization must, for instance, nowadays meet sustainability standards and comply with ESG criteria to be considered worthy of receiving financial resources. Companies are therefore increasingly committed to implementing a sustainability strategy that gives them a high ranking according to ESG criteria.

The adoption of these ESG strategies and an organization's sustainable development depend primarily on its human capital and how it is managed. According to human capital theory (Nafukho et al., 2004), people are the key factor in successfully implementing a competitive strategy. They represent an organization's core and distinctive assets by virtue of their knowledge, skills, and abilities (KSA) (Subramaniam & Youndt, 2005; Wright et al., 1994). Organizations can face challenges and seize opportunities thanks to their human capital (Chen & Chang, 2013). For instance, by institutional isomorphism, the ESG challenges become part of the corporate strategy and involve and require business changes focused on sustainability. This requires strategic management linked to human capital, specifically HRM. Despite its relevance and topicality, the literature has not definitively clarified how HRM can help organizations address the ESG criteria. As shown by previous studies (Anlesinya & Susomrith, 2020; Kramar & Mariappanadar, 2015), in the sustainable HRM literature, some research topics are inflated (e.g., green HRM) at the expense of others: for instance, the relationship between HRM and ESG strategies still seems unclear.

This study seeks to bridge this gap, starting with a literature review and exploring how HRM can contribute to ESG strategies. Specifically, we develop a bibliometric analysis and systematic literature review (SLR) (Bartolacci et al., 2020; Pizzi et al., 2020; Sassetti et al., 2018) to define the current scenario and build an explanatory framework.

6.2 Method

Conducting bibliometric analyses and a systematic literature review (SLR) is important for research development and represents a key tool in managing knowledge diversity about a specific research topic. Researchers can then map and assess existing studies but also deepen and develop the current structure further (Bartolacci et al., 2020; Donthu et al., 2021; Pizzi et al., 2020; Sassetti et al., 2018). A systematic literature review supported by a bibliometric analysis based on the visualization of similarities (VOS) technique (Van Eck & Waltman, 2010) was therefore done.

According to Page et al. (2020), the Preferred Reporting Items for Systematic Reviews and Meta-Analyses (PRISMA) protocol is a valuable tool for enhancing the reliability of such types of investigations: authors use it widely, and research journals endorse it for its high reproducibility and transparency. Considering the importance of PRISMA in research, we therefore took a systematic approach characterized by transparency and reproducibility by following Moher et al. (2009), Page et al. (2021), and Tranfield et al. (2003). The steps of identification, screening, eligibility, and inclusion of items are described in Fig. 6.1.

During the *identification* stage, we detected the most representative terms, i.e., "ESG"; "environmental, social, and governance"; "sustainability"; and "human resources." Thereafter we conducted a general keyword search on two bibliographic databases (Web of Science and Scopus®), selecting the following options to refine the results: English language, business and management categories, and document type such as journal articles and reviews. The search focused on the strings *("human resource" OR "HR" OR "HRM") AND ("sustainab*" OR "ESG" OR "environmental, social, and governance")*. Seeking the strings above in the title, abstract, and keywords, we obtained 1054 articles from Web of Science and 1988 from Scopus®. The search took place on October 13, 2023.

In the *screening* stage, following Arruda et al. (2022), conducting bibliometric analyses through VOSviewer software involves working on data from a single source. In accordance with Palumbo et al. (2022), we chose the database with wider coverage as the main one for our study: the values above led us to select Scopus®. We removed duplicates (4 items) and defined the inclusion/exclusion criteria. The relevance of the journal field for our research is the first criterion adopted, because we aimed to focus our study on the main business journal according to the Chartered Association of Business Schools (CABS, 2021) ranking. Figure 6.1 contains the list

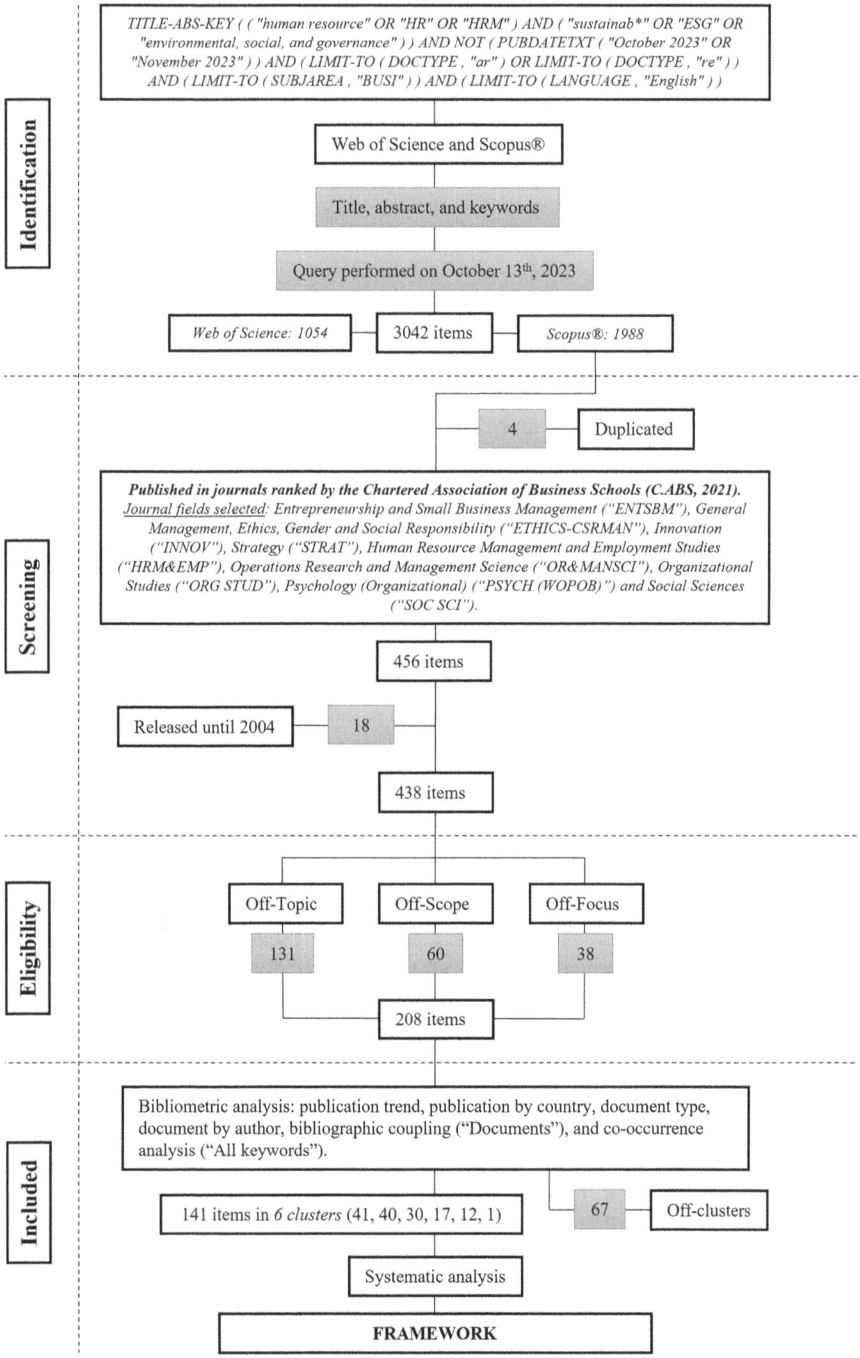

Fig. 6.1 PRISMA flow diagram

of the selected fields. The documents included numbered 456. Since ESG is the core concept of this research, we decided to only include articles published after the oldest extrapolated ESG paper (2004), whereafter the sample dropped to 438 articles.

To increase research accuracy, during the *eligibility* stage, we decided to exclude records that did not deal with (off-topic), emphasize (off-scope), or provide insights into how HRM contributes to ESG strategies (off-focus). Reading titles, keywords, as well as abstracts, and applying these criteria, allowed us to identify the most eligible papers (208), with 131 being off-topic, 60 off-scope, and 38 off-focus. Concluding with the *inclusion* stage, the filtering process described above allowed us to consider 208 documents in our bibliometric and systematic analyses.

After ensuring that the dataset only contained documents suitable for the purpose of this study, two types of bibliometric analysis were applied (Sassetti et al., 2018): bibliometric activity indicators and, having the single papers as units of analysis, bibliographic coupling. In detail, activity indicators provide data about the volume and impact of research, allowing one to observe the quantitative evolution of the literature. We specifically analyzed the publication trend, publication by country, document type, document citation, and co-occurrence analysis with "All keywords."

Based on Van Eck and Waltman (2010) and Brown et al. (2020), the bibliographic coupling was conducted through VOSviewer software (version 1.6.18). Bibliographic coupling occurs when two works refer to a common third work in their citations (two documents are considered bibliographically coupled if they both cite one or more documents). This results in a visual representation where the density of shading indicates the extent of common citations. Essentially, the distance between articles can be seen as a measure of the connection between cited references. Articles in the same cluster are strongly connected as a group due to their shared references, suggesting that a cluster represents a distinct research stream or topic. Following the process, six clusters based on bibliographic coupling were identified. Using the results of clustering found by VOSviewer, we systematically analyzed each paper in such clusters.

6.3 Results

In this section, we first present the main results of applying the activity indicators—the publication trend, publication by country, document citation, document type, and co-occurrence analysis with "All keywords." Thereafter the outcomes of the bibliographic coupling analysis will be examined.

6.3.1 *Activity Indicators*

The first analysis addressed the number of publications on HRM and ESG. Figure 6.2 confirms the growing interest in understanding this phenomenon in the last few years. The oldest ESG paper was published in 2005; more articles were only published after 2013. In particular, studies about the relationship between HRM and ESG started peaking in 2019, with more than 86 articles of the 208 in our dataset published after that year. This result confirms the novelty of the topic and the elevated interest by human resources scholars.

In the analysis of publication distribution across countries, Fig. 6.3 highlights the USA, India, and Australia as the leading contributors to the literature on the role of HRM in shaping ESG strategies. It is intriguing to notice that among European Union countries, only France actively engages in the discourse about HRM's contribution to the development of ESG strategies. It would confirm that the European literature predominantly emphasizes the development of ESG strategies, with a specific focus on accounting and governance perspectives. This underscores the need to broaden the discussion on this pivotal subject, particularly by incorporating HRM insights. The limited representation of European countries in the discourse presents an opportunity for increased collaboration and contribution to the evolving dialogue on ESG strategy development.

Figure 6.4 depicts the authors who have made the most significant contributions to our dataset. Charbel José Chiappetta Jabbour is at the forefront, with a substantial body of work on sustainability. Robin Kramar and Sugumar Mariappanadar also emerge as authors with noteworthy contributions, although the extent of their impact is comparatively less pronounced.

In our dataset, 5.8% of the documents are classified as reviews (Fig. 6.5). It is interesting to note that no literature reviews about ESG criteria in the HRM field

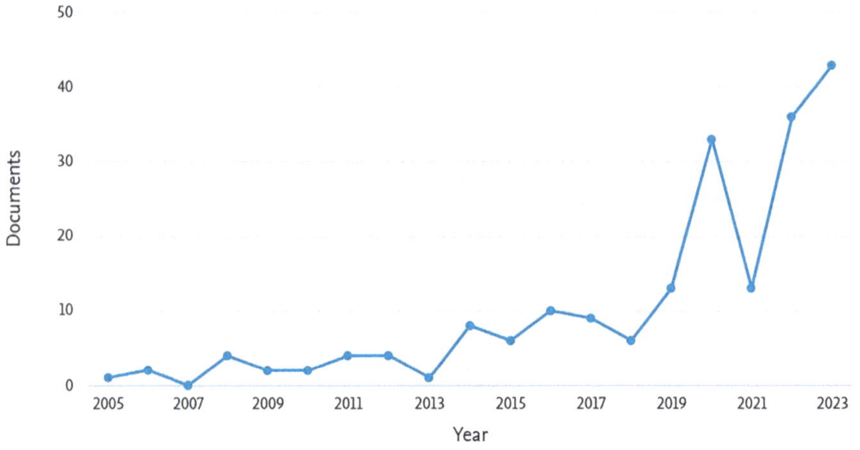

Fig. 6.2 Publication trend

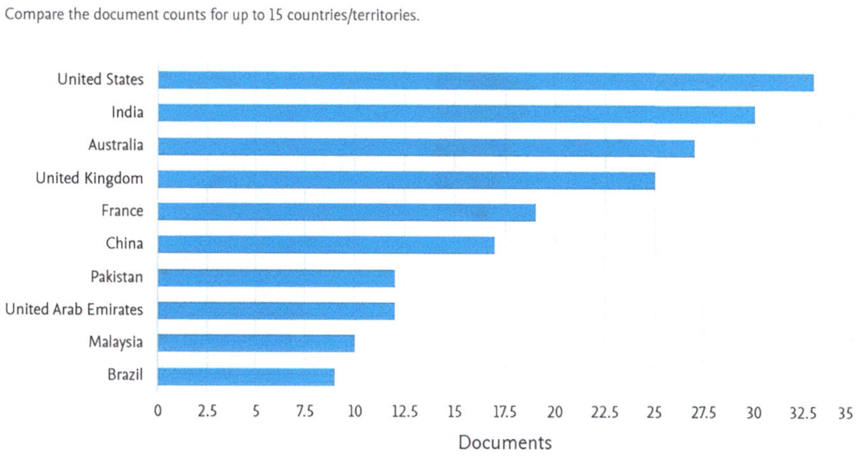

Fig. 6.3 Publication by country

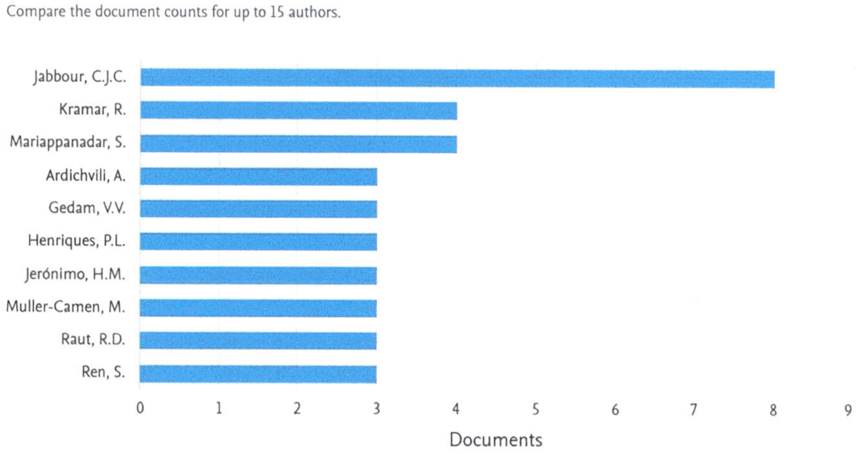

Fig. 6.4 Document by author

have been developed to date (Fig. 6.6). Although "environmental, social, and governance" and the abbreviation ESG were included in the keyword search, the co-occurrence analysis with "All keywords" does not show them. There are only references to environmental and social factors such as "environmental economics," "environmental management," "environmental sustainability," "environmental performance," "green human resource management," "GHRM," "circular economy," "social responsibility," and "corporate social responsibility." The only implicit reference to the concept of "governance" is in the keyword "leadership." This initial evidence strongly supports our research objective and underlines the need to conduct research on the topic.

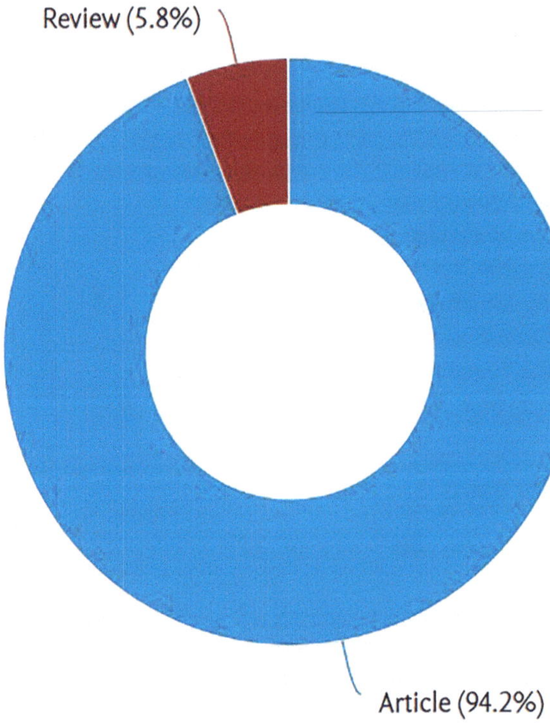

Fig. 6.5 Document type

6.3.2 Bibliographic Coupling

Exploring the core of this study, using bibliographic coupling in document analysis facilitated the formulation of the research stream's definition, pinpointing clusters in the realm of the relationship between HRM and ESG strategies (Fig. 6.7). The following section presents the six clusters and their associated themes, derived from a systematic analysis. Table 6.1 shows the six most influential documents per cluster. As the sixth cluster has only one document, it is not reported below.

The Multifaceted Relationship Between HRM Practices and Organizational Sustainability (Green Cluster)

The overarching theme that weaves through the green cluster (30 items) is the pivotal role of HRM and its associated practices in steering and reinforcing various facets of organizational sustainability. The narrative underscores the imperative for achieving a consensus between HR and sustainability managers, forming the bedrock for a resilient HRM system that can effectively propel sustainability-driven initiatives (Guerci & Pedrini, 2014). This theme extends to examining HRM impact on green innovation,

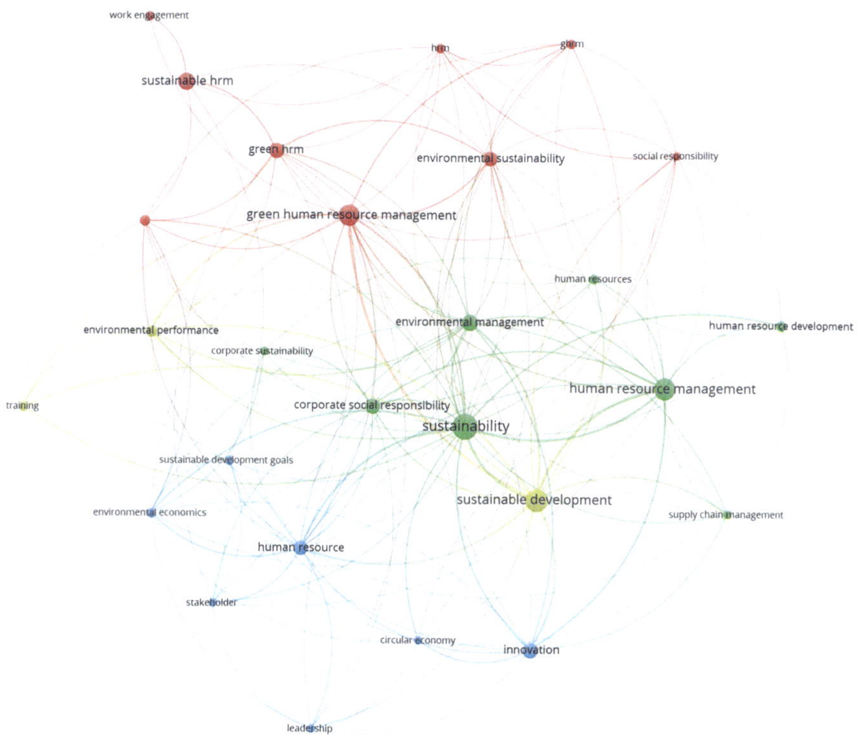

Fig. 6.6 Co-occurrence analysis with "All keywords" (the minimum number of occurrences for a document is 5)

the sustainable growth of small and medium-sized enterprises (SMEs), and the ever-evolving concept of organizational sustainability. This evolution includes a novel consideration—corporate spirituality—encompassed in the quadruple bottom line (QBL). Furthermore, the discussion traverses into the distinctive contributions of education and human resource development (HRD) in cultivating corporate social responsibility (CSR) and shaping talent management outcomes.

The main node of the green cluster is represented by the contribution of El-Kassar and Singh (2019), who investigated a holistic model that depicted and examined the relationships among green innovation and its drivers. They demonstrated that management commitment and human resource practices help overcome the technological challenges and influence an organization's performance and competitive advantage. Other recent research findings (Dwivedi et al., 2023) indicate that HR practices and theories directly impact organizational sustainability. However, with the introduction of innovation as a mediator, the initial relationship between these constructs weakened. This implies that human resource managers should cultivate an environment that encourages and supports employees' innovative thinking.

In the central part of the green cluster, most of the studies focused on the sustainable development of SMEs (Chowdhury et al., 2022; Dal Maso et al., 2020;

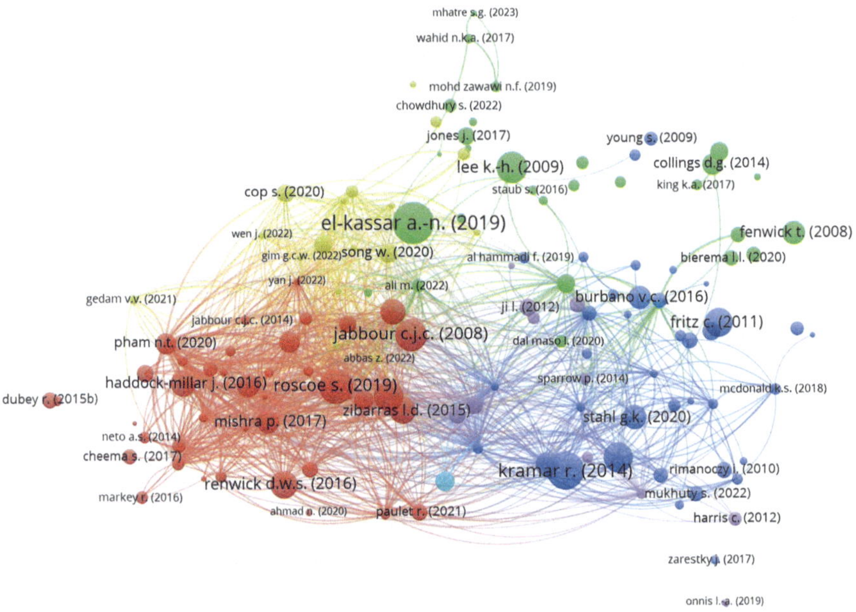

Fig. 6.7 VOS results of bibliographic coupling

Darmandieu et al., 2022; Jones & Corral de Zubielqui, 2017). In this context, the research indicated HRM as one of the critical factors needed to implement green management successfully (Ali et al., 2022; Lee, 2009). Shifting to the sustainability of SMEs' green corporate performance, general corporate culture and behavior have been indicated as drivers (Staub et al., 2016).

The upper level of the green cluster contains studies that started to focus on the recent evolution of the organizational sustainability concept with the consideration of the corporate spirituality construct. Some studies (Mhatre & Mehta, 2023; Mohd Zawawi & Abd Wahab, 2019; Wahid & Mohd. Mustamil, 2017) proposed a theoretical model by enriching the triple bottom line (TBL) concept with the inclusion of corporate spirituality, resulting in the new QBL paradigm. Beyond the conventional environmental, physical, social, and economic dimensions, these studies contend that organizational sustainability should also encompass corporate spirituality. It suggests that individuals with a heightened spiritual awareness may make more judicious choices concerning the environment, social well-being, and economic welfare of staff and the local community, fostering comprehensive and holistic sustainability.

Analyzing the right side of the green cluster, research results indicate that education in general (Camilleri, 2016) and HRD (Ardichvili, 2013; Jang & Ardichvili, 2020) can uniquely contribute to the CSR agenda through its developmental and reflective methods, fostering awareness among organizational members and involving a wider range of stakeholders (Collings, 2014).

Research by Fenwick and Bierema (2008) explored the role and challenges of HRD in promoting CSR in companies that declare a strong commitment to it. They

Table 6.1 The most influential paper per cluster (source: VOSviewer Software)

Authors	Publication year	Citations	Total link strength
Cluster 1 – Red			
Adjei-Bamfo P.; Bempong B.; Osei J.; Kusi-Sarpong S.	2020	21	380
Mishra P.	2017	136	464
Pham N.T.; Hoang H.T.; Phan Q.P.T.	2020	103	584
Roscoe S.; Subramanian N.; Jabbour C.J.C.; Chong T.	2019	336	379
Yong J.Y.; Yusliza M.-Y.; Ramayah T.; Jabbour C.J.C.; Sehnem S.; Mani V.	2020	243	500
Yusoff Y.M.; Nejati M.; Kee D.M.H.; Amran A.	2020	142	389
Cluster 2 – Blue			
Authors	*Publication year*	*Citations*	*Total link strength*
Anlesinya A.; Susomrith P.	2020	25	680
Aust I.; Matthews B.; Muller-Camen M.	2020	132	350
Jerónimo H.M.; de Lacerda T.C.; Henriques P.L.	2020	17	375
Kramar R.; Mariappanadar S.	2015	23	337
Podgorodnichenko N.; Edgar F.; Akmal A.	2022	54	437
Podgorodnichenko N.; Edgar F.; McAndrew I.	2020	12	406
Cluster 3 – Green			
Authors	*Publication year*	*Citations*	*Total link strength*
Ali M.; Puah C.-H.; Ali A.; Raza S.A.; Ayob N.	2022	39	285
Ardichvili A.	2013	56	74
Camilleri M.A.	2016	12	88
El-Kassar A.-N.; Singh S.K.	2019	535	69
Guerci M.; Pedrini M.	2014	92	187
Jang S.; Ardichvili A.	2020	18	312
Cluster 4 – Yellow			
Authors	*Publication year*	*Citations*	*Total link strength*
Abbas Z.; Sarwar S.; Rehman M.A.; Zámečník R.; Shoaib M.	2022	14	323
Abualigah A.; Koburtay T.; Bourini I.; Badar K.; Gerged A.M.	2023	10	330
Islam T.; Hussain D.; Ahmed I.; Sadiq M.	2021	87	406
Song W.; Yu H.; Xu H.	2020	85	296
Vázquez-Brust D.; Jabbour C.J.C.; Plaza-Úbeda J.A.; Perez-Valls M.; de Sousa Jabbour A.B.L.; Renwick D.W.S.	2023	8	303
Wen J.; Hussain H.; Waheed J.; Ali W.; Jamil I.	2022	11	246

(continued)

Table 6.1 (continued)

Authors	Publication year	Citations	Total link strength
Cluster 5 – Purple			
Authors	*Publication year*	*Citations*	*Total link strength*
Harris C.; Tregidga H.	2012	40	105
Ji L.; Huang J.; Liu Z.; Zhu H.; Cai Z.	2012	70	54
Kramar R.	2022	424	296
Lopez-Cabrales A.; Valle-Cabrera R.	2020	67	376
Merriman K.K.; Sen S.; Felo A.J.; Litzky B.E.	2016	33	73
Ren S.; Jackson S.E.	2020	69	201

concluded that HRD potentially offers an important voice, expertise, and services to achieve the fullest development of CSR and sustainable organizations (Bierema, 2020; Scully-Russ, 2012). By emphasizing a more inclusive and diverse assessment and development of talent management outcomes, Collings (2014) offered a more equitable comprehension of the impact of talent management on organizational performance sustainability. Finally, the study by Jang and Ardichvili (2020) identified four key areas where HRD-related strategies and practices, such as leadership development, education and training, culture change initiatives, and promoting critical reflection, were observed as playing a significant role in bolstering CSR initiatives.

Green HRM as a Tool for Environmental Sustainability Strategies (Red Cluster)

With 41 items, the red cluster is the largest one. The articles coupled bibliographically describe green HRM as a strategic lever for organizations to achieve sustainable development.

Pham et al. (2020) stated that green HRM refers to the integration of environmental management aspects in HRM, aiming to reduce and prevent pollution. Green HRM includes strategic aspects (policy-related) as well as more operational ones (practices-related) in a holistic approach that is able to align employees with the sustainable business strategy (Alcaraz et al., 2019; Mehrajunnisa et al., 2022). The significance of implementing eco-friendly HRM has been recognized over time until it became an independent research field.

Pursuing sustainable HRM development may have a positive impact in competitive terms. While green organizations help manage environmental impacts by innovating their products, services, and processes, they can gain a competitive advantage in terms of reputation, brand value, increased sales, talent acquisition, engaged workforce, better employee productivity, motivation, and loyalty (Mishra, 2017). Commitment to environmental sustainability therefore means competitive advantages not only in terms of green performance but also in social well-being and financial success (Khatoon et al., 2022; O'Donohue & Torugsa, 2016; Yusoff et al., 2020).

Adopting a strategy based on sustainability may be challenging for organizations because any green change must be introduced, developed, and accepted by the workforce. How employees perceive their organization's behavior toward environmental issues is important and influences their propensity to adopt sustainable behaviors (Haddock-Millar et al., 2016; Pellegrini et al., 2018). Mishra (2017) reported that several organizations adopt green HRM initiatives but some do not bother to formalize and follow those practices diligently (e.g., adoption of informal and cheaper means, such as posters and internal campaigns).

Formalizing green strategic actions as well as green HRM practices is however important for organizations to clarify employee engagement and roles in the greening process and encourage them to adopt eco-friendly behavior. Adjei-Bamfo et al. (2020); Khatoon et al. (2022); Subramanian and Suresh (2022); and Yusoff et al. (2020) stated that green recruitment and selection, green training and development, green rewards, and green performance management have a positive relationship with environmental business performance. Specifically, it was found that the best environmental performance is recorded when green HRM practices effectively support all green corporate activities, initiatives, and programs. Raut et al. (2020) identified ten green HRM indicators to consider for the effective implementation of sustainable environmental strategies. On the whole, developing green ability, motivating green employees, and providing green opportunities are the three main components of green HRM that organizations need to take into account (Pham et al., 2020).

The corporate development of eco-friendly skills starts from the recruitment and selection processes in which the environmental aspects should be highlighted (Adjei-Bamfo et al., 2020; Pham et al., 2020; Yusoff et al., 2020). Thereafter, training and development practices play a key role in increasing employees' environmental awareness and their green ability and expertise (Khatoon et al., 2022; Pham et al., 2020). According to Yong et al. (2020) and Mehrajunnisa et al. (2022), green recruitment and green training have a deeper impact on sustainability than all the other green HRM practices – they are best suited for improving the alignment between business strategy and the three dimensions of sustainability (economic, environmental, and social). However, Khatoon et al. (2022) stressed that the effective implementation of green HRM practices definitely has economic, social, and environmental benefits.

Organizations may adopt parameters to monitor and assess employees' performance in terms of achieving environmental goals and may consider financial and/or non-financial incentives to motivate employees to pursue corporate green aims (Pham et al., 2020). Yusoff et al. (2020) confirmed that reward systems are highly positive for corporate sustainability because they can maximize employee awareness and encourage behaviors to achieve corporate sustainable goals.

The development of a green organizational culture makes it possible to pursue sustainable goals: business principles, values, and symbols reflect and pull corporate commitment toward sustainability (Khatoon et al., 2022; Mehrajunnisa et al.,

2022; Pham et al., 2020). According to Roscoe et al. (2019), there are four main enablers of a sustainable organizational culture: peer involvement, employee empowerment, leadership emphasis, and message credibility. These key factors positively influence the relationship between green HRM practices and environmental business performance.

Mishra (2017) however warned that mere environmental vision/mission statements are not sufficient to promote eco-friendly behavior among employees; leaders play a crucial role instead (Mehrajunnisa et al., 2022; Zibarras & Coan, 2015). Pellegrini et al. (2018) found that employees are more likely to internalize, observe, and behave according to sustainability principles if their organization and managers enhance and promote sustainability. When the sustainability commitment of the company and managers is well-marked and promoted, it strongly influences the employee sentiment of belonging and impacts commitment to sustainability in the workplace. Employees become more inclined to participate in both in-role and extra-role sustainable activities (Pellegrini et al., 2018; Rayner & Morgan, 2018). Top management may in turn be encouraged to support the corporate green evolution through participating in awareness events and training courses on environmental issues as well as implementing government regulations, incentives, and ISO14000 (Khatoon et al., 2022; Mishra, 2017; Zibarras & Coan, 2015). Ren et al. (2020) and Mehrajunnisa et al. (2022) also remarked that leadership and green HRM seem to be positively linked to the top management's environmental commitment and the latter to the entire company's environmental performance.

Talking about green HRM does not mean only referring to environmental aspects of sustainability but also to social ones. According to Pham et al. (2020), green HRM practices also encompass the topics of work-life balance and employees' health and safety. The former refers to the equilibrium between professional and personal life concerning environmentally conscious values, attitudes, and behavior. The latter prioritizes employee well-being by implementing health and safety protocols aligned with environmental aspects.

Green HRM and Organizational Behavior Implications (Yellow Cluster)

The yellow cluster (17 items) includes research about the impact of green HRM on employee behavior and how it would be oriented to a more overarching vision of sustainable organization and performance. The core contributions focused on the role of leadership in supporting green and sustainable behavior in organizations. At the center of the yellow cluster, the studies by Islam et al. (2021a, b) are highlighted. They empirically demonstrated that ethical leadership serves as a predictor of green HRM, positively influencing employees' engagement in both green in-role and extra-role behavior.

These studies proposed that ethical leaders do not only exemplify organizational green HRM practices but also foster alignment between individuals' values and corporate values, encouraging corresponding behavior. Aligned to this study, the research by Ismail et al. (2022) and Khan and Khan (2022) emphasizes the crucial role of leaders being perceived as visionary for employees to positively respond to green HRM initiatives and have an impact on organizational citizenship behavior (OCB). Furthermore, spiritual (Abualigah et al., 2023) and authentic (Luu, 2023) leadership strengthens the positive relationship between green HRM and green work engagement. It creates a sense of belonging and reinforces the exchange relationship, highlighting the importance of leadership in promoting environmentally conscious behavior and creativity (Luu, 2023).

Other contributions underlined the pivotal role of specific green HRM practices in fostering sustainable behavior in various organizational contexts. The findings by Abbas et al. (2022) underscore the critical importance of green HRM, specifically green training and development as well as top management commitment to a greening workforce by promoting sustainability in higher education institutions in Pakistan.

Cop et al. (2020) come to the same findings, underscoring the positive impact of green training on both organizational citizenship behavior and environmental commitment in the tourism sector in Turkey. Consistent with Abbas et al. (2022), the findings by Wen et al. (2021) revealed that green HRM practices have a significant and positive relationship with environmental sustainability in Pakistan. This showed that, in addition to green training, better selection and recruitment practices also improve employee pro-environmental knowledge, while other practices, such as performance appraisal and reward systems, can motivate employees to achieve strategic organizational goals.

Some contributions focused on understanding how green HRM, through mechanisms such as green human capital, organizational responses to environmental pressures, communication of environmental commitment, and psychological factors like a sense of calling, play a crucial role in promoting sustainability and green behavior in organizational contexts. Song et al. (2021) explored the novel aspect of how green HRM influences green innovation, testing the indirect influence of green HRM on green innovation through green human capital and considering management environmental capital as a moderator in this indirect relationship.

The contribution by Vázquez-Brust et al. (2023) revealed green HRM systems as a crucial factor in explaining the intensity of the implementation of green practices in response to stakeholder environmental pressures. In the same vein, the research by Gim et al. (2022) demonstrated that companies adopting green HRM convey to their employees that a commitment to environmental sustainability goes beyond mere financial goals. Employees are consequently inclined to view these HRM practices as efforts aimed at enhancing their performance and overall well-being. The research by Zhang et al. (2021) addressed the unexplored relationship between a sense of calling and employee green behavior (EGB), revealing that a sense of calling positively influences EGB by increasing employees' prosocial motivation. This study contributed to a vocational psychology perspective to EGB literature, shedding light on the mechanisms and conditions influencing green behavior in the workplace.

Sustainable HRM (Blue Cluster)

The blue cluster (40 items) relates to the concept and features of sustainable HRM. In literature, there are several terms to describe the connection between HRM and sustainability (Kramar & Mariappanadar, 2015): "sustainable HRM" is the most widespread, as an umbrella term that captures the other concepts. The literature in this cluster can be traced back to five main research strands: sustainable HRM types (Anlesinya & Susomrith, 2020; Aust et al., 2020), sustainable HRM outcomes (Anlesinya & Susomrith, 2020; Jeronimo et al., 2020; Podgorodnichenko et al., 2020, 2022), evaluation and communication of sustainable HRM outcomes (Ehnert et al., 2016; Kramar, 2014; Stankevičiūtė & Savanevičienė, 2019), drivers for sustainable HRM adoption (Anlesinya & Susomrith, 2020; Kramar, 2014; Stahl et al., 2020), and sustainable HRM challenges (Anlesinya & Susomrith, 2020; Stankevičiūtė & Savanevičienė, 2019).

According to Aust et al. (2020), there are four types of sustainable HRM: socially responsible HRM, green HRM, triple bottom line (TBL) HRM, and common good HRM. The main difference between them lies in the purpose. The first one looks at economic and social goals, the second type looks at the economic and environmental ones, TBL HRM combines all three dimensions of sustainability (economic, social, and environmental purposes), while the fourth type seeks to contribute to the common good by trying to solve grand challenges. Anlesinya and Susomrith (2020) found that the literature on sustainable HRM is mainly oriented to green HRM (59.02%); articles about socially responsible HRM are about one quarter (25.41%), and the remaining percentage (15.57%) concerns TBL HRM. The authors did not highlight the last category because they believed it is not extrinsic to the other three, but intrinsic, representing the attention and sensitivity of each sustainable HRM type to the grand challenges. Although the prevalence of the green approach might have been shaped by escalating environmental corporate concerns, the social and economic dimensions are equally important.

Anlesinya and Susomrith (2020) found that sustainable HRM and the more traditional discipline generally base the definition of their practices on the same pillars, with some HRM practices being CSR-related. According to Podgorodnichenko et al. (2022), there is a nexus between corporate social responsibility/sustainability (CSR/S) and HRM that is important in attracting and retaining employees, engaging them in sustainability efforts, and enhancing organizational performance. The authors specifically considered the joint concept of CSR/S as "context-specific organizational actions and policies that take into account stakeholders' expectations and the triple bottom line of economic, social, and environmental performance" (Podgorodnichenko et al., 2022, p. 2).

Sustainable HRM practices result in positive outcomes for organizations (e.g., climate for sustainability and improved reputation) as well as employees (e.g., commitment, satisfaction, identification, pride, and loyalty) (Jeronimo et al., 2020; Podgorodnichenko et al., 2020). Anlesinya and Susomrith (2020) found that research on the macro-level and global implications of sustainable HRM is largely overlooked and limited attention is given to team-level and societal studies. Only a few studies investigated the potential impacts of sustainable HRM practices at a micro-level, aiming to assess how sustainable HRM practices influence employee behavior, commitment, trust, well-being, and mindset.

Generally, sustainable HRM practices have positive employee outcomes, improving green team creativity and the competitive advantage. The employee experience of sustainable HRM usually has positive social and environmental results (Podgorodnichenko et al., 2022). On the one hand, these desirable effects enhance corporate financial outcomes, environmental impact, human capital worth, organizational attractiveness, and possibilities of realizing the green supply chain; on the other hand, they seem to have the potential to lessen the income disparity among households (Anlesinya & Susomrith, 2020).

Sustainable HRM outcomes may be assessed by examining organizational, social, individual, and ecological impacts. According to Kramar (2014, pp. 1081, 1082), organizations should specifically evaluate the following aspects: "the quality of the employment relationship, the health and wellbeing of the workforce, productivity (organizational); the quality of relationships at work, organization being an employer of choice and being recognised among a range of potential sources of labour (social); and job satisfaction, employee motivation, and work-life balance (individual); use of resources, such as energy, paper, water use, production of green products and services and costs associated with work travel (ecological)."

Each organization should clarify which sustainable principles it intends to pursue, develop suitable metrics tailored to its specific needs, and then disseminate these throughout the workforce using HRM practices like role definition, performance assessments, and rewards. Stankevičiūtė and Savanevičienė (2019) demonstrated the importance of sustainability management in an organization, for instance, employees experiencing less work-related stress, burnout, and work-family conflict.

To demonstrate their commitment to sustainability, a growing number of organizations have drawn up sustainability reports. This document is benchmarked to the GRI framework and addressed to all stakeholders. In terms of disclosure, Ehnert et al. (2016) found that companies usually pay equal attention to communicating environmental and decent-work/human-rights indicators. However, they seem to prefer to mainly report HRM issues affecting their core workforce in developed countries compared to indicators about workforces in their supply chains (frequently in developing countries).

Researchers have also investigated the factors that prompt the adoption of sustainable HRM. Anlesinya and Susomrith (2020) classified them as internal or external drivers. The first category includes corporate figures, ethical leadership, company size, and expected benefits. Some roleplayers, such as employees and line and senior managers, play an important role in achieving sustainable HRM. For instance, the CEO grants credibility to HRM policies, allocates resources, and shapes consensus in the organizational hierarchy; managers play a vital role in executing HRM policies and strategies (Kramar, 2014). These roleplayers are pivotal in fostering employee dedication, involvement, and behavior aligned with sustainability.

In the other category, there are pressures from external stakeholders (e.g., customers, clients, regulatory agencies, governments, and research and educational institutions), legal regulations and policies, societal values, and adverse effects linked to employee work.

Organizations therefore have to cope with various interests from multiple internal and external stakeholders (Stahl et al., 2020). Implementing HRM is not impartial, but incorporates political, social, cultural, and power dynamics. HRM practices cannot be solely explained by rational decision-making, as those involved in formulating and executing HR policies navigate a landscape of conflicting pressures (Kramar, 2014).

There are many challenges around the adoption of sustainable HRM. Although a few studies investigated them, the successful implementation of sustainable HRM is possible only by addressing the related issues. Anlesinya and Susomrith (2020) and Stankevičiūtė and Savanevičienė (2019) reported that the key challenges are usually mainly related to shortcomings, such as a lack of a formalized system; negligence in integrating HRM with sustainability practices; limited commitment to green and sustainability training; incapacity to integrate sustainable HRM into recruitment, selection, performance appraisal, compensation, and reward systems; and insufficient employee involvement in designing sustainable HRM practices.

SHRM and Sustainable HR (Purple Cluster)

The purple cluster (12 items) concerns studies that adopt strategic human resource management (SHRM) as an organizational partner contributing to the implementation of diverse sustainability initiatives. The focal contribution is by Lopez-Cabrales and Valle-Cabrera (2020), who proposed a typology of sustainable corporate strategies, introducing four ideal types: reactive, compliant, analyzer, and proactive/innovative. The HRM role varies across sustainable corporate strategies. Reactive firms specifically lack a competitive strategy and are characterized by limited capacity responses to market changes, often neglecting sustainability concerns.

Consequently, HRM enables adaptability through flexible workforce practices and rapid responses to market changes that do not properly consider sustainability. Compliance strategy prioritizes legal requirements while seeking maximum shareholder returns, potentially leading to an imbalance in sustainability dimensions. In this regard, HRM ensures understanding and adherence to legal requirements, aligning practices with regulatory mandates. The analyzer strategy responds to competitors' actions, combining compliance and prospective approaches and reacting to external pressures. With an analyzer strategy, HRM balances compliance and prospective approaches, emphasizing continuous learning to stay abreast of sustainability trends.

Proactive and innovative firms regard sustainability as a decisive factor in competitiveness, with innovations in products, processes, and working conditions. This strategy is deemed to have the highest positive impact on the TBL, emphasizing environmental, social, and economic benefits (Lopez-Cabrales & Valle-Cabrera, 2020). In a proactive/innovative strategy, HRM fosters a culture of innovation, attracting and retaining talent aligned with sustainability goals. The contribution of

SHRM to the development of sustainable HRM is also pivotal in the theoretical contribution by Kramar (2022). She emphasized that while sustainable HRM is built on SHRM, it is more significant. This is attributed to its central focus, the processes adopted, the involvement with internal as well as external stakeholders, and the importance of embedded values and assumptions guiding the purpose of HRM.

In the same vein, the contribution by Shuang Ren and Jackson (2020) proposed a conceptualization of HRM-based change that actively supports sustainability as a form of institutional change. The article distinguished between strategic HRM roles aimed at aligning HRM systems with business objectives and the more challenging role of institutional entrepreneurship for sustainable change. Given HRM's organizational reach, professionals can play a pivotal role as institutional entrepreneurs (Shuang Ren & Jackson, 2020) and strategic leaders (Harris & Tregidga, 2012) in pursuing sustainability goals.

These theoretical contributions are supported by empirical studies that underscore the complexity of HRM practices influencing employee engagement in sustainable development. The work emphasizes the importance of aligning sustainability goals with financial objectives (Merriman et al., 2016), recognizing the impact of employee training (Ji et al., 2012), and considering organizational identity orientation (Li et al., 2012) in the implementation of sustainable strategies.

6.4 Discussion

In the current competitive environment, the intersection between ESG principles and HRM has emerged as a critical nexus, by shaping the strategic direction and sustainable practices of organizations worldwide. ESG factors, encompassing issues related to the environment, social responsibility, and governance practices, have increasingly become a compass for businesses that navigate the complexities of a globalized and interconnected world. HRM was traditionally viewed as the human capital steward of an organization, but is now recognized as a linchpin in driving ESG strategies. This symbiotic relationship between ESG and HRM reflects a paradigm shift in organizational priorities to achieve long-term success.

Nevertheless, the main result of the activity indicators shows a lack of specific references to ESG. This underscores the need to improve understanding of the interplay between ESG and HRM, accentuating the novelty and importance of our study in the literature. In the co-occurrence analysis, there is no explicit reference to the ESG strategies organizations adopt. The three dimensions (environment, society, and governance) are instead treated semi-independently, and the boundaries between them are nuanced rather than clear. From the bibliographic coupling and the consequent systematic literature review, a general interconnection of HRM and sustainability emerged, contributing to diverse aspects of organizational ESG strategies.

The green cluster mainly underscores the importance of consensus between HR and sustainability managers, forming a resilient HR management system that is crucial in driving sustainability initiatives. This aligns with the social aspect of

ESG, emphasizing the need for collaboration to foster social well-being in organizations.

The red cluster predominantly focuses on the development of green HRM for environmental strategic purposes, emphasizing strategic as well as operational aspects. This aligns with the environmental aspect of ESG, emphasizing the significance of environmental sustainability for competitive advantage and financial success.

Close to the red cluster, the yellow cluster directs attention to leadership and specific green HRM practices that foster sustainable behavior, including green human capital and organizational responses to environmental pressures. This is closely related to the overall ESG strategies, as effective leadership and HR practices contribute to the broader goals of sustainability across the E, S, and G aspects.

The blue cluster delves into sustainable HRM practices and their connection with CSR, recognizing a nexus between CSR, sustainability, and HRM. This aligns with the social and governance aspects of ESG, by emphasizing the importance of CSR and sustainable HRM practices in organizational performance and social impact.

The purple cluster highlights the contribution of SHRM to sustainable HRM, surpassing SHRM in significance. This integration is vital for achieving overall ESG strategies, as SHRM's central focus, stakeholder involvement, and embedded values align with broader sustainability goals across the E, S, and G dimensions.

Overall, it is clear from our review that there is no specific literature about HRM and ESG combined. The three strategic ESG components are however essential and relevant to sustainable HRM. Talking about HRM and ESG means reflecting on the strategic aspects of sustainability, recognizing the presence of various objectives, and identifying the emerging tensions and contradictions. HRM can undoubtedly support the recognition and simultaneous achievement of several sustainable corporate goals (Podgorodnichenko et al., 2020).

Poon and Law (2022) pointed out that tensions arise around the concept of sustainability and become the heart of sustainable HRM. Podgorodnichenko et al. (2020) identified two types of tensions that HR professionals should face: the paradoxes of belonging and performing. The former arises from the HRM function related to advancing a sustainability and ESG agenda, potentially intensifying existing HRM role tensions. It reflects conflicts among multiple identities, competing roles, values, and memberships. The latter emerges between corporate goals linked to sustainability and portrays conflicts around different goals and objectives related to stakeholder needs and interests.

All the roleplayers in and outside organizations can influence strategic decisions and concrete actions linked to managing sustainability interests, the related ESG strategies, and, consequently, tensions. This evolution ends up questioning the dominant and traditional models of strategic HRM in which "fit" and "alignment" are stressed and the responsibility for strategic decisions is only that of top management (Poon & Law, 2022).

Over the last four decades, strategic HRM has become the predominant approach to HRM policy, and in the last 20 years, sustainable HRM has evolved as a new strategic approach (Kramar, 2014). In fact, the primary emphasis of strategic HRM lies in advancing organizational performance, especially in economic terms. Sustainable HRM instead goes beyond mere economic gains by also pursuing social and environmental outcomes. An integrative and multidimensional view on sustainability has emerged in the literature: it recognized that organizations should take into account inevitable tensions and trade-offs between economic, environmental, and social pillars of sustainability with different temporal (long-term versus short-term) and spatial (local versus global) dimensions (Stahl et al., 2020). Kramar and Mariappanadar (2015) claimed that sustainable HRM is refocusing strategic HRM and specifically that all HRM actions contribute to the sustainability of organizations and communities.

For an effective SHRM approach and a real application of sustainable HRM, a better understanding of how governance is addressed in sustainable HRM literature is needed. Unlike social and environmental ones, this aspect cannot be structured and systematized in an absolute way—it is not possible to identify a model of organizational structure or corporate bodies that are universally considered sustainable. A new corporate governance role for sustainability is undoubtedly emerging in organizations, but the literature on the sustainability manager is still in its infancy.

As shown in several clusters, governance aspects are crucial for the effective implementation of environmental, social, and economic strategies and by extension for successful corporate sustainability. This consideration allowed us to overcome the classical TBL approach and integrate it with ESG strategies (Fig. 6.8). Although the TBL approach is one of the most extensively used definitions of sustainability in business practices, it looks only at an organization's environmental, social, and economic aspects (Dyllick & Hockerts, 2002; Elkington, 1998; McWilliams et al., 2016; Montiel & Delgado-Ceballos, 2014; Norman & MacDonald, 2004; Yu & Zhao, 2015).

When combining HRM and ESG strategies, the further (and complementary) dimension of sustainability must be considered. An emerging line of research considers the concept of spirituality as the fourth element of sustainability, but in the managerial field and especially in the ESG field, this does not seem to be sufficient.

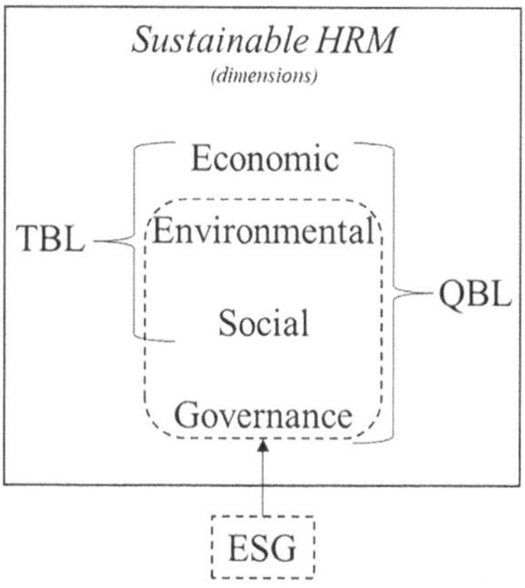

Fig. 6.8 Theoretical framework

According to the CSRD, organizations have to supply information about the characteristics of governance bodies, organizational structure, corporate ethics, and culture, among other aspects. It seems logical that overcoming the concept of corporate spirituality is necessary.

Another factor seems to stand out with a particular emphasis on being the most suitable to fulfill the role of the fourth sustainability dimension: governance. This does not only entail its narrow meaning but involves and connects the concept of corporate spirituality and organizational aspects such as business value, ethics, and culture. Moreover, it is an essential element in achieving long-term strategic objectives (Budsaratragoon & Jitmaneeroj, 2019).

Integrating the governance dimension into the TBL approach becomes crucial to obtain a more comprehensive evaluation of corporate sustainability. The global business context also stresses the need to move to a QBL approach: organizations are experiencing an evolution of the concept of TBL sustainability toward QBL sustainability (Aust et al., 2020). The QBL approach therefore becomes the frame of reference, when corporate sustainability is considered as an all-inclusive concept of environmental, social, governance, and economic aspects. It stresses the important role of all four pillars to achieve corporate sustainability. The core values and ultimate purpose of an organization are not compromised to pursue the other three goals.

6.5 Conclusion and Future Research

In the current economic context, the intricate interconnection between ESG principles and HRM is emerging as a decisive force that is shaping the strategic trajectory and sustainable practices of organizations globally. ESG increasingly serves as a navigational compass for businesses that face the complexities of a globalized world. The symbiotic relationship between ESG and HRM entails a paradigm shift in organizational priorities, by emphasizing the integral role of HRM in driving ESG strategies for long-term success. Our analysis however revealed a lack of specific references to ESG in sustainable HRM literature and a nuanced discussion on the relationship between ESG and HRM.

The core implication of our review is that the three components of ESG strategies are essential and strongly connected to sustainable HRM, although there is no specific literature on HRM and ESG combined. The tensions and contradictions identified in HRM (such as the paradoxes of belonging and performing) emphasize the evolving nature of HRM practices in pursuing sustainability and ESG goals. This evolution challenges traditional strategic HRM models, shifting the emphasis from mere economic gains to a multidimensional view of sustainability that includes social and environmental outcomes.

Future research could contribute to the development of a new research field capable of integrating the ESG topic with the HRM field. Empirical studies might be developed to verify the symbiotic relationship between ESG and HRM and answer the following questions: How does HRM lead ESG practices for long-term success? How is HRM evolving to address the paradoxes of belonging and performing and to pursue ESG goals?

Moving forward, an effective transition from SHRM to sustainable HRM requires a deeper understanding of how governance is addressed in sustainable HRM literature. Unlike social and environmental aspects, governance cannot be universally structured, and the emergence of the sustainability manager adds a new dimension. Governance aspects play a crucial role in the effective implementation of environmental, social, and economic strategies toward achieving corporate sustainability. This demands the integration of the TBL approach with ESG strategies, particularly emphasizing the role of the governance pillar. This is another aspect that future research could explore further. Empirical studies may, for instance, clarify the main changes needed for the convergence between sustainable HRM and the governance dimension of sustainability, as well as the resulting effects in terms of performance.

Interpreting corporate sustainability according to the QBL approach encapsulates the integration of environmental, social, governance, and economic performance, also highlighting the multifaceted nature of sustainability. This study shows that QBL HRM is still a nascent research field. Given its relevance from both a practical and academic standpoint, future research could attend to this branch of sustainable HRM.

References

Abbas, Z., Sarwar, S., Rehman, M. A., Zámečník, R., & Shoaib, M. (2022). Green HRM promotes higher education sustainability: A mediated-moderated analysis. *International Journal of Manpower, 43*(3), 827–843.

Abualigah, A., Koburtay, T., Bourini, I., Badar, K., & Gerged, A. M. (2023). Towards sustainable development in the hospitality sector: Does green human resource management stimulate green creativity? A moderated mediation model. *Business Strategy and the Environment, 32*(6), 3217–3232.

Adjei-Bamfo, P., Bempong, B., Osei, J., & Kusi-Sarpong, S. (2020). Green candidate selection for organizational environmental management. *International Journal of Manpower, 41*(7), 1081–1096.

Alcaraz, J. M., Susaeta, L., Suarez, E., Colón, C., Gutiérrez-Martínez, I., Cunha, R., et al. (2019). The human resources management contribution to social responsibility and environmental sustainability: Explorations from Ibero-America. *International Journal of Human Resource Management, 30*(22), 3166–3189.

Ali, M., Puah, C.-H., Ali, A., Raza, S. A., & Ayob, N. (2022). Green intellectual capital, green HRM and green social identity toward sustainable environment: A new integrated framework for Islamic banks. *International Journal of Manpower, 43*(3), 614–638.

Anlesinya, A., & Susomrith, P. (2020). Sustainable human resource management: A systematic review of a developing field. *Journal of Global Responsibility, 11*(3), 295–324.

Ardichvili, A. (2013). The role of HRD in CSR, sustainability, and ethics: A relational model. *Human Resource Development Review, 12*(4), 456–473.

Arruda, H., Silva, E. R., Lessa, M., Proença, D., Jr., & Bartholo, R. (2022). VOSviewer and bibliometrix. *Journal of the Medical Library Association: JMLA, 110*(3), 392.
Aust, I., Matthews, B., & Muller-Camen, M. (2020). Common Good HRM: A paradigm shift in Sustainable HRM? *Human Resource Management Review, 30*(3).
Bartolacci, F., Caputo, A., & Soverchia, M. (2020). Sustainability and financial performance of small and medium sized enterprises: A bibliometric and systematic literature review. *Business Strategy and the Environment, 29*(3), 1297–1309.
Bierema, L. L. (2020). HRD research and practice after 'The Great COVID-19 Pause': The time is now for bold, critical, research. *Human Resource Development International, 23*(4), 347–360.
Brown, T., Park, A., & Pitt, L. (2020). A 60-year bibliographic review of the Journal of Advertising Research: Perspectives on trends in authorship, influences, and research impact. *Journal of Advertising Research, 60*(4), 353–360.
Budsaratragoon, P., & Jitmaneeroj, B. (2019). Measuring causal relations and identifying critical drivers for corporate sustainability: The quadruple bottom line approach. *Measuring Business Excellence, 23*(3), 292–316.
Camilleri, M. A. (2016). Corporate sustainability and responsibility toward education. *Journal of Global Responsibility, 7*(1), 56–71.
Chen, Y.-S., & Chang, K.-C. (2013). The nonlinear effect of green innovation on the corporate competitive advantage. *Quality and Quantity, 47*, 271–286.
Chowdhury, S., Dey, P. K., Rodríguez-Espíndola, O., Parkes, G., Tuyet, N. T. A., Long, D. D., & Ha, T. P. (2022). Impact of organisational factors on the circular economy practices and sustainable performance of small and medium-sized enterprises in Vietnam. *Journal of Business Research, 147*, 362–378.
Collings, D. G. (2014). Toward mature talent management: Beyond shareholder value. *Human Resource Development Quarterly, 25*(3), 301–319.
Cop, S., Alola, U. V., & Alola, A. A. (2020). Perceived behavioral control as a mediator of hotels' green training, environmental commitment, and organizational citizenship behavior: A sustainable environmental practice. *Business Strategy and the Environment, 29*(8), 3495–3508.
Dal Maso, L., Basco, R., Bassetti, T., & Lattanzi, N. (2020). Family ownership and environmental performance: The mediation effect of human resource practices. *Business Strategy and the Environment, 29*(3), 1548–1562.
Darmandieu, A., Garcés-Ayerbe, C., Renucci, A., & Rivera-Torres, P. (2022). How does it pay to be circular in production processes? Eco-innovativeness and green jobs as moderators of a cost-efficiency advantage in European small and medium enterprises. *Business Strategy and the Environment, 31*(3), 1184–1203.
DiMaggio, P. J., & Powell, W. W. (1983). The iron cage revisited: Institutional isomorphism and collective rationality in organizational fields. *American Sociological Review, 48*, 147–160.
Donthu, N., Kumar, S., Mukherjee, D., Pandey, N., & Lim, W. M. (2021). How to conduct a bibliometric analysis: An overview and guidelines. *Journal of Business Research, 133*, 285–296.
Dwivedi, P., Chaturvedi, V., & Vashist, J. K. (2023). Innovation for organizational sustainability: The role of HR practices and theories. *International Journal of Organizational Analysis, 31*(3), 759–776.
Dyllick, T., & Hockerts, K. (2002). Beyond the business case for corporate sustainability. *Business Strategy and the Environment, 11*(2), 130–141.
Ehnert, I., Parsa, S., Roper, I., Wagner, M., & Muller-Camen, M. (2016). Reporting on sustainability and HRM: A comparative study of sustainability reporting practices by the world's largest companies. *International Journal of Human Resource Management, 27*(1), 88–108.
El-Kassar, A.-N., & Singh, S. K. (2019). Green innovation and organizational performance: The influence of big data and the moderating role of management commitment and HR practices. *Technological Forecasting and Social Change, 144*, 483–498.
Elkington, J. (1998). Partnerships from cannibals with forks: The triple bottom line of 21st-century business. *Environmental Quality Management, 8*(1), 37–51.

Fenwick, T., & Bierema, L. (2008). Corporate social responsibility: Issues for human resource development professionals. *International Journal of Training and Development, 12*(1), 24–35.

Gim, G. C. W., Ooi, S. K., Teoh, S. T., Lim, H. L., & Yeap, J. A. L. (2022). Green human resource management, leader–member exchange, core self-evaluations and work engagement: The mediating role of human resource management performance attributions. *International Journal of Manpower, 43*(3), 682–700.

Guerci, M., & Pedrini, M. (2014). The consensus between Italian HR and sustainability managers on HR management for sustainability-driven change – Towards a 'strong' HR management system. *The International Journal of Human Resource Management, 25*(13), 1787–1814.

Haddock-Millar, J., Sanyal, C., & Müller-Camen, M. (2016). Green human resource management: A comparative qualitative case study of a United States multinational corporation. *International Journal of Human Resource Management, 27*(2), 192–211.

Harris, C., & Tregidga, H. (2012). HR managers and environmental sustainability: Strategic leaders or passive observers? *The International Journal of Human Resource Management, 23*(2), 236–254.

Islam, T., Hussain, D., Ahmed, I., & Sadiq, M. (2021a). Ethical leadership and environment specific discretionary behaviour: The mediating role of green human resource management and moderating role of individual green values. *Canadian Journal of Administrative Sciences/Revue Canadienne des Sciences de l'Administration, 38*(4), 442–459.

Islam, T., Khan, M. M., Ahmed, I., & Mahmood, K. (2021b). Promoting in-role and extra-role green behavior through ethical leadership: Mediating role of green HRM and moderating role of individual green values. *International Journal of Manpower, 42*(6), 1102–1123.

Ismail, H., El Irani, M., & Kertechian, K. S. (2022). Green HRM and nongreen outcomes: The mediating role of visionary leadership in Asia. *International Journal of Manpower, 43*(3), 660–681.

Jang, S., & Ardichvili, A. (2020). Examining the Link Between Corporate Social Responsibility and Human Resources: Implications for HRD Research and Practice. *Human Resource Development Review, 19*(2), 183–211.

Jeronimo, H. M., de Lacerda, T. C., & Henriques, P. L. (2020). From sustainable HRM to employee performance: A complex and intertwined road. *European Management Review, 17*(4), 871–884.

Ji, L., Huang, J., Liu, Z., Zhu, H., & Cai, Z. (2012). The effects of employee training on the relationship between environmental attitude and firms' performance in sustainable development. *The International Journal of Human Resource Management, 23*(14), 2995–3008.

Jones, J., & Corral de Zubielqui, G. (2017). Doing well by doing good: A study of university-industry interactions, innovationess and firm performance in sustainability-oriented Australian SMEs. *Technological Forecasting and Social Change, 123*, 262–270.

Khan, A. N., & Khan, N. A. (2022). The nexuses between transformational leadership and employee green organisational citizenship behaviour: Role of environmental attitude and green dedication. *Business Strategy and the Environment, 31*(3), 921–933.

Khatoon, A., Khan, N. A., Parvin, F., Wahid, M. S., Jamal, M. T., & Azhar, S. (2022). Green HRM: Pathway towards environmental sustainability using AHP and FAHP in a nascent parsimony. *International Journal of Manpower, 43*(3), 805–826.

Kramar, R. (2014). Beyond strategic human resource management: Is sustainable human resource management the next approach? *International Journal of Human Resource Management, 25*(8), 1069–1089.

Kramar, R. (2022). Sustainable human resource management: Six defining characteristics. *Asia Pacific Journal of Human Resources, 60*(1), 146–170.

Kramar, R., & Mariappanadar, S. (2015). Call for papers for a Special Issue: Sustainable human resource management. *Asia Pacific Journal of Human Resources, 53*(3), 389–392.

Lee, K. H. (2009). Why and how to adopt green management into business organizations? *Management Decision, 47*(7), 1101–1121.

Lewis, A. C., Cardy, R. L., & Huang, L. S. (2019). Institutional theory and HRM: A new look. *Human Resource Management Review, 29*(3), 316–335.

Li, J., Tang, G., & Chen, Y. (2012). Firms' human resource in information system and sustainable performance: Does their organizational identity matter? *The International Journal of Human Resource Management, 23*(18), 3838–3855.

Lopez-Cabrales, A., & Valle-Cabrera, R. (2020). Sustainable HRM strategies and employment relationships as drivers of the triple bottom line. *Human Resource Management Review, 30*(3), 100689.

Luu, T. T. (2023). Can green creativity be fostered? Unfolding the roles of perceived green human resource management practices, dual mediation paths, and perceived environmentally-specific authentic leadership. *The International Journal of Human Resource Management, 34*(6), 1246–1273.

McWilliams, A., Parhankangas, A., Coupet, J., Welch, E., & Barnum, D. T. (2016). Strategic decision making for the triple bottom line. *Business Strategy and the Environment, 25*(3), 193–204.

Mehrajunnisa, M., Jabeen, F., Faisal, M. N., & Mehmood, K. (2022). Prioritizing Green HRM practices from policymaker's perspective. *International Journal of Organizational Analysis, 30*(3), 652–678.

Merriman, K. K., Sen, S., Felo, A. J., & Litzky, B. E. (2016). Employees and sustainability: The role of incentives. *Journal of Managerial Psychology, 31*(4), 820–836.

Meyer, J. W., & Rowan, B. (1977). Institutionalized organizations: Formal structure as myth and ceremony. *American Journal of Sociology, 83*(2), 340–363.

Mhatre, S. G., & Mehta, N. K. (2023). A review of workplace spirituality: Identifying present development and future research agenda. *Management Research Review, 46*(9), 1185–1206.

Mishra, P. (2017). Green human resource management: A framework for sustainable organizational development in an emerging economy. *International Journal of Organizational Analysis, 25*(5), 762–788.

Mohd Zawawi, N. F., & Abd Wahab, S. (2019). Organizational sustainability: A redefinition? *Journal of Strategy and Management, 12*(3), 397–408.

Moher, D., Liberati, A., Tetzlaff, J., & Altman, D., Group, T. P. (2009). *Preferred reporting items for systematic reviews and metaanalyses: The PRISMA statement* (reprinted from annals of internal medicine). *Physical Therapy,* 89.

Montiel, I., & Delgado-Ceballos, J. (2014). Defining and measuring corporate sustainability: Are we there yet? *Organization and Environment, 27*(2), 113–139.

Mukhuty, S., Upadhyay, A., & Rothwell, H. (2022). Strategic sustainable development of Industry 4.0 through the lens of social responsibility: The role of human resource practices. *Business Strategy and the Environment, 31*(5), 2068–2081.

Nafukho, F. M., Hairston, N., & Brooks, K. (2004). Human capital theory: Implications for human resource development. *Human Resource Development International, 7*(4), 545–551.

Norman, W., & MacDonald, C. (2004). Getting to the bottom of "triple bottom line". *Business Ethics Quarterly, 14*(2), 243–262.

Obrecht, A., Pham, M., Spehn, E., Payne, D., Brémond, A. C., Altermatt, F., et al. (2021). *Achieving the SDGs with biodiversity.*

O'Donohue, W., & Torugsa, N. (2016). The moderating effect of 'Green' HRM on the association between proactive environmental management and financial performance in small firms. *International Journal of Human Resource Management, 27*(2), 239–261.

Page, M. J., McKenzie, J. E., Bossuyt, P. M., Boutron, I., Hoffmann, T., Mulrow, C. D., et al. (2020). Mapping of reporting guidance for systematic reviews and meta-analyses generated a comprehensive item bank for future reporting guidelines. *Journal of Clinical Epidemiology, 118*, 60–68.

Page, M. J., McKenzie, J. E., Bossuyt, P. M., Boutron, I., Hoffmann, T. C., Mulrow, C. D., et al. (2021). The PRISMA 2020 statement: An updated guideline for reporting systematic reviews. *International Journal of Surgery, 88*, 105906.

Palumbo, R., Fakhar Manesh, M., & Petrolo, D. (2022). What makes work smart in the public sector? Insights from a bibliometric analysis and interpretive literature review. *Public Management Review*, 1–26.

Papalexandris, N. (2022). Sustainable development and the critical role of HRM. *Studia Universitatis Babes Bolyai-Oeconomica, 67*(3), 27–36.

Pellegrini, C., Rizzi, F., & Frey, M. (2018). The role of sustainable human resource practices in influencing employee behavior for corporate sustainability. *Business Strategy and the Environment (John Wiley & Sons, Inc), 27*(8), 1221–1232.

Pham, N. T., Hoang, H. T., & Phan, Q. P. T. (2020). Green human resource management: A comprehensive review and future research agenda. *International Journal of Manpower, 41*(7), 845–878.

Pizzi, S., Caputo, A., Corvino, A., & Venturelli, A. (2020). Management research and the UN sustainable development goals (SDGs): A bibliometric investigation and systematic review. *Journal of Cleaner Production, 276*, 124033.

Podgorodnichenko, N., Edgar, F., & McAndrew, I. (2020). The role of HRM in developing sustainable organizations: Contemporary challenges and contradictions. *Human Resource Management Review, 30*(3).

Podgorodnichenko, N., Edgar, F., & Akmal, A. (2022). An integrative literature review of the CSR-HRM nexus: Learning from research-practice gaps. *Human Resource Management Review, 32*(3).

Poon, T. S.-C., & Law, K. K. (2022). Sustainable HRM: An extension of the paradox perspective. *Human Resource Management Review, 32*(2).

Raut, R. D., Gardas, B., Luthra, S., Narkhede, B., & Kumar Mangla, S. (2020). Analysing green human resource management indicators of automotive service sector. *International Journal of Manpower, 41*(7), 925–944.

Rayner, J., & Morgan, D. (2018). An empirical study of 'green' workplace behaviours: Ability, motivation and opportunity. *Asia Pacific Journal of Human Resources, 56*(1), 56–78.

Ren, S., & Jackson, S. E. (2020). HRM institutional entrepreneurship for sustainable business organizations. *Human Resource Management Review, 30*(3), 100691.

Ren, S., Tang, G., & Jackson, S. E. (2020). Effects of Green HRM and CEO ethical leadership on organizations' environmental performance. *International Journal of Manpower, 42*(6), 961–983.

Roscoe, S., Subramanian, N., Jabbour, C. J. C., & Chong, T. (2019). Green human resource management and the enablers of green organisational culture: Enhancing a firm's environmental performance for sustainable development. *Business Strategy & the Environment (John Wiley & Sons, Inc), 28*(5), 737–749.

Santana, M., & Lopez-Cabrales, A. (2019). Sustainable development and human resource management: A science mapping approach. *Corporate Social Responsibility and Environmental Management, 26*(6), 1171–1183.

Sassetti, S., Marzi, G., Cavaliere, V., & Ciappei, C. (2018). Entrepreneurial cognition and socially situated approach: A systematic and bibliometric analysis. *Scientometrics, 116*, 1675–1718.

Scully-Russ, E. (2012). Human resource development and sustainability: Beyond sustainable organizations. *Human Resource Development International, 15*(4), 399–415.

Song, W., Yu, H., & Xu, H. (2021). Effects of green human resource management and managerial environmental concern on green innovation. *European Journal of Innovation Management, 24*(3), 951–967.

Stahl, G. K., Brewster, C. J., Collings, D. G., & Hajro, A. (2020). Enhancing the role of human resource management in corporate sustainability and social responsibility: A multi-stakeholder, multidimensional approach to HRM. *Human Resource Management Review, 30*(3).

Stankevičiūtė, Ž., & Savanevičienė, A. (2019). Can sustainable HRM reduce work-related stress, work-family conflict, and burnout? *International Studies of Management and Organization, 49*(1), 79–98.

Staub, S., Kaynak, R., & Gok, T. (2016). What affects sustainability and innovation — Hard or soft corporate identity? *Technological Forecasting and Social Change, 102*, 72–79.

Subramaniam, M., & Youndt, M. A. (2005). The influence of intellectual capital on the types of innovative capabilities. *Academy of Management Journal, 48*(3), 450–463.

Subramanian, N., & Suresh, M. (2022). The contribution of organizational learning and green human resource management practices to the circular economy: A relational analysis - Part I. *Learning Organization, 29*(5), 428–442.

Tranfield, D., Denyer, D., & Smart, P. (2003). Towards a methodology for developing evidence-informed management knowledge by means of systematic review. *British Journal of Management, 14*(3), 207–222.

Van Eck, N., & Waltman, L. (2010). Software survey: VOSviewer, a computer program for bibliometric mapping. *Scientometrics, 84*(2), 523–538.

Vázquez-Brust, D., Jabbour, C. J. C., Plaza-Úbeda, J. A., Perez-Valls, M., de Sousa Jabbour, A. B. L., & Renwick, D. W. (2023). The role of green human resource management in the translation of greening pressures into environmental protection practices. *Business Strategy and the Environment, 32*(6), 3628–3648.

Wahid, N. K. A., & Mohd. Mustamil, N. (2017). Ways to maximize the triple bottom line of the telecommunication industry in Malaysia. *Journal of Organizational Change Management, 30*(2), 263–280.

Wen, J., Hussain, H., Waheed, J., Ali, W., & Jamil, I. (2021). Pathway toward environmental sustainability: Mediating role of corporate social responsibility in green human resource management practices in small and medium enterprises. *International Journal of Manpower.*

Wright, P. M., McMahan, G. C., & McWilliams, A. (1994). Human resources and sustained competitive advantage: A resource-based perspective. *International Journal of Human Resource Management, 5*(2), 301–326.

Yong, J. Y., Yusliza, M. Y., Ramayah, T., Chiappetta Jabbour, C. J., Sehnem, S., & Mani, V. (2020). Pathways towards sustainability in manufacturing organizations: Empirical evidence on the role of green human resource management. *Business Strategy and the Environment (John Wiley & Sons, Inc), 29*(1), 212–228.

Yu, M., & Zhao, R. (2015). Sustainability and firm valuation: An international investigation. *International Journal of Accounting and Information Management, 23*(3), 289–307.

Yusoff, Y. M., Nejati, M., Kee, D. M. H., & Amran, A. (2020). Linking green human resource management practices to environmental performance in hotel industry. *Global Business Review, 21*(3), 663–680.

Zhang, Z., Zhang, Y., & Jia, M. (2021). Does a sense of calling facilitate sustainability? Research on the influence of calling on employee green behavior. *Business Strategy and the Environment, 30*(7), 3145–3159.

Zibarras, L. D., & Coan, P. (2015). HRM practices used to promote pro-environmental behavior: A UK survey. *International Journal of Human Resource Management, 26*(16), 2121–2142.

Chapter 7
Exploring the Tax Avoidance–CSR Interplay: Insights from ESG Components

Alessandro Gabrielli, Francesco Pistolesi, Giulio Greco, and Emanuele Teti

7.1 Introduction

The relationship between corporate social responsibility (CSR) and tax avoidance has become a central focus in contemporary research on ethical corporate conduct in the field of taxation. Prior research provides ample evidence that firms employ a variety of tax avoidance strategies, from tax planning to more aggressive tactics like evasion and sheltering, aimed at reducing tax burdens (Hanlon & Heitzman, 2010). Studies exploring the link between tax avoidance and CSR present conflicting evidence, revealing a complex interaction or even no interaction at all (Davis et al., 2016; Jemiolo & Farnsel, 2023; Timbate, 2023). In line with corporate culture theory (CCT) and stakeholder theory (SKT), some studies find a negative correlation, with firms engaging in tax avoidance showing less commitment to CSR. By contrast, other research suggests that tax avoidance can prompt CSR activities (a positive relationship), as predicted by the resource-based view (RBV) and shareholder theory (ST). In addition, theories like legitimacy theory (LT) and risk management theory (RMT) suggest that firms strategically use CSR to mitigate risks associated with aggressive tax avoidance, supporting a positive relationship.

Despite these insights, the evidence remains inconclusive and fragmented, with a lack of comprehensive insight into the specific dimensions of CSR, particularly those related to the environment, society, and governance. This research seeks to address these gaps by delving deeper into the relationship between tax avoidance and CSR, investigating the impact of different dimensions of CSR. Indeed, tax

---

A. Gabrielli (✉) · F. Pistolesi · G. Greco · E. Teti
Department of Economics and Management, University of Pisa, Pisa, Italy
e-mail: alessandro.gabrielli@unipi.it; francesco.pistolesi@phd.unipi.it; giulio.greco@unipi.it; emanuele.teti@unipi.it

F. Bernini (ed.), *Creating Value Through Sustainability*, SIDREA Series in Accounting and Business Administration,
https://doi.org/10.1007/978-3-031-74292-7_7

avoidance likely affects specific CSR aspects differently, such as environmental, social, and governance (ESG) components. We use ESG scores to explore the complexity of the tax avoidance–CSR relationship across these various dimensions.

In this chapter, following a literature review, we develop hypotheses concerning the relationship between tax avoidance and components of the ESG score among US companies listed on the NYSE and the Nasdaq. The findings show variations in the statistical significance and/or direction of the association between tax avoidance and CSR across ESG components. Specifically, tax avoidance has a positive significant association with the environmental and social components of the ESG score, while it shows no significant association with the governance component. The findings suggest that environmental concerns may interact with tax avoidance through tax incentives for green investments and initiatives. Also, deeper investigations show that concerns regarding human rights and the workforce likely interact with tax avoidance through tax incentives for philanthropic initiatives or via the reputation management channel.

This study contributes to prior studies on tax avoidance and CSR by highlighting the complexity of the relationship, which warrants more in-depth investigation (Jemiolo & Farnsel, 2023; Timbate, 2023). While several theories may predict either a positive or a negative relationship, the channels through which CSR affects tax avoidance (and vice versa) remain largely unexplored. In this respect, our findings on the environmental component of the ESG scores suggest that specific tax incentives might facilitate a "substitution effect" between green investment and initiatives, on the one hand, and CSR, on the other hand. A similar substitution effect may be present for aspects of the social component of the ESG.

This study also has practical implications. It suggests that policymakers and stakeholders could use tax incentives to promote ethical corporate conduct. Such incentives might be useful in aligning profit and equity value maximization with sustainable and responsible management.

7.2 Tax Avoidance and CSR: Theoretical Background and Literature Review

Minor and Morgan (2011, p. 40) argue that "for many firms, the most precious asset lies not on the balance sheet, nor in the human capital of the workforce, but rather in its reputation." However, a firm's reputation is a delicate asset that can be easily damaged by unethical practices, stakeholder dissatisfaction, and negative media coverage (Carroll & Joulfaian, 2005; Menicacci & Simoni, 2024). Therefore, active commitment to CSR and ESG practices can provide companies with "insurance-like benefits," thereby mitigating the risk of reputational damage (Minor & Morgan, 2011).

In the current CSR debate, taxation plays a central role (see, e.g., PwC, 2023; Bilicka et al., 2024; Caglio et al., 2022; Gandullia & Piserà, 2020; Kovermann & Velte, 2021). Companies can manifest their commitment to societal causes through direct CSR activities like philanthropy or indirectly by fulfilling their tax obligations (Jemiolo & Farnsel, 2023; Fourati et al., 2019). Decisions aimed at minimizing tax expenditures (i.e., tax avoidance) can significantly influence a firm's CSR policies and public perception as "good corporate citizens," leading to potential reputational concerns and negative media coverage (Shin et al., 2023; Sikka, 2012; Menicacci & Simoni, 2024). Therefore, firms should balance the potential benefits of engaging in a higher level of tax avoidance against the potential costs and risks associated with such decisions (Scholes & Wolfson, 2014; Dyreng et al., 2016).

Corporate tax avoidance involves employing various strategies aimed at reducing tax expenditures (Dyreng et al., 2008; Wang et al., 2020). Hanlon and Heitzman (2010) contend that "tax avoidance represents a continuum of tax planning strategies." While investments like municipal bonds lower explicit taxes and are perfectly legal, other practices such as "sheltering," "evasion," and "aggressiveness" are more prone to scrutiny during tax audits. Despite the potential public benefits of both tax payments and CSR activities, studies linking tax avoidance with CSR[1] provide conflicting evidence, highlighting that they can either complement, substitute, or exhibit no association at all (Davis et al., 2016; Jemiolo & Farnsel, 2023; Timbate, 2023).[2]

Several studies show that tax avoidance and CSR are negatively related. This view is consistent with a substantial incongruence between being a "tax avoider" and a "socially responsible" company, with corporate tax contributions forming an integral part of CSR commitments (Weisbach, 2002). This perspective aligns with the predictions of corporate culture theory (CCT) and stakeholder theory (SKT).

According to CCT, this negative link stems from the shared belief within an organization that a company's purpose extends beyond profit maximization, encompassing broader social and environmental considerations (Kreps, 1990; Jones Christensen et al., 2014; Lanis & Richardson, 2012). Hence, tax avoidance is likely to negatively relate to CSR, as it redirects relevant resources from society to the firm (Desai & Dharmapala, 2009; Hoi et al., 2013). Hoi et al. (2013) find a higher level of tax avoidance in firms with more CSR irresponsible activities, supporting the notion that corporate culture influences both tax avoidance and CSR. Similarly, SKT advocates creating value for all stakeholders and external parties beyond just the shareholders as the path to sustained business success (Donaldson & Preston, 1995). From this standpoint, fulfilling tax obligations can be seen as a vital responsibility for maintaining a solid relationship with a crucial stakeholder: the

[1] McWilliams and Siegel (2001) argue that CSR can be defined as the firm's commitment and engagement toward a set of "actions that appear to further some social good, beyond the interests of the firms and that which is required by the law."

[2] Early findings by Huseynov and Klamm (2012) suggest that the relationship between tax avoidance and CSR is highly complex. Their research shows that the relationship between the tax fees paid for auditor-provided tax services and the firm's level of tax avoidance is influenced by the level of CSR. Specifically, firms with robust governance or diversity issues tend to exhibit higher levels of tax aggressiveness. Conversely, firms with more community concerns show lower levels of tax avoidance.

government.[3] Tax avoidance can also be perceived as an unethical practice by the media, stakeholders, and the public, potentially increasing the firms' reputational costs (Graham et al., 2014; Dyreng et al., 2016). As a result, reputational concerns and negative media coverage can reduce managerial inclination toward tax avoidance activities, acting as a "deterrent factor" (Kanagaretnam et al., 2018; Hoi et al., 2022; Menicacci & Simoni, 2024).

In line with these expectations, empirical research provides evidence that companies with higher CSR rankings exhibit greater tax compliance in various countries, such as Nigeria (Mgbame et al., 2017), South Korea (Park, 2017), and France (Chouaibi et al., 2022). Moreover, a related body of literature supports a consistent negative association when examining specific internal and external characteristics of firms, such as the presence of outside directors (Lanis & Richardson, 2018), directors with foreign experience (Wen et al., 2020), women on the board (Rakia et al., 2023), specific ownership structures such as chaebol affiliation (Yoon et al., 2021) and state ownership (Liu & Lee, 2019), stricter tax enforcement (Zhao, 2022), the establishment of corporate foundations (Wang et al., 2022), and the use of tax havens as preferred headquarter locations (Lee, 2020; Lei & Zhang, 2020; Lee et al., 2021).

Although the aforementioned literature supports the idea that tax avoidance and CSR serve as substitutes, with tax avoider businesses showing lower commitment to CSR, other studies fail to uncover similar evidence. For example, Mayberry and Watson (2021) found no discernible correlation between tax avoidance and CSR, using the passage of constituency statutes in US states as a quasi-experimental setting. Vacca et al. (2020) and Pranata et al. (2021) reached the same conclusion when examining samples of Italian and Indonesian firms, respectively. Similarly, Mohanadas et al. (2020) fail to find a connection between tax aggressiveness and CSR performance in their analysis of a sample of Malaysian companies. These studies suggest that a firm's level of tax avoidance is not influenced by its CSR commitment, challenging the idea that tax avoidance plays a role in assessing a firm's dedication to acting in a socially responsible way. This idea is further supported by studies showing limited evidence (Hanlon & Slemrod, 2009) or even no association between a firm's reputation and tax avoidance (Gallemore et al., 2014; Chen et al., 2019).

Another strand of the literature empirically supports a positive association between tax avoidance and CSR. This evidence contrasts with the idea that tax avoidance is incompatible with being a socially responsible firm and can be

[3] In this regard, Kovermann and Velte (2021, p. 22) argue that: "Since tax payments benefit a wide range of stakeholders, especially the upper-echelons-perspective would imply that CSR is negatively associated with tax avoidance." However, an alternative interpretation of SKT, based on the agency framework (Hill & Jones, 1992), suggests that firms strategically balance their engagement in CSR or tax avoidance activities to benefit certain classes of stakeholders while penalizing others. This would lead to the opposite conclusion that tax avoidance is positively related to CSR. Indeed, as Kovermann and Velte (2021, p. 22) clarify: "Since CSR can be directly aimed at the more powerful and thus important stakeholders, whereas tax payments cannot, management can be expected to prefer CSR overpaying taxes." For similar considerations, see also Zeng (2016).

interpreted through different theoretical frameworks. According to the resource-based view (RBV) framework (Penrose, 2009), tax payment reductions can be viewed as a powerful funding source, potentially increasing the pool of resources available to support CSR-related activities (Branco & Rodrigues, 2006; Hasan et al., 2017; Al-Hadi et al., 2019). Drawing on the RBV-based slack resource theory, Watson (2015) suggests that the mixed relationship between CSR and tax avoidance can be explained by pre-tax earnings performance (i.e., a proxy for resource availability). This theory suggests a positive relationship with the current or future earnings performance is high, which is consistent with the idea that firms with more resources are better equipped to engage in CSR activities (Penrose, 2009). Similarly, shareholder theory (ST) suggests that corporate tax minimization and CSR activities can be complementary, as both are expected to enhance shareholder value (Mao, 2019).[4] In line with these predictions, several empirical studies demonstrate a positive association between tax avoidance and CSR in various settings, including developing economies such as Brazil (Kim & Im, 2017) and China (Gulzar et al., 2018; Mao, 2019).[5]

Alternatively, a positive CSR–tax avoidance link implies that firms strategically utilize CSR disclosure and practices to mitigate the risks associated with engaging in aggressive tax avoidance behaviors (see, e.g., Mamede de Andrade et al., 2020; Kim & Im, 2017). This perspective aligns with the predictions of both legitimacy theory (LT) and risk management theory (RMT) (Godfrey, 2005; Godfrey et al., 2009; Deegan, 2002; Col & Patel, 2019). Drawing on LT, Richardson et al., (2013) empirically establish a positive and statistically significant link between corporate tax aggressiveness and CSR disclosure. Abdelfattah and Aboud (2020) also provide evidence that Egyptian firms mitigate the impact of corporate tax avoidance activities by increasing CSR disclosure, especially those with a more diversified board of directors. Examining the correlation between tax avoidance and CSR report readability within Chinese companies, Xu et al. (2022) find positive and significant evidence.[6] Schochet et al. (2022) discover a positive relationship between corporate tax avoidance and employee treatment, an important aspect of the firm's CSR, while Alsaadi (2020) suggests that tax avoidance increases not only CSR disclosure but also CSR commitments, as shown by the investigation of firms in countries with

[4] For example, Mao (2019, p. 50) states that "firms may also engage in tax avoidance for the same reason of engaging in CSR – to achieve shareholder wealth maximization." While this could suggest a complementarity of tax avoidance and CSR activities, leading to a positive association between the two constructs, it can also occur that tax avoidance and CSR contribute to maximizing shareholders' value separately and are, therefore, "unrelated" (Mao, 2019).

[5] Specifically, Gulzar et al. (2018) employ CSR ratings provided by the Rankins (RKS) agency. Their findings indicate a negative correlation between CSR and both the current and cash ETRs, which are proxies of corporate tax avoidance, thus indicating that companies demonstrating higher levels of CSR are more likely to aggressively engage in tax avoidance than those with lower CSR levels.

[6] However, the research of Xu et al. (2022) also finds that such relationships are weaker for state-owned firms and firms located in less developed areas of China.

different levels of tax-financial reporting conformity.[7] Col and Patel (2019) also confirm a positive association between tax avoidance and CSR, particularly in companies relying on tax havens. Using the enactment of the Controlled Foreign Corporations look-through rule by Congress in 2016, they show that firms affected by the new regulation increased CSR practices in response.

It should also be noted that most of the CSR/ESG ratings[8] used in the literature are composite scores that include several distinct components, each capturing a particular facet of a firm's CSR commitment. For instance, the ESG score encompasses three main components (also referred to as "pillars" or "dimensions"): the environmental component (E), the social component (S), and the governance component (G).[9] Each pillar can be further broken down into individual sub-indices, which capture the specific activities and commitments undertaken by a firm with respect to each dimension (Madhavan et al., 2021).

Prior literature suggests that the relationship between tax avoidance and CSR/ESG scores may vary across the different CSR/ESG dimensions (Fallan & Fallan, 2019). For instance, Lanis and Richardson (2015) discovered a negative association between tax avoidance and CSR categories related to community relations and diversity. Laguir et al. (2015) also show a negative correlation between the social dimension of CSR and tax avoidance, alongside a positive correlation between tax avoidance and the economic component of CSR. Similarly, Park (2017) identifies a negative link between tax avoidance and certain components of a firm's CSR, such as social services, employee satisfaction, and contribution to economic growth. Mohanadas et al. (2020) find a negative connection between tax aggressiveness and "community-related" CSR performance and a positive one with "workplace-related" CSR performance.

Although these studies have attempted to disentangle the correlation between tax avoidance and CSR/ESG scores according to their dimensions, the evidence remains incomplete. Accordingly, recent studies call for a more in-depth analysis of how each component is associated with corporate tax avoidance (e.g., Abdelfattah & Aboud, 2020). The benefit of analyzing specific CSR/ESG dimensions is twofold. On the one hand, it helps obtain more granular information on specific aspects of corporate sustainability that are influenced by tax avoidance. On the other hand, it reduces the risk of losing explanatory power on certain components or sub-indices of the CSR/ESG score compared with a pooled analysis (Abid & Dammak, 2022).

---

[7] Building on this line of inquiry, additional research has also explored the role of auditing (Abid & Dammak, 2022) and the utilization of tax havens by firms (Preuss, 2010; Col & Patel, 2019), consistently confirming a positive association between the two constructs.

[8] In this chapter, ESG is used as a substitute for CSR, and the terms are used interchangeably, as suggested by Gillan et al. (2021).

[9] For example, the "E" component provided by Refinitiv Datastream can be broken down into the following sub-indices: (i) emissions; (ii) product innovation, and (iii) resource use. Similarly, the "S" dimension encompasses four individual sub-indices: (i) community; (ii) human rights; (iii) product responsibility; and (iv) workforce. Likewise, the "G" pillar is decomposable into three specific sub-indices: (i) CSR strategy; (ii) management; and (iii) shareholders.

Notably, most existing studies mainly focus on the macro-pillars of the CSR/ESG score, while there remains limited evidence on how individual sub-indices relate to tax avoidance. Recently, Yoon et al. (2021) examined the association between tax avoidance and ESG in a sample of South Korean firms using ESG data from the Korean Corporate Governance Services (KCGS) but did not provide evidence of how single sub-indices of ESG dimensions relate to tax avoidance. Moreover, they captured tax avoidance by using book-tax differences but did not examine effective tax rates (ETRs), which is the most commonly used proxy for tax avoidance (Hanlon & Heitzman, 2010). In this study, we answer the recent call for research by Abdelfattah and Aboud (2020) and attempt to advance this literature by investigating how ETRs relate to each single sub-index of the ESG score's components in a sample of US public firms. In the next section, we develop our research hypotheses that relate tax avoidance to the ESG score, its constituent dimensions, and individual sub-indices.

7.3 Hypothesis Development

Prior literature on CSR and tax avoidance provides conflicting results (Jemiolo & Farnsel, 2023; Timbate, 2023). On the one hand, studies grounded in CCT and SKT suggest a negative correlation between tax avoidance and CSR. This aligns with the idea that tax payments are an integral element of a firm's CSR commitment (e.g., Hoi et al., 2013). On the other hand, studies drawing on the RBV and ST suggest that tax avoidance may be positively linked to a firm's commitment to CSR, as both activities can be seen as value-enhancing tools for the firm and its shareholders (Al-Hadi et al., 2019; Wagner, 2019). Alternatively, another stream of the literature based on LT and RMT suggests a positive tax avoidance–CSR relationship, indicating that aggressive tax avoider firms strategically commit to CSR disclosure and practices to hedge against the risks and societal costs that may arise from such practices (Richardson et al., 2013). This view is consistent with the idea that firms use CSR as an "insurance-like" tool (Godfrey et al., 2009; De Roeck et al., 2023; Shiu & Yang, 2017). Finally, a third line of the literature under-emphasizes the relevance of tax avoidance for CSR and shows no association between the two (Mayberry & Watson, 2021). The irrelevance of tax avoidance for CSR can also be predicted based on ST, assuming the two activities independently lead to shareholders' wealth maximization (Kovermann & Velte, 2021). In summary, the literature provides conflicting views regarding the impact of tax avoidance on a firm's CSR. Whether and how CSR is related to tax avoidance is an open empirical question. Accordingly, we posit the following non-directional research hypothesis (see H1):

H1: The ESG score is related to corporate tax avoidance.

In the realm of literature providing empirical support for an association between tax avoidance and CSR/ESG scores, certain scholars have expanded the horizon of their analyses by investigating the specific dimensions of the CSR/ESG score and how they relate to tax avoidance (e.g., Lanis & Richardson, 2015; Park, 2017; Yoon et al., 2021). Collectively, this literature indicates that the association between tax avoidance and CSR/ESG scores can change in significance and/or direction across CSR dimensions. The reason for such a heterogeneous relation is that corporate tax decisions and CSR practices are intertwined with multiple aspects of a firm's choices and activities, including operational activities, investment, and employment decisions (Gillan et al., 2021; Jemiolo & Farnsel, 2023). Therefore, the influence that tax avoidance has on each CSR/ESG component is likely to vary depending on the degree of alignment between a firm's tax strategy and CSR commitment.

However, predicting how tax avoidance relates to each component of the CSR/ESG dimensions is ex ante ambiguous because firms operate within legal frameworks that allow them to align their tax planning strategies to be consistent with achieving "socially desirable outcomes" (Inger & Stekelberg, 2022). For example, it can be said that tax avoider firms would be more likely to prioritize short-term financial goals versus long-term sustainability and, as such, disregard costly environmental efficiency strategies, thereby reducing their CSR commitment. However, firms may also invest in tax advantages activities aimed at fostering energy efficiency and lowering carbon emissions, thus aligning the corporate tax strategy with CSR commitment.[10] In this case, a positive association with tax avoidance and the E dimension should be expected.

Similarly, the influence of tax avoidance on the components of the S dimension may also vary. If firms benefit from tax deductions because of philanthropic activities, donations, or adherence to labor laws incentivizing diversity and inclusion among the workforce (e.g., hiring of people with disabilities), a positive association between tax avoidance and the S dimension should be expected (Arco-Castro et al., 2020). By contrast, the association between tax avoidance and the S dimension should be negative, if the community or its workforce does not perceive that the company is paying its fair share of taxes (Makni et al., 2019).

Relatedly, the literature indicates that tax avoidance can increase the firm's value due to higher expected cash flow (Lin et al., 2014), but it can also reduce it as a result of managerial discretion, reporting and governance opacity, and/or increased risk of tax audits (Desai et al., 2007; Hasan et al., 2014; Shevlin et al., 2020). Therefore, it remains uncertain whether and how tax avoidance influences the sub-indices of the G dimension.

To sum up, previous literature supporting an association between tax avoidance and CSR/ESG components suggests that this association is likely to vary across the sub-indices of the CSR/ESG dimensions. However, evidence provided by extant research on this point is mixed, and to the best of our knowledge, no prior study has linked tax avoidance to the individual indices of ESG components. Accordingly, we posit these two related research hypotheses:

[10] Inger and Stekelberg (2022) refer to the consistency between tax avoidance and CSR as "socially responsible tax avoidance" and distinguish it from other forms of tax reduction activities that are not related to a positive CSR commitment.

H2a: If an association between tax avoidance and the ESG score exists, this association varies across each individual dimension of the ESG score.

H2b: If an association between tax avoidance and the individual dimensions of the ESG score exists, this association varies across the sub-indices of the ESG score's individual dimensions.

7.4 Research Methodology

7.4.1 Sample and Data

For this analysis, we used data extracted from Refinitiv Datastream. We focused on the 17-year time window from 2005 to 2021 to analyze a comprehensive sample of all companies listed on the NYSE and the Nasdaq at the time the analysis was made.

We then identified 6291 enterprises (2280 from the NYSE and 4011 from the Nasdaq). The USA can provide an interesting and suitable setting for our investigation for several reasons. First, the US institutional environment embeds a robust regulatory framework on ESG and corporate sustainability, including the recently SEC-mandated disclosure of material information concerning ESG-related and climate-related risks and practices (Karpoff et al., 2022),[11] several policies aimed at enhancing social responsibility and human rights protection like the Dodd–Frank Wall Street Reform and Consumer Protection Act (Christensen et al., 2017), and other public initiatives undertaken over the years to foster sustainable corporate practices (e.g., Clean Air Act set by the Environmental Protection Agency,[12] as well as other renewable energy initiatives).[13] Second, US public companies are subject to stringent scrutiny by the media, regulatory market authorities, and the IRS (Internal Revenue Service); this, in turn, could provide an interesting setting to examine how firms balance their tax and CSR practices (see, e.g., Rego, 2003; Kubick et al., 2016; Bozanic et al., 2017; Lartey et al., 2022). Third, the Nasdaq and the NYSE are the two largest stock exchanges in the world by market capitalization, holding economic and societal relevance not only for the USA but also globally.[14] Finally, a single-country investigation can mitigate the issue that differences across jurisdictions—such as cultural factors (Ortas & Gallego-Álvarez, 2020), book-tax conformity levels (Alsaadi, 2020), and country-level governance (Zeng, 2019)—found to influence the tax avoidance–CSR association by prior studies would drive our findings.

---

[11] See PwC (2024): https://www.pwc.com/us/en/services/esg/library/sec-climate-disclosures.html

[12] See: https://www.epa.gov/regulatory-information-topic/regulatory-and-guidance-information-topic-air

[13] See: https://www.epa.gov/energy/clean-energy-programs#renewable

[14] See: https://www.edudwar.com/top-10-stock-exchanges-in-the-world/

Table 7.1 Screening criteria. This table outlines the screening process used in this study, detailing the reduction from all US-listed firms to those with complete data for regression analysis

Screening step	Criteria applied	Firms remaining
1	All listed firms in the US market (active firms on the NYSE and the Nasdaq)	6291
2	Firms with a fiscal year ending on 31 December during the analysis period	5018
3	Firms with complete data available for regression analysis	670–671 (firm-year observation: 3945–3981)

To avoid bias in the results of the analysis, we eliminated all companies with tax years different from 31/12, reducing the number of companies to 5018. The dataset panel takes an unbalanced form since we did not remove all companies without full coverage of the information needed to conduct the analysis. After removing all missing data, the number of enterprise-year observations used in regression models is in the range of 3945–3981. The sample selection strategy is summarized in Table 7.1.

7.4.2 *Model Specification and Variables*

To observe the relationship between the CSR/ESG scores and the long-term ETR, we have specified the following model:

$$\text{ESG} = \beta_0 + \beta_x\left(\text{ETR}\right) + \beta_z\left(\text{Controls}\right) + \varepsilon$$

We used Pooled OLS to perform the regression analysis on the panel dataset. In line with the assumptions of the Pooled OLS estimator, we carried out specific diagnostic tests for heteroscedasticity and serial correlation. The tests confirm the presence of both heteroscedasticity and serial correlation. Thus, we used cluster-robust standard errors to accommodate both issues (Verbeek, 2021).

Dependent Variables

The dependent variables of our analysis are the ESG overall score (esg_score), the three main pillars—environmental (e_score), social (s_score), and governance (g_score)—and the 10 ESG/CSR sub-indices that form the three main pillars and the comprehensive score: emissions score, product innovation score, resource use score, community score, human rights score, product responsibility score, workforce score, CSR strategy score, management score, and shareholders score. For more details about all the variables used, see Table 7.2. Refinitiv Datastream provided independent assessments of ESG scores, and these scores take values between 0 and 1, following an order of increasing sustainability.

Table 7.2 Variable description. This table collects and describes all the dependent, independent, and control variables used in empirical analysis

Name	Description
ETR (1)	The lagged 5-year average of the ratio between total income tax expenses and total pre-tax income
ESG score (2)	ESG overall score: measures the company's ESG performance based on verifiable, publicly reported data. For each observation, we calculated the lagged 5-year average
e score (3)	Environmental pillar score: measures the company's environmental performance using the three environmental category scores (emissions score, product innovation score, and resource use score). For each observation, we calculated the lagged 5-year average
e score (emissions) (4)	Emission reduction score: assesses the firm's commitment and efficacy in mitigating environmental emissions from its production and operational processes. For each observation, we calculated the lagged 5-year average
e score (product innovation) (5)	Innovation score: measures a firm's efforts to reduce environmental impacts and burdens for its clients, generating new market opportunities through the adoption of new eco-designed environmental technologies, processes, or products. For each observation, we calculated the lagged 5-year average
e score (resource use) (6)	Resource use score; considers the company's effective or capable consumption minimization of materials, energy, or water or the adoption of environmentally efficient solutions through enhanced supply chain management. For each observation, we calculated the lagged 5-year average
s score (7)	Social pillar score: measures the company's social performance, based on the four social category scores (community score, human rights score, product responsibility score, and workforce score). For each observation, we calculated the lagged 5-year average
s score (community) (8)	Community score: measures the company's commitment to being a good citizen, oriented by public health policies and adopting ethical business practices. For each observation, we calculated the lagged 5-year average
s score (human rights) (9)	Human rights score: assesses a company's proficiency in promoting and defending human rights principles as outlined in international human rights conventions. For each observation, we calculated the lagged 5-year average
s score (product responsibility) (10)	Product responsibility score: reflects a firm's capacity to ensure the health and safety of customers, integrity, and data quality in its goods and services. For each observation, we calculated the lagged 5-year average
s score (workforce) (11)	Workforce score: measures a company's commitment to job satisfaction, a healthy and safe workplace for the employees, diversity inclusion, equal opportunities, and career development opportunities for its workforce. For each observation, we calculated the lagged 5-year average
g score (12)	Governance pillar score: measures the company's governance performance, based on the three governance category scores (CSR strategy score, management score, and shareholders score). For each observation, we calculated the lagged 5-year average
g score (CSR strategy) (13)	CSR strategy score: reflects how a company integrates economic (financial), social, and environmental aspects into its everyday decision-making processes. For each observation, we calculated the lagged 5-year average

(continued)

Table 7.2 (continued)

Name	Description
g score (management) (14)	Management score: measures a company's application of best practices in corporate governance principles. For each observation, we calculated the lagged 5-year average
g score (shareholders) (15)	Shareholders score: measures a company's proficiency in ensuring equal treatment for all shareholders and implementing mechanisms to prevent hostile takeovers. For each observation, we calculated the lagged 5-year average
leverage (16)	The lagged 5-year average of the ratio between total liabilities and total assets
ln(Total Asset) (17)	The lagged 5-year average of the Total Asset natural logarithm
growth(Total Asset) (18)	The lagged 5-year average of the annual growth rate of Total Asset
ROA (19)	Return on Assets, a performance index, is calculated as the ratio between Net Income and Total Asset. For each observation, we calculated the lagged 5-year average
Current Ratio (20)	A liquidity index is calculated as the ratio between Current Assets and Current Liabilities. For each observation, we calculated the lagged 5-year average

For each dependent variable, we calculate the lagged average of the previous 5 years, as our analysis focuses on the long term.

Independent Variable

The independent variable of our analysis is the long-term ETR (Hanlon & Heitzman, 2010; Badertscher et al., 2019), calculated as the ratio between total income tax expenses and total pre-tax income, using the following formula:

$$\mathrm{ETR} = \frac{\text{Total income tax expenses}}{\text{PreTax Income}}$$

Since we study the long-term ETR, we calculate the lagged average of the previous 5 years. Moreover, as observed by Gebhart (2017), truncation bias occurs when pre-tax income is negative. To accommodate the truncation bias, in line with previous studies, we drop loss years, since it is challenging to interpret negative ETR (Henry & Sansing, 2018).

Regarding possible simultaneity issues (e.g., not only does the ETR have an impact on ESG scores, but vice versa), we do not believe this kind of endogeneity exists. In our opinion, it is highly improbable that ESG/CSR scores will have a direct impact on firms' ETR.

Control Variables

In building the regression models, we also considered several classic accounting control variables: total liabilities to total assets ratio (leverage), as a proxy for the financial leverage; the natural logarithm of total assets (ln(Total Asset)), as a proxy for the firm's size; the firm's growth orientation (growth(Total Asset)) calculated in the annual change in total assets; return on assets (ROA), calculated as the ratio between the net income and total assets, to consider the financial performance dimension; liquidity index; and the current ratio (Current Ratio), which is calculated as the ratio between current assets and current liabilities. We have also included fixed effects for years and industries. As for the dependent and independent variables, for each control, we calculate the lagged average of the previous 5 years.

7.5 Results and Discussion

7.5.1 Descriptive Statistics and Bivariate Analysis

Table 7.3 shows the descriptive statistics of the variables used in this analysis for the whole sample. All variables have been winsorized at 5% to replace outliers with less extreme values.

Table 7.4 shows the Pearson correlation matrix. In column 1, we observe that correlation coefficients between ETR and ESG/CSR scores are generally negative and statistically significant at the p value level < 0.05. The only coefficient that turns out to be positive and statistically insignificant is the one associated with the shareholders score variable. Although preliminary, this result supports our non-directional hypothesis H1, according to which ESG ratings are significantly associated with corporate tax avoidance. More specifically, a negative correlation has been identified, consistent with literature suggesting that companies managing to save on taxes have better CSR (Fig. 7.1).

The Pearson matrix is also useful for observing whether there is an excessive correlation between the regression model's explanatory variables, which could lead to multicollinearity problems. Correlation coefficients do not appear to raise suspicions of multicollinearity.

As part of the preliminary analysis, we reported in Figs. 7.2, 7.3, 7.4, and 7.5 the mean and median of the ESG/CSR scores in the decile ranges of the independent variable ETR. Generally, we can observe that the traced lines of tendency hint at a decreasing linear relation, confirming H1. However, we cannot always detect a clear decreasing linear relation according to H2a and H2b, i.e., if an association between tax avoidance and the ESG score exists, this association varies across each individual dimension of the ESG score and the sub-indices of the ESG score's individual dimensions.

Table 7.3 Descriptive statistics. This table shows the descriptive statistics for the variables used in empirical analysis. Standard deviation, distribution (minimum, 25th percentile, median, 75th percentile, and maximum), skewness, kurtosis, and number of observations are reported for each variable mean. All variables have been winsorized to the 5% level to replace the extreme values of distribution tails with less extreme values

Variables (5-year average)	Mean	SD	p05 (min)	p25	p50 (median)	p75	p95 (max)	Skewness	Kurtosis	Obs.
ETR	0.269	0.124	−0.001	0.207	0.298	0.36	0.444	−0.843	2.844	8811
esg_score	0.46	0.184	0.164	0.306	0.448	0.612	0.781	0.126	1.903	5827
e_score	0.361	0.268	0	0.111	0.335	0.592	0.82	0.214	1.74	5827
e score (emissions)	0.399	0.309	0	0.1	0.375	0.67	0.916	0.205	1.677	5799
e score (product innovation)	0.237	0.272	0	0	0.12	0.44	0.804	0.783	2.225	5793
e score (resource use)	0.4	0.319	0	0.085	0.367	0.689	0.926	0.209	1.619	5799
s_score	0.463	0.2	0.167	0.293	0.44	0.622	0.836	0.286	1.961	5822
s score (community)	0.68	0.191	0.302	0.539	0.698	0.841	0.954	−0.374	2.102	5799
s score (human rights)	0.254	0.286	0	0	0.13	0.482	0.838	0.763	2.16	5799
s score (product responsibility)	0.427	0.267	0.033	0.2	0.369	0.657	0.898	0.309	1.843	5799
s score (workforce)	0.503	0.247	0.12	0.288	0.491	0.709	0.925	0.121	1.829	5799
g_score	0.545	0.189	0.182	0.405	0.568	0.695	0.841	−0.299	2.112	5827
g score (CSR strategy)	0.36	0.327	0	0.026	0.283	0.668	0.926	0.387	1.671	5799
g score (management)	0.58	0.23	0.147	0.409	0.603	0.768	0.928	−0.286	2.039	5799
g score (shareholders)	0.556	0.252	0.095	0.357	0.584	0.772	0.929	−0.274	1.941	5799
leverage	0.541	0.215	0.15	0.381	0.558	0.696	0.928	−0.119	2.173	13,125
ln(Total Asset)	14.303	1.959	10.495	12.92	14.363	15.756	17.595	−0.154	2.237	13,190
growth(Total Asset)	0.129	0.155	−0.059	0.027	0.084	0.183	0.559	1.365	4.334	12,105
ROA	0.054	0.056	−0.061	0.022	0.048	0.084	0.176	0.233	3.016	12,891
Current Ratio	2.295	1.534	0.702	1.216	1.797	2.821	6.525	1.422	4.3	12,760

Table 7.4 Pearson correlation matrix. This table shows the results of the Pearson correlation matrix for the variables used in empirical analysis (*p value < 0.05)

	(1)	(2)	(3)	(4)	(5)	(6)	(7)	(8)	(9)	(10)	(11)	(12)	(13)	(14)	(15)	(16)	(17)	(18)	(19)	(20)
ETR (1)	1																			
esg score (2)	−0.117*	1																		
e score (3)	−0.115*	0.899*	1																	
e score (emissions) (4)	−0.089*	0.852*	0.920*	1																
e score (product innovation) (5)	−0.135*	0.538*	0.667*	0.447*	1															
e score (resource use) (6)	−0.105*	0.875*	0.925*	0.865*	0.471*	1														
s score (7)	−0.114*	0.912*	0.785*	0.753*	0.422*	0.801*	1													
s score (community) (8)	−0.030	0.744*	0.679*	0.678*	0.345*	0.669*	0.762*	1												
s score (human rights) (9)	−0.130*	0.706*	0.618*	0.550*	0.366*	0.658*	0.783*	0.465*	1											
s score (product responsibility) (10)	−0.099*	0.643*	0.547*	0.494*	0.402*	0.527*	0.732*	0.414*	0.473*	1										
s score (workforce) (11)	−0.072*	0.814*	0.735*	0.758*	0.308*	0.762*	0.844*	0.697*	0.528*	0.502*	1									
g score (12)	−0.039*	0.656*	0.450*	0.462*	0.255*	0.434*	0.401*	0.368*	0.302*	0.266*	0.385*	1								
g score (CSR strategy) (13)	−0.077*	0.823*	0.836*	0.843*	0.442*	0.828*	0.736*	0.659*	0.589*	0.475*	0.715*	0.518*	1							

(continued)

Table 7.4 (continued)

	(1)	(2)	(3)	(4)	(5)	(6)	(7)	(8)	(9)	(10)	(11)	(12)	(13)	(14)	(15)	(16)	(17)	(18)	(19)	(20)
g score (management) (14)	−0.034*	0.508*	0.285*	0.284*	0.189*	0.271*	0.261*	0.236*	0.191*	0.181*	0.240*	0.936*	0.301*	1						
g score (shareholders) (15)	0.029	0.286*	0.160*	0.201*	0.031*	0.149*	0.142*	0.153*	0.089*	0.081*	0.157*	0.536*	0.238*	0.289*	1					
leverage (16)	0.012	0.167*	0.176*	0.184*	0.111*	0.175*	0.137*	0.156*	0.119*	0.114*	0.107*	0.089*	0.197*	0.031*	0.093*	1				
ln(Total Asset) (17)	0.036*	0.523*	0.566*	0.588*	0.263*	0.548*	0.471*	0.500*	0.316*	0.262*	0.525*	0.269*	0.550*	0.133*	0.136*	0.093*	1			
growth(Total Asset) (18)	−0.058*	−0.220*	−0.241*	−0.214*	−0.168*	−0.230*	−0.161*	−0.155*	−0.155*	−0.122*	−0.117*	−0.182*	−0.215*	−0.139*	−0.086*	0.136*	0.416*	1		
ROA (19)	−0.127*	0.033*	−0.002	−0.002	0.023	0.015	0.060*	0.025	0.069*	0.078*	0.055*	0.005	−0.044*	0.035*	−0.042*	−0.086*	−0.139*	−0.177*	1	
Current Ratio (20)	−0.057*	−0.215*	−0.213*	−0.249*	−0.097*	−0.208*	−0.171*	−0.204*	−0.106*	−0.086*	−0.192*	−0.147*	−0.276*	−0.066*	−0.127*	−0.042*	−0.251*	−0.017*	0.055*	1

Theoretical Framework	Main Assumption	Predicted Relation between Tax Avoidance and CSR	Interpretation
Corporate Culture Theory (CCT)	Each organization is a system of shared beliefs among its members	Negative	CSR-committed firms are less likely to engage in tax avoidance due to potential reputational risks and ethical concerns
Stakeholder Theory (SKT)[1]	Organizations should consider and manage the interests of all stakeholders, not just shareholders	Negative	Tax payments are integral to a firm's CSR commitment; non-compliance can harm the interests of local communities and governments, who are key stakeholders
Resource-Based View (RBV)/ **Slack Resource Theory**	Each organization is a bundle of unique resources and capabilities	Positive	Cash tax savings from tax avoidance can increase a firm's resources, which can be used to further CSR investments
Shareholder Theory (ST)	A firm's primary purpose is to maximize shareholder wealth	Positive or Unrelated	Tax avoidance can complement a firm's CSR activities, as both are expected to increase the enhance shareholder value
Legitimacy Theory (LT) and **Risk Management Theory** (RMT)	Organizations need to maintain a certain level of social acceptance and recognition to operate effectively	Positive	Corporations may use increased CSR commitment and disclosure practices to hedge against risks stemming from tax avoidance

Fig. 7.1 Theoretical frameworks to interpret the relation between tax avoidance and CSR. Assuming CSR activities are not strategically employed by managers to direct resources toward certain, more powerful, stakeholders—a concept that reframes stakeholder theory based on agency theory, often referred to as "stakeholder–agency theory" (see Hill & Jones, 1992)

7.5.2 Multivariate Regression

Table 7.5 shows the results of the main analysis. Dependent variables are the overall ESG score (model 1), the E score (model 2), the S score (model 3), and the G score (model 4). From regression analysis, it is possible to observe a negative and statistically significant coefficient associated with the main ETR variable, except for model 4, where the dependent variable is the G score: −0.128 for the overall ESG score, −0.270 for the E score, −0.122 for the S score, and −0.0265 for the G score.

Thus, the results confirm H1, according to which tax avoidance has an impact on an enterprise's ESG score. In particular, as already noted in the preliminary analyses, there seems to be a negative relationship between the ETR and firms' ESG/CSR scores (in other words, the higher the tax avoidance, the higher the firms' ESG/CSR scores). According to the model's estimates, when the ETR drops by 1%, it would be reflected in an overall ESG score on average greater than 0.00128 (in a range from 0 to 1). Similarly, when the ETR drops by 1%, firms' E and S scores increase by 0.0027 and 0.00122, respectively. The result supports the line of authors who claim there is a positive relationship between tax avoidance and CSR. The phenomenon can be explained through two different perspectives.

According to the first view, tax avoidance is not incompatible with firms' ESG/CSR score; instead, consistent with RBV, minimizing tax payments can be considered a source of funding available to support CSR-related activities (Branco & Rodrigues, 2006; Hasan et al., 2017; Al-Hadi et al., 2019). Alternatively, according to ST, corporate tax minimization and CSR activities can be complementary, as both are expected to enhance shareholder value.

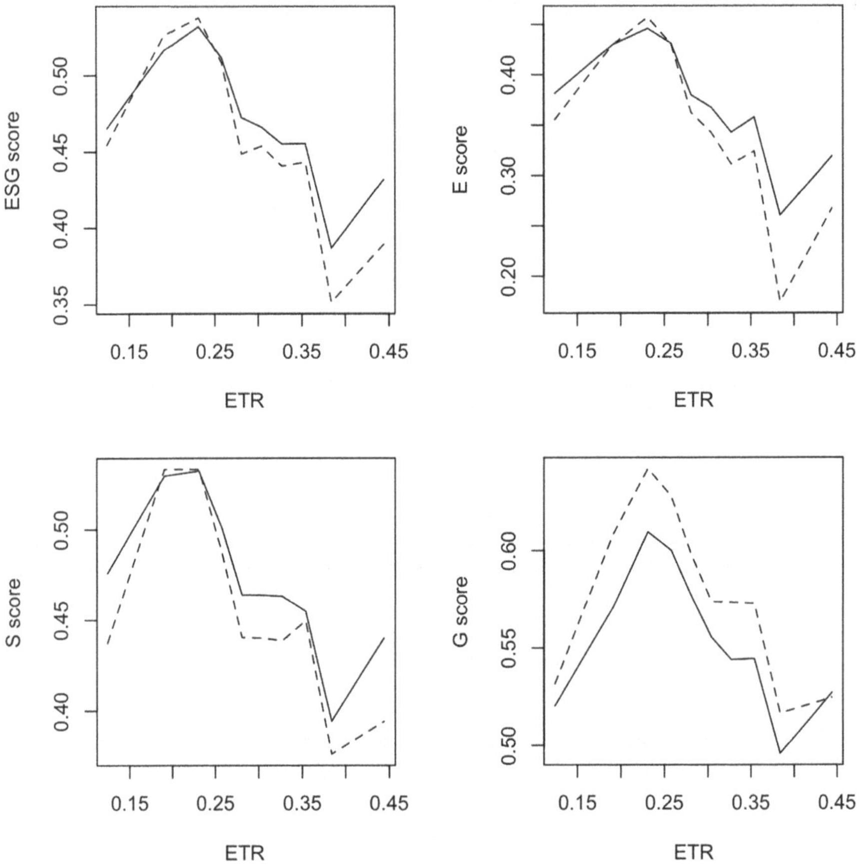

Fig. 7.2 ESG overall score and three main pillars as a function of ETR. This figure shows the mean (solid line) and median (dashed line) ESG score, E score, S score, and G score (dependent variables) of the decile ranges of the ETR, the independent variable

However, according to the second possible interpretation of the phenomenon and consistent with LT and RMT (Godfrey et al., 2009), a positive association between tax avoidance and CSR may suggest that firms strategically employ CSR disclosure and practices to mitigate the risks associated with aggressive tax avoidance behaviors (see, e.g., Mamede de Andrade et al., 2020).

The fact that the Pillar G score is not statistically significant confirms H2b, which posits that the association between ESG/CSR scores and the ETR varies across each individual dimension of the ESG score. More specifically, only the Pillar E and S scores are negatively affected by the ETR, while the Pillar G score is not. Prima facie, a non-association between the ETR and Pillar G of the ESG/CSR score can contrast with prior theoretical and empirical research positing that effective corporate governance mechanisms steer tax avoidance (Desai & Dharmapala, 2006, 2009; Desai et al., 2007; Kovermann & Velte, 2019). However, the firms included in our

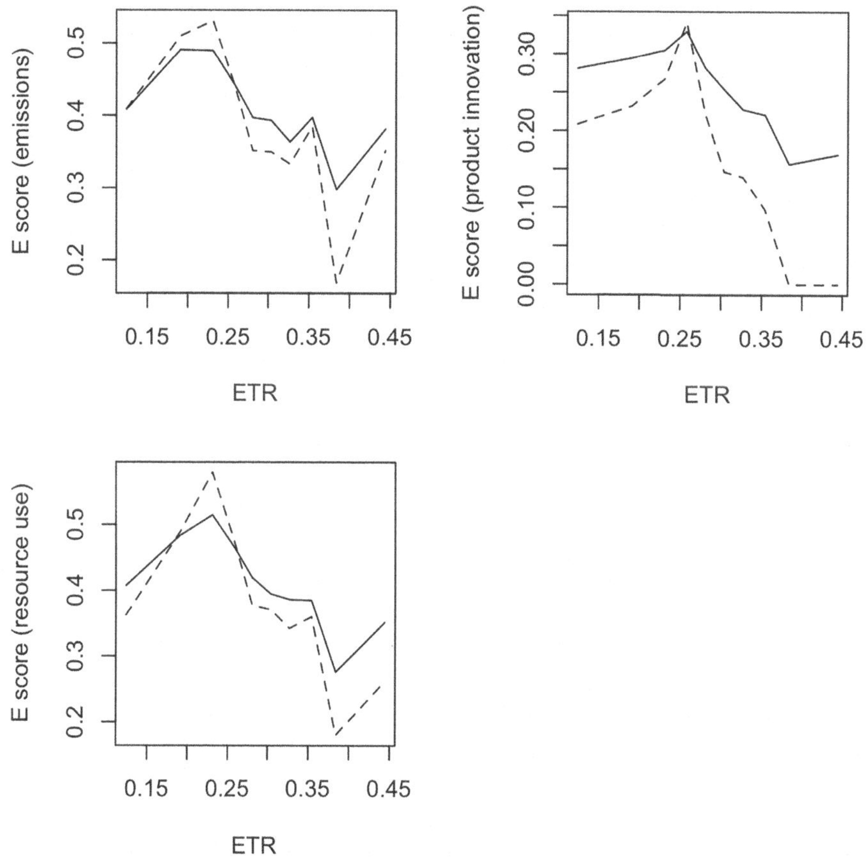

Fig. 7.3 Environmental measures as a function of ETR. This figure shows the mean (solid line) and median (dashed line) environmental category scores (emissions score, product innovation score, and resource use score) of the decile ranges of the ETR

sample are likely to exhibit high-quality corporate governance due to their strong scrutiny by the market and regulators. As a result, our finding could reflect the mixed effects that tax avoidance activities have on stakeholders' interests, benefiting residuals versus fixed-claimants and minority shareholders (De Vito, 2024).

To analyze the topic more deeply, Table 7.6 shows the results at the disaggregated level, replacing the category scores as dependent variables with the overall score and the three main pillars.

From the results, we see that all three coefficients associated with the Pillar E category scores are negative and statistically significant. As for Pillar S, the coefficients are all negative, but only the coefficients associated with the Human Rights and Workforce scores are statistically significant, with p values of <0.1 and <0.05, respectively. Finally, regarding Pillar G, only the coefficient associated with the CSR strategy score is negative and statistically significant at the p value level <0.01.

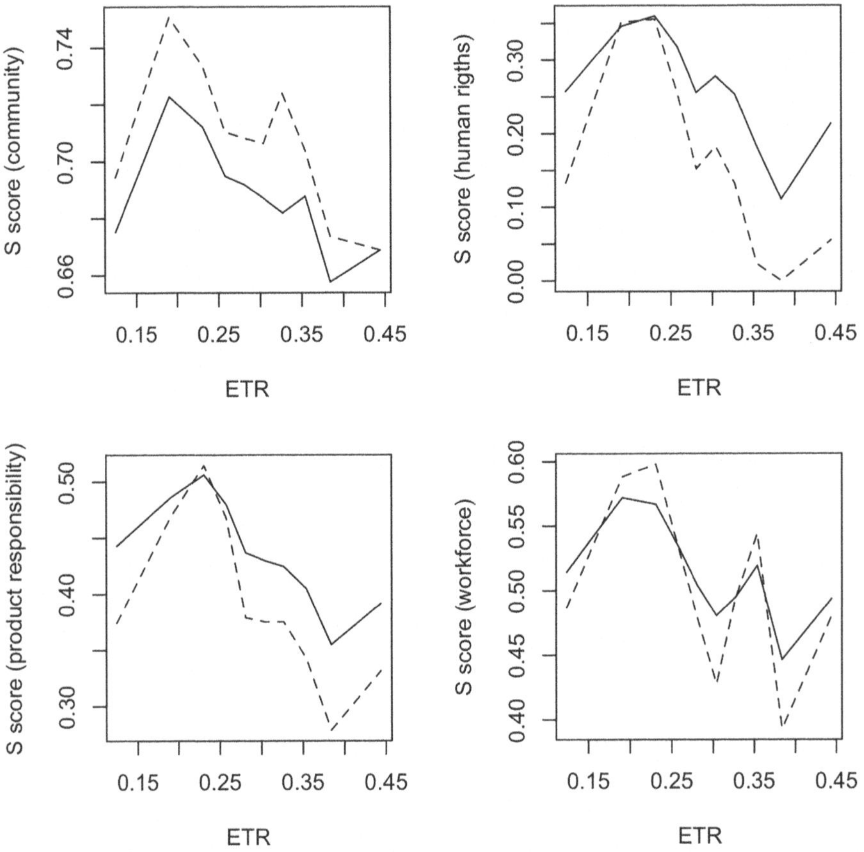

Fig. 7.4 Social measures as a function of ETR. This figure shows the mean (solid line) and median (dashed line) social category scores (community score, human rights score, product responsibility score, and workforce score) of the decile ranges of the ETR

From Table 7.6, we can deduce that companies' tax avoidance activities do not affect all areas of CSR in the same way. More specifically, it seems that mainly investments in Pillar E are influenced by tax avoidance, while Pillars S and G are only partially affected. These results confirm H2b, according to which the association between ESG/CSR scores and ETR varies across the sub-indices of the ESG score's individual dimensions.

The evidence supports several studies that investigate how the specific dimensions of the CSR/ESG score are related to tax avoidance and find that the association between tax avoidance and CSR/ESG scores can change in the level of statistical significance and/or the direction across various CSR dimensions (Lanis & Richardson, 2015; Park, 2017; Yoon et al., 2021).

Pillar E's higher sensitivity to ETR could be explained by the increasing number of tax incentives aimed at encouraging companies to adopt sustainable practices and

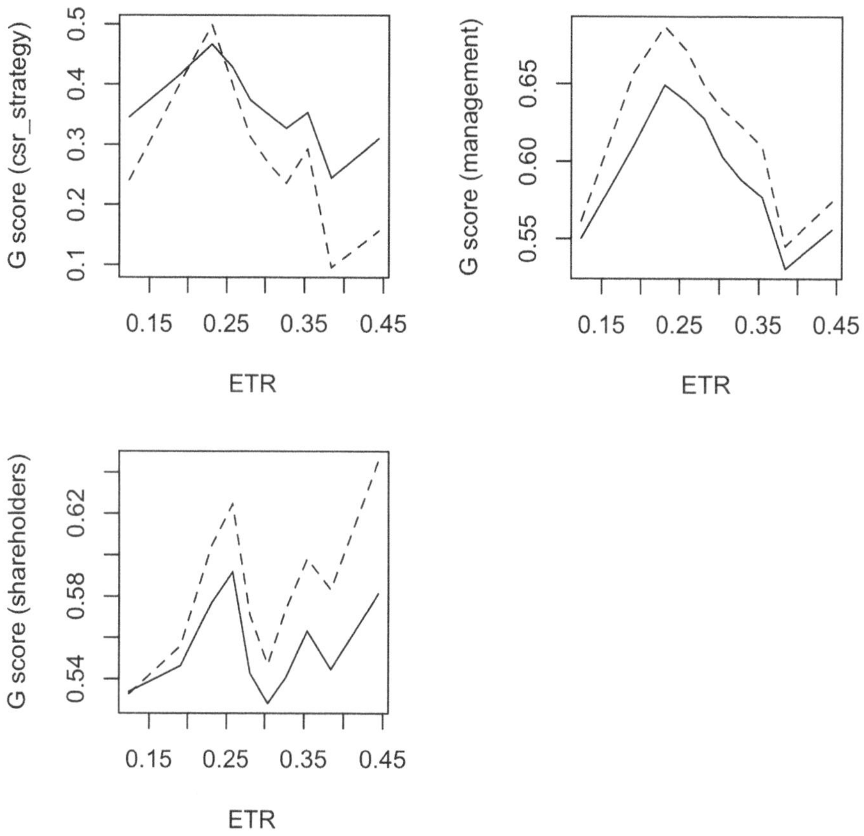

Fig. 7.5 Governance measures as a function of ETR. This figure shows the mean (solid line) and median (dashed line) governance category scores (CSR strategy score, management score, and shareholders score) of the decile ranges of the ETR

reduce their environmental impact. Examples from our context of analysis (i.e., the USA) include the Federal Solar Investment Tax Credit, the Renewable Electricity Production Tax Credit, the Electric Vehicle Tax Credit, the Federal Renewable Fuel Standard, the Deductions for Energy Efficiency in Buildings, and the Energy-Efficient Commercial Buildings Tax Deduction, among others.

Such incentives push companies to invest more in sustainable technologies and practices, reducing their environmental impact and improving corporate reputation. This demonstrates a concrete commitment to environmental sustainability and makes companies more favorably perceived by the public and investors. In addition, these incentives increase regulatory compliance, encouraging companies to adhere to more stringent environmental standards required by law. All these motivations would contribute to explaining the link between tax avoidance and Pillar E; more than anything else, it would seem from the results to be the pillar that is more sensitive to enterprises' tax avoidance activity.

Table 7.5 Main ESG pillar regression results. This table shows the coefficients estimated by the pooled OLS estimator. Model 1, ESG score = *f*(ETR, controls); model 2, E score = *f*(ETR, controls); model 3, S score = *f*(ETR, controls); model 4, G score = *f*(ETR, controls). Cluster-robust standard errors in parentheses. *$p < 0.1$; **$p < 0.05$; ***$p < 0.01$

	(1)	(2)	(3)	(4)
Variables	ESG score	E score	S score	G score
Constant	−1.031***	−1.909***	−1.163***	−0.0747
	(0.0809)	(0.123)	(0.0929)	(0.0983)
ETR	−0.128**	−0.270***	−0.122**	−0.0265
	(0.0547)	(0.0730)	(0.0566)	(0.0645)
leverage	−0.0592*	−0.0679	−0.0888**	−0.00884
	(0.0339)	(0.0563)	(0.0387)	(0.0413)
ln(TA)	0.0898***	0.138***	0.0974***	0.0391***
	(0.00433)	(0.00669)	(0.00508)	(0.00517)
growth(TA)	−0.209***	−0.329***	−0.149***	−0.223***
	(0.0377)	(0.0527)	(0.0417)	(0.0468)
ROA	0.578***	0.628***	0.701***	0.353**
	(0.134)	(0.207)	(0.157)	(0.161)
CR	−0.0141***	−0.00178	−0.0221***	−0.00105
	(0.00513)	(0.00825)	(0.00567)	(0.00660)
Year fixed effects	Yes	Yes	Yes	Yes
Industry fixed effects	Yes	Yes	Yes	Yes
VIF	2.63	2.63	2.63	2.63
Observations	3949	3949	3945	3949
R-squared	0.471	0.476	0.440	0.202

Robust standard errors in parentheses
***$p < 0.01$, **$p < 0.05$, *$p < 0.1$

Concerning the S dimension, the result that only the Human Rights and Workforce scores are statistically significant can be explained by the tax deductions related to philanthropic activities, donations, or adherence to labor laws that promote diversity and inclusion among the workforce (Arco-Castro et al., 2020).

In sum, this analysis indicates that tax avoidance is significantly associated only with those ESG sub-components that are usually targeted by policymakers with tax incentives and other forms of advantageous tax waivers. This result is consistent with the prediction of the RBV and ST that firms can align their tax planning strategies with socially and environmentally sustainable practices. Although LT and RMT can also support a positive association between tax avoidance and ESG, our sub-components analysis suggests it is unlikely that firms purposely engage in CSR activities to counteract aggressive tax planning strategies.

Table 7.6 Specific score regression results. This table focuses on specific score regressions and shows the coefficients estimated by the pooled OLS estimator. Model 1, emissions score = *f*(ETR, controls); model 2, product innovation score = *f*(ETR, controls); model 3, resource use score = *f*(ETR, controls); model 4, community score = *f*(ETR, controls); model 5, human rights score = *f*(ETR, controls); model 6, product responsibility score = *f*(ETR, controls); model 7, workforce score = *f*(ETR, controls); model 8, CSR strategy score = *f*(ETR, controls); model 9, management score = *f*(ETR, controls); model 10, shareholders score = *f*(ETR, controls). Cluster-robust standard errors in parentheses. $^{*}p < 0.1$; $^{**}p < 0.05$; $^{***}p < 0.01$

	(1)	(2)	(3)	(4)	(5)	(6)	(7)	(8)	(9)	(10)
Variables	(E score) emissions	(E score) product innovation	(E score) resource use	(S score) community	(S score) human rights	(S score) product responsibility	(S score) workforce	(G score) CSR strategy	(G score) Management	(G score) Shareholders
Constant	−2.204***	−1.144***	−2.287***	−0.718***	−1.602***	−1.198***	−1.305***	−1.989***	0.200	0.177
	(0.133)	(0.166)	(0.144)	(0.0993)	(0.150)	(0.141)	(0.120)	(0.149)	(0.127)	(0.161)
ETR	−0.247***	−0.326***	−0.252***	−0.0538	−0.145*	−0.108	−0.161**	−0.227***	−0.00302	0.0639
	(0.0749)	(0.0873)	(0.0903)	(0.0549)	(0.0820)	(0.0773)	(0.0641)	(0.0842)	(0.0774)	(0.0838)
leverage	−0.0655	−0.0941	−0.0799	−0.0271	−0.0661	−0.0584	−0.110**	−0.0825	−0.0120	0.0743
	(0.0656)	(0.0638)	(0.0685)	(0.0420)	(0.0664)	(0.0601)	(0.0542)	(0.0662)	(0.0515)	(0.0702)
ln(TA)	0.163***	0.0773***	0.163***	0.0846***	0.108***	0.0862***	0.120***	0.149***	0.0239***	0.0214**
	(0.00740)	(0.00918)	(0.00754)	(0.00536)	(0.00879)	(0.00754)	(0.00631)	(0.00809)	(0.00658)	(0.00879)
growth(TA)	−0.326***	−0.192***	−0.399***	−0.0914**	−0.274***	−0.139**	−0.145***	−0.340***	−0.233***	−0.118*
	(0.0581)	(0.0621)	(0.0629)	(0.0412)	(0.0584)	(0.0616)	(0.0507)	(0.0624)	(0.0590)	(0.0649)
ROA	1.004***	0.0676	0.951***	0.508***	0.879***	0.866***	0.749***	0.702***	0.353*	0.217
	(0.218)	(0.255)	(0.248)	(0.161)	(0.239)	(0.234)	(0.183)	(0.232)	(0.207)	(0.245)
CR	−0.00842	0.00896	−0.00781	−0.0104	−0.0172**	−0.0168*	−0.0242***	−0.0291***	0.00497	−0.00149
	(0.00957)	(0.0107)	(0.00993)	(0.00681)	(0.00854)	(0.00873)	(0.00769)	(0.00969)	(0.00859)	(0.0113)
Year fixed effects	Yes	Yes	Yes	Yes	Yes	Yes	Yes	Yes	Yes	Yes
Industry fixed effects	Yes	Yes	Yes	Yes	Yes	Yes	Yes	Yes	Yes	Yes
VIF	2.64	2.64	2.64	2.64	2.64	2.64	2.64	2.64	2.64	2.64

(continued)

Table 7.6 (continued)

	(1)	(2)	(3)	(4)	(5)	(6)	(7)	(8)	(9)	(10)
Observations	3981	3977	3981	3981	3981	3981	3981	3981	3981	3981
R-squared	0.485	0.247	0.436	0.328	0.352	0.261	0.408	0.458	0.107	0.099

Robust standard errors in parentheses
$^{***}p < 0.01$, $^{**}p < 0.05$, $^{*}p < 0.1$

7.6 Conclusion

The relationship between CSR and tax avoidance is a key topic in contemporary academic research on ethical corporate behavior. However, the existing evidence is mixed and lacks comprehensive insights into specific CSR dimensions. This research addressed the gap by exploring the impact of different CSR dimensions. For this purpose, it investigated how tax avoidance influences various components of the ESG score.

Our study examined the relationship between tax avoidance and ESG score components in US-listed companies. The research provides the association between tax avoidance and CSR changes in significance and direction across ESG components. Tax avoidance displays a significant negative association with the environmental and social components but no significant relation with the governance component. The findings suggest that tax incentives might influence the interaction between environmental concerns and tax avoidance through incentives for green investments, among others. Similarly, tax incentives for philanthropic initiatives and related reputation management may affect human rights and workforce concerns, as captured by the ESG score's society component.

This study contributes to prior research on tax avoidance and CSR by highlighting how complex and multifaceted this relationship is. Our research examined the channels through which CSR might influence tax avoidance and vice versa. For example, regarding the environmental component of ESG scores, it suggests that specific tax incentives are channels for a possible "substitution effect" between green initiatives and CSR.

Overall, our in-depth analyses of the ESG components provide evidence consistent with the RBV and ST (e.g., Watson, 2015; Branco & Rodrigues, 2006; Hasan et al., 2017; Al-Hadi et al., 2019) that public policies designed to incentivize corporate green initiatives or philanthropic activities can provide companies with the opportunity to conceal tax avoidance practices and CSR/ESG commitment. This finding aligns with the notion of "socially responsible tax avoidance" recently introduced by Inger and Stekelberg (2022).

Our study has practical implications, suggesting to policymakers and stakeholders that tax incentives can promote ethical corporate conduct. Tax incentives might serve as a useful tool to align value maximization with sustainable and responsible management. Despite the valuable insights provided by this study, several limitations must be acknowledged. First, although untabulated robustness checks are broadly consistent with the main findings, there remain concerns regarding potential endogeneity between ESG scores and tax avoidance practices. Future research should employ advanced econometric techniques to address this issue and focus on specific tax incentives as channels for a possible "substitution effect" between green initiatives and CSR. Moreover, the institutional setting of this study is confined to the US context, which may limit the findings' generalizability. Finally, a breakdown of the sample by industry would enhance the robustness of the results and provide interesting sector-specific insights.

References

Abdelfattah, T., & Aboud, A. (2020). Tax avoidance, corporate governance, and corporate social responsibility: The case of the Egyptian capital market. *Journal of International Acçounting, Auditing and Taxation, 38*, 100304.

Abid, S., & Dammak, S. (2022). Corporate social responsibility and tax avoidance: The case of French companies. *Journal of Financial Reporting and Accounting, 20*(3/4), 618–638.

Al-Hadi, A., Chatterjee, B., Yaftian, A., Taylor, G., & Monzur Hasan, M. (2019). Corporate social responsibility performance, financial distress and firm life cycle: Evidence from Australia. *Accounting and Finance, 59*(2), 961–989.

Alsaadi, A. (2020). Financial-tax reporting conformity, tax avoidance and corporate social responsibility. *Journal of Financial Reporting and Accounting, 18*(3), 639–659.

Arco-Castro, L., López-Pérez, M. V., Pérez-López, M. C., & Rodríguez-Ariza, L. (2020). Corporate philanthropy and employee engagement. *Review of Managerial Science, 14*, 705–725.

Badertscher, B. A., Katz, S. P., Rego, S. O., & Wilson, R. J. (2019). Conforming tax avoidance and capital market pressure. *The Accounting Review, 94*, 1–30. https://doi.org/10.2308/accr-52359

Bilicka, K. A., Casi-Eberhard, E., Seregni, C., & Stage, B. (2024). *Tax strategy disclosure: A greenwashing mandate?* TRR 266 accounting for transparency working paper series no. 40. Available at SSRN: https://ssrn.com/abstract=3672420 or doi:https://doi.org/10.2139/ssrn.3672420.

Bozanic, Z., Hoopes, J. L., Thornock, J. R., & Williams, B. M. (2017). IRS attention. *Journal of Accounting Research, 55*(1), 79–114.

Branco, M. C., & Rodrigues, L. L. (2006). Corporate social responsibility and resource-based perspectives. *Journal of Business Ethics, 69*, 111–132.

Caglio, A., Melloni, G., & Su, J. (2022). The end of greenwashing? A renewed infrastructure for CSR information in the new normal. *Academy of Management Annual Meeting Proceedings*, (1).

Carroll, R., & Joulfaian, D. (2005). Taxes and corporate giving to charity. *Public Finance Review, 33*(3), 300–317.

Chen, S., Schuchard, K., & Stomberg, B. (2019). Media coverage of corporate taxes. *The Accounting Review, 94*(5), 83.

Chouaibi, J., Rossi, M., & Abdessamed, N. (2022). The effect of corporate social responsibility practices on tax avoidance: An empirical study in the French context. *Competitiveness Review: An International Business Journal, 32*(3), 326–349.

Christensen, H. B., Floyd, E., Liu, L. Y., & Maffett, M. (2017). The real effects of mandated information on social responsibility in financial reports: Evidence from mine-safety records. *Journal of Accounting and Economics, 64*(2–3), 284–304.

Col, B., & Patel, S. (2019). Going to haven? Corporate social responsibility and tax avoidance. *Journal of Business Ethics, 154*(4), 1033–1050.

Davis, A. K., Guenther, D. A., Krull, L. K., & Williams, B. M. (2016). Do socially responsible firms pay more taxes? *The Accounting Review, 91*(1), 47–68.

De Roeck, K., Raineri, N., Jones, D. A., & Scheidler, S. (2023). Giving the benefit of the doubt: Investigating the insurance-like effect of csr in mitigating negative employee reactions to psychological contract breach. *Journal of Management Studies*.

De Vito, A. (2024). Minority shareholders and tax avoidance. *Journal of Accounting and Public Policy, 44*, 107179.

Deegan, C. (2002). Introduction: The legitimising effect of social and environmental disclosures–a theoretical foundation. *Accounting, Auditing & Accountability Journal, 15*(3), 282–311.

Desai, M. A., & Dharmapala, D. (2006). Corporate tax avoidance and high-powered incentives. *Journal of Financial Economics, 79*(1), 145–179.

Desai, M. A., & Dharmapala, D. (2009). Corporate tax avoidance and firm value. *The Review of Economics and Statistics, 91*(3), 537–546.

Desai, M., Dyck, I., & Zingales, L. (2007). Theft and taxes. *Journal of Financial Economics, 84*, 591–623. https://doi.org/10.1016/j.jfineco.2006.05.005

Donaldson, T., & Preston, L. E. (1995). The stakeholder theory of the corporation: Concepts, evidence, and implications. *Academy of Management Review, 20*(1), 65–91.
Dyreng, S. D., Hanlon, M., & Maydew, E. L. (2008). Long-run corporate tax avoidance. *The Accounting Review, 83*(1), 61–82.
Dyreng, S. D., Hoopes, J. L., & Wilde, J. H. (2016). Public pressure and corporate tax behavior. *Journal of Accounting Research, 54*(1), 147–186.
Fallan, E., & Fallan, L. (2019). Corporate tax behaviour and environmental disclosure: Strategic trade-offs across elements of CSR? *Scandinavian Journal of Management, 35*(3), 101042.
Fourati, Y. M., Affes, H., & Trigui, I. (2019). Do socially responsible firms pay their right part of taxes? Evidence from the European Union. *The Journal of Applied Business and Economics, 21*(1), 24–48.
Gallemore, J., Maydew, E. L., & Thornock, J. R. (2014). The reputational costs of tax avoidance. *Contemporary Accounting Research, 31*(4), 1103–1133.
Gandullia, L., & Piserà, S. (2020). Do income taxes affect corporate social responsibility? Evidence from European-listed companies. *Corporate Social Responsibility and Environmental Management, 27*(2), 1017–1027.
Gebhart, M. S. (2017). Measuring corporate tax avoidance – An analysis of different measures. *Junior Management Science*, 43–60 Seiten. doi:https://doi.org/10.5282/JUMS/V2I2PP43-60.
Gillan, S. L., Koch, A., & Starks, L. T. (2021). Firms and social responsibility: A review of ESG and CSR research in corporate finance. *Journal of Corporate Finance, 66*, 101889.
Godfrey, P. C. (2005). The relationship between corporate philanthropy and shareholder wealth: A risk management perspective. *Academy of Management Review, 30*(4), 777–798.
Godfrey, P. C., Merrill, C. B., & Hansen, J. M. (2009). The relationship between corporate social responsibility and shareholder value: An empirical test of the risk management hypothesis. *Strategic Management Journal, 30*(4), 425–445.
Graham, J. R., Hanlon, M., Shevlin, T., & Shroff, N. (2014). Incentives for tax planning and avoidance: Evidence from the field. *The Accounting Review, 89*(3), 991–1023.
Gulzar, M. A., Cherian, J., Sial, M. S., Badulescu, A., Thu, P. A., Badulescu, D., & Khuong, N. V. (2018). Does corporate social responsibility influence corporate tax avoidance of Chinese listed companies? *Sustainability, 10*(12), 4549.
Hanlon, M., & Heitzman, S. (2010). A review of tax research. *Journal of Accounting and Economics, 50*(2–3), 127–178.
Hanlon, M., & Slemrod, J. (2009). What does tax aggressiveness signal? Evidence from stock price reactions to news about tax shelter involvement. *Journal of Public Economics, 93*(1–2), 126–141.
Hasan, I., Hoi, C. K. S., Wu, Q., & Zhang, H. (2014). Beauty is in the eye of the beholder: The effect of corporate tax avoidance on the cost of bank loans. *Journal of Financial Economics, 113*(1), 109–130.
Hasan, M. M., Al-Hadi, A., Taylor, G., & Richardson, G. (2017). Does a firm's life cycle explain its propensity to engage in corporate tax avoidance? *European Accounting Review, 26*(3), 469–501.
Henry, E., & Sansing, R. (2018). Corporate tax avoidance: Data truncation and loss firms. *Review of Accounting Studies, 23*, 1042–1070. https://doi.org/10.1007/s11142-018-9448-0
Hill, C. W., & Jones, T. M. (1992). *Stakeholder-agency theory. Journal of management studies, 29*(2), 131–154.
Hoi, C. K., Wu, Q., & Zhang, H. (2013). Is corporate social responsibility (CSR) associated with tax avoidance? Evidence from irresponsible CSR activities. *The Accounting Review, 88*(6), 2025–2059.
Hoi, C. K., Ke, Y., Wu, Q., & Zhang, H. (2022). Does public scrutiny on corporate tax decisions affect directors? Effects of responsible (irresponsible) corporate tax practices on director reputation. *Accounting and Business Research*, 1–22.
Huseynov, F., & Klamm, B. K. (2012). Tax avoidance, tax management and corporate social responsibility. *Journal of Corporate Finance, 18*(4), 804–827.

Inger, K., & Stekelberg, J. (2022). Valuation implications of socially responsible tax avoidance: Evidence from the electricity industry. *Journal of Accounting and Public Policy, 41*(4), 106959.

Jemiolo, S., & Farnsel, C. (2023). Complements, substitutes or neither? A review of the relation between corporate social responsibility and corporate tax avoidance. *Journal of Accounting Literature*.

Jones Christensen, L. I. S. A., Mackey, A., & Whetten, D. (2014). Taking responsibility for corporate social responsibility: The role of leaders in creating, implementing, sustaining, or avoiding socially responsible firm behaviors. *Academy of Management Perspectives, 28*(2), 164–178.

Kanagaretnam, K., Lee, J., Lim, C. Y., & Lobo, G. (2018). Societal trust and corporate tax avoidance. *Review of Accounting Studies, 23*, 1588–1628.

Karpoff, J. M., Litan, R., Schrand, C., & Weil, R. L. (2022). What ESG-related disclosures should the SEC mandate? *Financial Analysts Journal, 78*(2), 9–18.

Kim, J., & Im, C. (2017). Study on corporate social responsibility (CSR): Focus on tax avoidance and financial ratio analysis. *Sustainability, 9*(10), 1710.

Kovermann, J., & Velte, P. (2019). The impact of corporate governance on corporate tax avoidance—A literature review. *Journal of International Accounting, Auditing and Taxation, 36*, 100270.

Kovermann, J., & Velte, P. (2021). CSR and tax avoidance: A review of empirical research. *Corporate Ownership and Control, 18*(2), 20–39.

Kreps, D. M. (1990). Corporate culture and economic theory. *Perspectives on Positive Political Economy, 90*(109–110), 8.

Kubick, T. R., Lynch, D. P., Mayberry, M. A., & Omer, T. C. (2016). The effects of regulatory scrutiny on tax avoidance: An examination of SEC comment letters. *The Accounting Review, 91*(6), 1751–1780.

Laguir, I., Staglianò, R., & Elbaz, J. (2015). Does corporate social responsibility affect corporate tax aggressiveness? *Journal of Cleaner Production, 107*, 662–675.

Lanis, R., & Richardson, G. (2012). Corporate social responsibility and tax aggressiveness: A test of legitimacy theory. *Accounting, Auditing and Accountability Journal, 26*(1), 75–100.

Lanis, R., & Richardson, G. (2015). Is corporate social responsibility performance associated with tax avoidance? *Journal of Business Ethics, 127*, 439–457.

Lanis, R., & Richardson, G. (2018). Outside directors, corporate social responsibility performance, and corporate tax aggressiveness: An empirical analysis. *Journal of Accounting, Auditing and Finance, 33*(2), 228–251.

Lartey, T., Uddin, M., Danso, A., & Wood, G. (2022). CEO overconfidence and IRS attention. *Journal of Financial Stability, 61*, 101035.

Lee, D. (2020). Corporate social responsibility of US-listed firms headquartered in tax havens. *Strategic Management Journal, 41*(9), 1547–1571.

Lee, Y., Ng, S., Shevlin, T., & Venkat, A. (2021). The effects of tax avoidance news on employee perceptions of managers and firms: Evidence from glassdoor. com ratings. *The Accounting Review, 96*(3), 343–372.

Lei, S., & Zhang, Y. (2020). The role of the media in socially responsible investing. *International Journal of Bank Marketing, 38*(4), 823–841.

Lin, S., Tong, N., & Tucker, A. L. (2014). Corporate tax aggression and debt. *Journal of Banking and Finance, 40*, 227–241.

Liu, H., & Lee, H. A. (2019). The effect of corporate social responsibility on earnings management and tax avoidance in Chinese listed companies. *International Journal of Accounting and Information Management, 27*(4), 632–652.

Madhavan, A., Sobczyk, A., & Ang, A. (2021). Toward ESG alpha: Analyzing ESG exposures through a factor lens. *Financial Analysts Journal, 77*(1), 69–88.

Makni, Y., Affes, H., & Trigui, I. (2019). do socially responsible firms pay their right part of taxes? Evidence from the European Union. *Journal of Applied Business and Economics, 21*(1), 24–48.

Mamede de Andrade, E., Rodrigues, L. L., & Cosenza, J. P. (2020). Corporate behavior: An exploratory study of the Brazilian tax management from a corporate social responsibility perspective. *Sustainability, 12*(11), 4404.

Mao, C. W. (2019). Effect of corporate social responsibility on corporate tax avoidance: Evidence from a matching approach. *Quality and Quantity, 53*(1), 49–67.

Mayberry, M. A., & Watson, L. (2021). Is corporate social responsibility related to corporate tax avoidance? Evidence from a natural experiment. *The Journal of the American Taxation Association, 43*(1), 79–106.

McWilliams, A., & Siegel, D. (2001). Profit maximizing corporate social responsibility. *Academy of Management Review, 26*(4), 504–505.

Menicacci, L., & Simoni, L. (2024). Negative media coverage of ESG issues and corporate tax avoidance. *Sustainability Accounting, Management and Policy Journal, 15*(7), 1–33.

Mgbame, C. O., Chijoke-Mgbame, M. A., Yekini, S., & Yekini, C. K. (2017). Corporate social responsibility performance and tax aggressiveness. *Journal of Accounting and Taxation, 9*(8), 101–108.

Minor, D., & Morgan, J. (2011). CSR as reputation insurance: Primum non nocere. *California Management Review, 53*(3), 40–59.

Mohanadas, N. D., Abdullah Salim, A. S., & Pheng, L. K. (2020). CSR and tax aggressiveness of Malaysian listed companies: Evidence from an emerging economy. *Social Responsibility Journal, 16*(5), 597–612.

Ortas, E., & Gallego-Álvarez, I. (2020). Bridging the gap between corporate social responsibility performance and tax aggressiveness: The moderating role of national culture. *Accounting, Auditing, and Accountability Journal, 33*(4), 825–855.

Park, S. (2017). Corporate social responsibility and tax avoidance: Evidence from Korean firms. *Journal of Applied Business Research, 33*(6), 1059–1068.

Penrose, E. T. (2009). *The Theory of the Growth of the Firm*. Oxford University Press.

Pranata, I. P. A. A., Adhitanaya, K., Rizaldi, M. F., Winanda, G. B. E., Lestari, N. M. I. D., & Astuti, P. D. (2021). The effect of corporate social responsibility, firm size, and leverage on tax aggressiveness: An empirical evidence. *Universal Journal of Accounting and Finance, 9*(6), 1478–1486.

Preuss, L. (2010). Tax avoidance and corporate social responsibility: You can't do both, or can you? *Corporate Governance: The international journal of business in society, 10*(4), 365–374.

PwC. (2023). *Tax is a crucial part of the ESG conversation*. Available at: https://www.pwc.com/gx/en/services/tax/publications/tax-is-a-crucial-part-of-esg-reporting.html

Rakia, R., Kachouri, M., & Jarboui, A. (2023). The moderating effect of women directors on the relationship between corporate social responsibility and corporate tax avoidance? Evidence from Malaysia. *Journal of Accounting in Emerging Economies*.

Rego, S. (2003). Tax-avoidance activities of US multinational corporations. *Contemporary Accounting Research, 20*(4), 805–833.

Richardson, G., Taylor, G., & Lanis, R. (2013). The impact of board of director oversight characteristics on corporate tax aggressiveness: An empirical analysis. *Journal of Accounting and Public Policy, 32*(3), 68–88.

Schochet, S., Benlemlih, M., & Jaballah, J. (2022). Is corporate tax avoidance related to employee treatment? *Journal of Empirical Finance, 69*, 63–80.

Scholes, M. S., Wolfson, M. A., Erickson, M., Maydew, E., & Shevlin, T. (2014). *Taxes and business strategy*. Prentice Hall.

Shevlin, T., Urcan, O., & Vasvari, F. P. (2020). Corporate tax avoidance and debt costs. *The Journal of the American Taxation Association, 42*(2), 117–143.

Shin, J., Moon, J. J., & Kang, J. (2023). Where does ESG pay? The role of national culture in moderating the relationship between ESG performance and financial performance. *International Business Review, 32*(3), 102071.

Shiu, Y. M., & Yang, S. L. (2017). Does engagement in corporate social responsibility provide strategic insurance-like effects? *Strategic Management Journal, 38*(2), 455–470.

Sikka, P. (2012). Smoke and mirrors: Corporate social responsibility and tax avoidance. In *Corporate Social Responsibility* (pp. 53–84). Routledge.

Timbate, L. (2023). CSR and corporate taxes: Substitutes or complements? *BRQ Business Research Quarterly, 26*(4), 327–346.

Vacca, A., Iazzi, A., Vrontis, D., & Fait, M. (2020). The role of gender diversity on tax aggressiveness and corporate social responsibility: Evidence from Italian listed companies. *Sustainability, 12*(5), 2007.

Verbeek, M. (2021). *Panel methods for finance: A guide to panel data econometrics for financial applications*. De Gruyter.

Wagner, F. W. (2019). Business taxation and corporate social responsibility. *Schmalenbachs Zeitschrift für betriebswirtschaftliche Forschung, 71*, 347–380.

Wang, C. L., Lu, C. H., & Kuo, T. T. (2022). Corporate foundations: Tax avoidance or corporate social responsibility. *Journal of Accounting Review, 74*(1).

Wang, F., Xu, S., Sun, J., & Cullinan, C. P. (2020). Corporate tax avoidance: A literature review and research agenda. *Journal of Economic Surveys, 34*(4), 793–811.

Watson, L. (2015). Corporate social responsibility, tax avoidance, and earnings performance. *Journal of the American Taxation Association, 37*(2), 1–21.

Weisbach, D. A. (2002). An economic analysis of anti-tax-avoidance doctrines. *American Law and Economics Review, 4*(1), 88–115.

Wen, W., Cui, H., & Ke, Y. (2020). Directors with foreign experience and corporate tax avoidance. *Journal of Corporate Finance, 62*, 101624.

Xu, S., Wang, F., Cullinan, C. P., & Dong, N. (2022). Corporate tax avoidance and corporate social responsibility disclosure readability: Evidence from China. *Australian Accounting Review, 32*(2), 267–289.

Yoon, B., Lee, J. H., & Cho, J. H. (2021). The effect of ESG performance on tax avoidance—Evidence from Korea. *Sustainability, 13*(12), 6729.

Zeng, T. (2016). Corporate social responsibility, tax aggressiveness, and firm market value. *Accounting Perspectives, 15*(1), 7–30.

Zeng, T. (2019). Relationship between corporate social responsibility and tax avoidance: International evidence. *Social Responsibility Journal, 15*(2), 244–257.

Zhao, L. (2022). Corporate philanthropy as a response to greater tax enforcement. *Accounting and Business Research*, 1–22.

Chapter 8
Italian Benefit Company (Società Benefit) and Default Risk: An Empirical Analysis of the Italian Context

Enrico Gonnella and Lucia Talarico

8.1 Introduction

In recent years, a new entrepreneurial paradigm has emerged, where the traditional business goal of profit creation for shareholders is accompanied by a further commitment to public benefit and environmental and social issues are targeted. This hybrid business model (Corsi et al., 2020; Rawhouser et al., 2015; Blount & Offei-Danso, 2013, p. 620) has evolved from a growing awareness of the importance, if not the need, to re-evaluate shareholders' priorities in favor of other categories of stakeholders, to the point of proposing a balanced approach to stakeholder interests.

In response, Italian lawmakers have introduced a new legal business structure, informed by laws in various US states, among others (Baudot et al., 2020; Alexander, 2020), and the experience of B Corps—companies that the US non-profit organization B Lab certifies as meeting high standards of social and environmental sustainability (Corsi et al., 2020; Parker et al., 2019; Moroz et al., 2018; Cao et al., 2017). Unlike the B Corps, however, benefit companies are legally required to combine profit and common benefit.

In this paper, we focus on Italian benefit companies to analyze whether the benefit nature affects the risk of lender insolvency. Specifically, it examines lenders' perception of risk toward benefit companies. Thus, the paper contributes new insights into a relatively unexplored area in the literature.

The following section details the primary characteristics of this new business model as regulated by Italian law and reviews the literature before undertaking an empirical investigation into the cost of debt for Italian benefit companies.

E. Gonnella (✉) · L. Talarico
Department of Economics and Management, University of Pisa, Pisa, Italy
e-mail: enrico.gonnella@unipi.it; lucia.talarico@unipi.it

F. Bernini (ed.), *Creating Value Through Sustainability*, SIDREA Series in Accounting and Business Administration,
https://doi.org/10.1007/978-3-031-74292-7_8

The literature relating to the topic is still developing, partly due to the recent enactment of the law concerning Italian benefit companies. Given that benefit corporations institutionalize a company's commitment to social and environmental practices, it seemed helpful to examine studies that, following stakeholder theory, have analyzed the possible relationship between corporate social responsibility (CSR) and the cost of capital, particularly the cost of debt.

In light of this paper's focus and the findings from existing studies, a research hypothesis is formulated and tested through empirical analysis. This analysis involves a sample of Italian companies divided into two groups: Italian benefit companies and comparable Italian profit companies. A hierarchical multiple linear regression analysis is conducted with the default spread as the response variable, the company's status as an Italian benefit company (dummy variable) as the explanatory variable, and four control variables.

The paper is structured as follows: After outlining the defining characteristics of the benefit company as regulated by Italian law (§ 8.2), it reviews the most significant literature concerning the relationship between CSR, benefit companies, and the cost of debt and then formulates the scientific hypothesis to be tested (§ 8.3). The subsequent section describes the statistical methodology adopted in the empirical research (§ 8.4). The results of the analysis are presented next (§ 8.5), followed by the concluding remarks (§ 8.6).

8.2 Italian Benefit Company: Main Characteristics

The Italian benefit company was introduced by paragraphs 376–384 of Sole Article, Law No. 208, of 28 December 2015, in force since 2016. Italian legislators acted swiftly, inspired by earlier models, specifically in Maryland, where benefit companies were introduced in 2010 (Baudot et al., 2020; Alexander, 2020).

According to paragraph 376 of Sole Article, Law 208/2015, corporations are classified as benefit companies, "which, in carrying out their economic activities, not only aim to distribute profits but also pursue one or more objectives of common benefit." Paragraph 378(a) further clarifies that common benefit involves "the pursuit, in the course of the benefit corporation's economic activities, of one or more positive effects, or the reduction of negative effects" on one or more categories referred to in paragraph 376 or "individuals, communities, territories and the environment, cultural and social heritage, entities and associations, as well as other stakeholders" (paragraph 376, Sole Article, Law 208/2015).

Given the sweep of the provision and to address potential ambiguities in defining these objectives (Toffoletti, 2022, p. 186), the law requires a company to clearly state the "specific" benefit purposes in their corporate objectives, in addition to the aim of distributing profits (Mosco, 2018, p. 89; Denozza & Stabilini, 2017, p. 6).

Despite its hybrid nature, a benefit company maintains the traditional patrimonial and administrative rights of shareholders, including the right to dividends and reserves and to be reimbursed for the value of shares in the event of the company's liquidation (Capelli, 2020, p. 569; Bianchini & Sertoli, 2018, p. 202; Denozza & Stabilini, 2017, p. 6). However, the company's commitment to benefit aims is both constitutive and permanent.

This is further supported by paragraph 377 of the law mentioned above, which mandates that the beneficial purposes "shall be pursued through an administration aimed at balancing the interests of the shareholders and the interests of those who may be impacted by the company's business activity" (paragraph 377, Sole Article, Law 208/2015). Thus, balancing involves not only the profit motive and common benefit purposes but also the interests of the different stakeholders (Angelici, 2017, p. 6; Denozza & Stabilini, 2017, p. 6; Zoppini, 2017, p. 6; Capelli, 2020, p. 569), including, as stated in paragraph 378(b), "the individuals or groups of individuals directly or indirectly involved in, or affected by, the activities of the benefit corporation, being, inter alia: workers, clients, suppliers, lenders, creditors, public administration and civil society" (paragraph 378(b), Sole Article, Law 208/2015).

The legislative use of "balancing" for this broad spectrum of interests signifies a shift away from shareholder primacy (Sneirson, 2019; Sjåfjell, 2019; Codazzi, 2020, p. 594; Rossi, 2017, p. 5) and introduces a powerful innovation in the company's mission and vision. It also produces a very controversial modulation of the responsibilities of company directors, who are required to respect this hybrid purpose (Nori, 2021, pp. 794–796; Rossi, 2017, pp. 8–9; Palmieri, 2017, pp. 218–223; Cian, 2021, pp. 1131–1148).

An Italian benefit company must operate "in a responsible, sustainable, and transparent manner" (paragraph 376, Sole Article, Law 208/2015). To this end, one or more individuals responsible for pursuing the common benefit must be designated (paragraph 380, Sole Article, Law 208/2015). Companies that are established and managed in compliance with the regulations mentioned above may use the designation "benefit company," abbreviated as "SB," which they may choose to include in their company name (paragraph 379, Sole Article, Law 208/2015).

Italian legislation determines that a benefit company can adopt any corporate form already available to commercial companies. However, its corporate purpose must specify the common benefit or benefits it intends to pursue alongside profit making (Codazzi, 2021, p. 1248; Richter Jr., 2017, pp. 272–275). The law also allows the company to adopt the benefit model at its founding or at any subsequent time.

Owing to their specific characteristics, Italian benefit companies must comply with specific and additional obligations compared with non-benefit companies – in particular, the drafting and publication of an impact report. This report, which includes both reporting and programmatic content (Taffari, 2023; Maggi & Rossi, 2022; Drisaldi, 2022), must cover four specified areas: corporate governance, workers, other stakeholders, and the environment (Annex 5, paragraph 378, Sole Article, Law 208/2015). It must be drawn up according to standards developed by a third party with multidisciplinary expertise and capable of using a scientific method (Annex 4, paragraph 378, Sole Article, Law 208/2015, Nos. 2, 3, and 4).

8.3 Literature Review and Development of the Hypothesis

In this study, we analyze the relationship between benefit companies and lenders in the Italian context, specifically regarding the risk of insolvency that lenders associate with benefit companies compared with non-benefit companies. Given that the cost of debt varies depending on the perceived risk of the capital lender, the size and dynamics of the former reflect those of the latter.

Studies on the relationship between the benefit corporation and the cost of debt have been limited, as this new business model was only legislated in Italy in 2016. However, it is possible to consider the results of earlier studies that indirectly inform this present study. As mentioned earlier, Italian benefit companies embody a hybrid business model where the commitment to CSR is institutionalized alongside the traditional profit objective. The literature has long explored the existence, significance, and meaning of a possible relationship between CSR and corporate value (Di Giulio et al., 2011, p. 132).

More specifically, corporate social performance (CSP) may influence corporate value in two ways: the relationship between CSR and corporate financial performance (CFP) and the relationship between CSR and the risk/cost of capital. For this study, the latter is particularly noteworthy as it provides a valuable framework for understanding the more limited relationship between the Italian benefit company and the cost of debt.

The literature review shows that the relationship between CSR and the cost of capital still requires further investigation (Eichholtz et al., 2019, p. 19). The findings, however, are occasionally ambiguous, partly because of geographical and cultural differences in the contexts where the companies operate (Jones, 1995, p. 387). In addition, variability arises from the different periods considered and the diversity of indicators used to measure both CSR—sometimes focusing solely on the environmental dimension, sometimes on broader dimensions—and the cost of debt, whether accounting-based or market-based measures.

Added to this is the interaction among various factors, such as the reference industry, managerial motivations, the nature of the chosen and implemented social projects, and the specific capabilities within the company (Baird et al., 2012), which make the model's parameterization very complex.

In particular, concerning the cost of equity, EI Ghoul et al. (2011) conclude from a large sample of US companies that a commitment to CSR initiatives leads to a reduction in the cost of equity. Similarly, Girerd-Potin et al. (2014) analyze the relationship between the environmental, social, and governance (ESG) dimensions of CSR and the market value of companies within the Stoxx Europe 600 index and find that companies with positive ESG performance have a lower cost of equity.

Di Giulio et al. (2011) consider all the companies listed in the Dow Jones Sustainability World Index (DJSWI) from 2000 to 2005. For each of them, they select the CSP scores assigned each year by the Sustainable Asset Management (SAM) Group and analyze the annual financial performance (Di Giulio et al., 2011, p. 139). Their study identifies a negative relationship between the CSP of the previous year and the weighted average cost of capital of the subsequent period.

Oikonomou et al. (2012) focus on the relationship between CSP and financial risk in a sample of S&P 500 companies between 1992 and 2009. They find that CSR is negatively, albeit weakly, related to systematic corporate risk and that poor social responsibility performance is strongly and positively correlated with financial risk. These relationships are also influenced by the degree of market volatility.

Focusing on the environmental profile, La Rosa and Bernini analyze a sample of European companies from the S&P Euro 350 index and find that negative environmental, social, and governance (ESG) performance, particularly concerning environmental controversies, is associated with an increase in the cost of equity capital. However, this effect can be mitigated by further company activities that positively influence the environment (La Rosa & Bernini, 2022).

Regarding the relationship between CSR and the cost of debt, which is the primary interest of this article, some studies detect effects that are either insignificant or absent (Hoepner et al., 2016; Goss & Roberts, 2011; Menz, 2010; D'Antonio et al., 1997). However, most of the literature suggests a reduction in the cost of debt when companies engage in socially responsible behavior.

Some authors like Sharfman and Fernando (2008) note an asymmetric behavior between the cost of debt and the cost of equity. Their examination of US companies in the S&P 500 index shows that improved environmental risk management not only reduces the cost of equity, mainly through decreased stock volatility as measured by beta, and increases the debt capacity of companies but also raises the cost of debt. However, this higher cost of debt, offset by the tax shield, ultimately enhances the firm's overall economic performance.

Chava (2014) also considers both the cost of equity and debt, which show a symmetrical trend; both costs increase for companies judged positively from an environmental point of view and decrease for companies where the environmental dimension may represent a vulnerability.

Eichholtz et al. (2019, p. 20) focus on a particular economic sector (i.e., real estate) to isolate the effect environmental efficiency can have on the cost of debt. Their analysis of companies managing real estate portfolios—specifically, real estate investment trusts and their assets—finds that commercial mortgages on assets certified by Energy Star and LEED have lower spreads than those on non-certified assets. Similar trends are evident in corporate bond spreads, where companies with environmentally screened real estate portfolios benefit from significantly lower bond spreads.

Bauer and Hann (2010) examine the impact of corporate environmental management on the cost of debt for companies issuing bonds. They note that companies with environmental concerns have lower credit ratings and a higher cost of debt than more environmentally responsible companies, which enjoy better credit ratings (Bauer & Hann, 2010, p. 24).

Oikonomou et al. (2014) follow a similar research path and deduce from their empirical analysis that companies with more responsible behavior are rewarded with lower corporate bond yield spreads, while those with negative environmental performance face higher spreads. This pattern is consistent when focusing on the bond ratings assigned to specific debt issues.

Ge and Liu (2015) also analyze bond issues and conclude that better CSR performances allow for issuance at lower costs. They highlight that investors are interested not only in the company's commitment to social responsibility issues but also in the weaknesses it has shown.

Chava (2014) and Schneider (2010) further support these findings. Chava notes that firms with environmental concerns have higher costs of debt than those without such concerns. Schneider, whose study focuses on US companies in the chemical and paper sectors, confirms that good environmental performance helps reduce a company's bond yields.

Concerning the relationship between borrowers and banks, Kim et al. (2014) find that the ethical behavior of borrowers encourages banks to lend at lower rates. La Rosa et al. (2018) reach similar conclusions. Analyzing a sample of European non-financial companies listed from 2005 to 2012, they find a negative relationship between corporate social performance and interest rates and a positive relationship between corporate social performance and credit ratings.

Generally, when a company's behavior aligns with CSR values, there tends to be a reduction in the cost of debt; the effect may be modest but is still statistically significant (Goss & Roberts, 2011). This correlation is often attributed to the mitigation of various types of risk—financial, reputational, and legal—through positive performances in ESG fields (Bellavite Pellegrini et al., 2023, p. 62; Cooper & Uzun, 2015; Bauer & Hann, 2010). However, some studies present contrary findings, such as Magnanelli and Izzo (2017), who, despite acknowledging the prevailing view of a negative relationship between CSR and the cost of debt, analyze a sample of 332 companies from 2005 to 2009 and reveal an opposite trend, specifically noting a lack of attention from credit institutions toward companies engaged in socially responsible practices (Magnanelli & Izzo, 2017).

It is important to reiterate that this paper focuses on an area where research is limited: the analysis of the cost of capital in benefit corporations. The studies most relevant to this topic include those by Everett (2013) and Bellavite Pellegrini et al. (2023). Everett conducts telephone surveys with the founders of 94 benefit corporations and finds that their cost of equity is significantly lower than that of for-profit companies, with a differential of around 35%. Bellavite Pellegrini et al. (2023) limit their study to the Italian context. They analyze a sample of 152 active benefit companies in Italy and, by using accounting metrics, conclude that being recognized as a benefit company is perceived as a risk-reducing factor and, therefore, leads to a lower cost of capital, also thanks to "better and more transparent risk management" (Bellavite Pellegrini et al., 2023, p. 71).

In conclusion, there is a prevailing body of scientific evidence suggesting that better performance in ESG fields generates a lower cost of capital by reducing the risk perceived by investors and lenders (Bellavite Pellegrini et al., 2023, p. 62; Cooper & Uzun, 2015, p. 13).

This research aligns with these findings but is specifically tailored to benefit companies in the Italian context and focuses on the risk of insolvency that lenders attribute to them. It uses stakeholder theory as its theoretical framework.

Among the three approaches identified by Donaldson and Preston (1995), the instrumental approach is chosen for this research. This approach, as per Donaldson and Preston (1995; Riso et al., 2023, p. 3; Steurer, 2006), provides a valuable framework for analyzing the potential connection between benefit purposes, responsible stakeholder management, and conditions of access to credit. The corporate perspective is also adopted (Steurer, 2006, pp. 57–58).

In light of the considerations above, we intend to test the following hypothesis:

H: Being an Italian benefit company has a negative and statistically significant impact on the risk of insolvency (measured by the default spread).

8.4 Methodology

This research aims to determine whether the risk of insolvency attributed by lenders to Italian benefit companies differs from that attributed to comparable Italian profit companies and, if so, whether it is perceived as lower or higher. The interest rates charged on loans are calculated by adding a spread to the base rate (e.g., Euribor, ECB, IRS) to reflect a company's estimated likelihood of default, hence the term "default spread."

The default spread compensates the lender for the risk that the borrower will fail to meet their debt obligations within a defined period. Furthermore, it varies according to the different technical forms of financing, each with its own risk profile.

An estimate of the average default spread that banks apply to borrowers can be calculated by subtracting the risk-free rate from the average cost of borrowing,[1] determined by using accounting-based measures (return on debt). This is the estimation method used in this study.

The research hypothesis was tested through an empirical analysis of a sample of Italian companies divided into two groups: Italian benefit companies and comparable Italian profit companies. A hierarchical multiple linear regression analysis was performed, with the default spread as the response variable and the company's status as a benefit company as the explanatory variable.

The first methodological step was to select a sample of Italian benefit companies to determine the default spread. The Aida database, managed by Bureau van Dijk, was used to extract the sample. The selection criteria included Italian companies with the legal form of joint stock companies and limited liability companies, identifiable as benefit companies by the addition of the acronym SB (*Società Benefit*) to their corporate name. These companies were required to have 2021 sales between 2 million and 50 million euros and to have filed all financial statements for the years 2017–2021, which ensured the sampled companies were beyond the startup phase.

[1] Please refer to Damodaran (2018, pp. 204 and 207–208).

The initial sample comprised 230 companies classified by an ATECO code.[22] Further screening was carried out to exclude companies that did not have financial debt or lacked the necessary information to calculate the default spread, which reduced the sample to 102 benefit companies.

An initial descriptive analysis of the sampled companies was performed based on ATECO codes, which were grouped into three groups: primary and manufacturing industry (group 1), commercial industry (group 2), and service industry (group 3).

The chosen parameters took into account factors that significantly affect company risk and, therefore, the default spread. These factors included the industry's cyclicality (ATECO code), size (sales), operational risk (operating leverage), and financial risk (financial leverage).

To assess the delayed effect on the 2021 default spread, the levers were calculated based on values in fiscal year 2020.[33] In the absence of cost classification into fixed and variable ones, the ratio of fixed to current assets was used as a proxy to determine operating leverage. Financial leverage was calculated as the ratio between the net financial position and shareholders' equity.

The default spread was calculated by subtracting the risk-free rate from the return on debt (ROD). The ROD was derived from the ratio of the financial charges in 2021 to the average bank indebtedness at the beginning and end of 2021. The risk-free rate was estimated by using the yield of Italy's 10-year treasury bonds issued in 2021.

A second sample of Italian profit companies was then selected based on the same criteria as for the benefit companies: ATECO code, 2021 sales between 2 million and 50 million euros, and filing all financial statements for the 2017–2021 period.

The initial pool of comparable companies comprised 25,395 units. It was decided to compare each Italian benefit company with three Italian profit companies selected through a 1:3 propensity score matching. This selection was based on the following control parameters: ATECO code, sales, operating leverage, and financial leverage.[4] This approach aimed to minimize the selection bias inherent in the nature of the phenomenon, which precluded conducting a randomized controlled trial (RCT), where assignments to groups occur randomly.

Before propensity score matching, a screening was necessary to remove any profit companies from the sample where it was impossible to calculate one of the control variables or the default spread due to missing information. This reduced the number of comparable units from 25,395 to 14,258.

Following this, 1:3 propensity score matching based on the mentioned control variables was conducted. The decision for a company to classify itself as a benefit company is not random but depends on its own initiative and the fulfillment of specific requirements. Therefore, this study design is observational, i.e., non-randomized.

---

[2] ATECO serves as the classification system for economic activities in Italy, which ISTAT (National Institute of Statistics) has adopted for statistical purposes.

[3] This research is based on the hypothesis that any effects produced by the pandemic crisis on the data used in the survey are similar for benefit and profit companies.

[4] See, for example, Dehejia and Wahba (2002), Austin (2008), and Benedetto et al. (2018).

In this context, propensity score matching was applied as a statistical method to build a control group comparable to the treated group. This approach helps mitigate the possible confounding effects due to the intrinsic endogeneity of individual companies, thus more accurately isolating the real impact of being a benefit company on the spread.

Specifically, a model based on a logit function was developed to estimate the likelihood of observations being assigned to the benefit company group.

$$p(x) = \text{prob}(D = 1|x) = E(D|x)$$

where:

- D is a dummy variable that takes 1 if the company is part of the BENEFIT group and 0 otherwise
- x represents the variables that may influence the probability of a company being assigned to the benefit group
- prob ($D = 1|x$) denotes the probability that D equals 1 given x
- $E(D|x)$ is the expected value of D given x

Since not all 102 benefit companies found three comparable Italian profit companies as per the criteria of the propensity score matching based on the control variables, the benefit sample was reduced to 91 companies and the comparable sample to 273.

These companies were then added to the previously formed sample of benefit companies, resulting in a final sample of 364 companies, divided as follows:

- The benefit group, which includes the 91 Italian benefit companies
- The comparable group, which includes the 273 Italian profit companies

After applying a winsorization at the 1st and 99th percentiles, a descriptive comparison of the two groups was carried out regarding the control variables. A hierarchical linear regression model was then constructed to determine the statistically significant relationships with the default spread.

Given the right-hand asymmetry observed in all the quantitative variables, it was decided to express the value in logarithmic form during the construction of the regression model, thus resulting in a log-log regression model.

The dependent variable in all the regressions analyzed is the logarithm of the default spread, while the business structure (benefit or profit) serves as the independent variable. The logarithms of sales, operating leverage, and financial leverage, along with the ATECO code classified into the three groups already indicated, are considered control variables.

To test the research hypothesis, the following hierarchical regression model was built:

1. log(DefaultSpread)t = a + b1*DummyBenefit
2. log(DefaultSpread) t = a + b1* DummyBenefit + b2*log(OperatingLeverage) t-1 + b3*DummyIndustry + b4*log(FinancialLeverage)t-1 + b5* log(Sales) t-1

The dataset used for this analysis was prepared using information extracted from the Aida database and processed with IBM Statistics software, version 28.

8.5 Results

After matching, the sample consists of 364 companies, including 91 benefit companies and 273 comparable companies.

Among the industries in which these companies operate, the primary and manufacturing industry is the most populated (49.6% in the comparable group, 54.9% in the benefit group), followed by the commercial industry in the comparable group (40.9%) and the service industry in the benefit group (30.8%). The least represented industry includes service companies in the comparable group (9.4%) and commercial companies in the benefit group (14.3%).

Table 8.1 reports the minimum and maximum values, average, and standard deviation of the economic-financial control parameters used in the model: sales, operating leverage, financial leverage for 2020, and default spread for 2021. Notably, the variables were winsorized at the 1st and 99th percentiles to exclude outliers that could invalidate the statistics.

For 2020, the sales of the sampled benefit companies fluctuated between a minimum value of 466,612 and a maximum of 51,368,088, with an average of 12,289,772 (SD = 11,336,562).

By contrast, the sales of comparable companies were higher, averaging 36,879,908, but exhibited less variability (SD = 8,870,992). The operating leverage

Table 8.1 Statistics

		Minimum	Maximum	Average	Std dev.
Benefit	Sales2020V.I	466,612	51,368,088	12,289,772	11,336,562
	Operating leverage2020V.I	0.007896301	16.9950502	1.167056692	2.15458676
	Financial leverage2020V.I	−1.5059127	5.3326643	0.6837673	1.1793006
	Default spread	0.0020433	0.0745008	0.0207611	0.0153283
Comparable	Sales2020V.I	9,335,939	78,523,000	36,879,908	8,870,992
	Operating leverage2020V.I	0	8.101694028	0.574486884	0.746116722
	Financial leverage2020V.I	−3.7443581	20.3714417	0.7016053	1.5863346
	Default spread	−0.001	0.1365220	0.0283986	0.0261180

for benefit companies varied from 0.008 to 16.995, with an average of 1.17 and greater variability (SD = 2.15458676). Meanwhile, comparable companies demonstrated a range from 0 to 8.102 with an average of 0.57.

Regarding financial leverage, the indicator for benefit companies varied between −1.5 and + 5.3 (average = 0.68), while for the comparable companies, it fluctuated more significantly, with scores ranging from −3.74 to +20.37 (average = 0.70).

The default spread for benefit companies was between 0.002 and 0.074 (average = 0.02), and for comparable companies, it ranged between −0.001 and + 0.136 (average = 0.03). Overall, the benefit companies exhibit lower financial risk than the profit companies.

A hierarchical multiple regression model was constructed to evaluate whether adding control variables modifies the relationship between being a benefit corporation and the logarithm of the default spread. The results of each regression model are displayed in Tables 8.2, 8.3, and 8.4.

The linearity of the relationship was evaluated by using partial regression plots and a plot of studentized residuals against unstandardized predicted values. The residuals' independence was confirmed by the Durbin–Watson statistic, which produced a value of 2.028, close to 2 (Draper & Smith, 1998).

Homoscedasticity is visually assessed by plotting the studentized residuals versus non-standardized predicted values. There was no multicollinearity, as indicated by tolerance values all greater than 0.1 (Hair et al., 2014). No influential values were detected, with Cook's distances all being less than 1 (Cook & Weisberg, 1982).

The simple linear regression model $F(1;362) = 7.020$; $p = 0.008$, R-squared = 0.019) shows that being a benefit corporation has a statistically significant impact on the logarithm of the default spread ($b = -0.006$; $p = 0.008$).

From the full regression model incorporating all variables $F(5;357) = 1.497$; $p = 0.026$, adjusted R-squared = 0.023), it emerges that the only two variables with a statistically significant impact on the logarithm of the default spread are the logarithm of sales (beta = −0.173; $p = 0.039$) and being a benefit company (beta = −0.260, $p = 0.002$).

Specifically, being a benefit company shows the most significant impact on the model, having the highest standardized regression coefficient in absolute values. Analyzing the non-standardized coefficients, it is evident that benefit companies, on average, have a default spread that is 0.011 lower than that of profit companies, even when accounting for the same ATECO group, logarithms of sales, operating leverage, and financial leverage. The inclusion of control variables, therefore, leads to an increased impact of being a benefit company, as the relative regression coefficient shifts from $b = -0.006$ to $b = -0.011$.

Since both the dependent and quantitative independent variables are expressed in logarithmic form, the regression coefficients of the log-log model can be interpreted in percentage terms: a 1% increase in the sales results in a 0.009% decrease in the logarithm of the default spread.

Table 8.2 Model summary

Model	R	R-squared	Adjusted R-squared	Std. error of the estimate	Change statistics					Durbin-Watson
					R-squared change	F change	df1	df2	Sig. F change	
1	0.138[a]	0.019	0.016	0.018997440206391	0.019	7.020	1	362	0.008	
2	0.198[b]	0.039	0.023	0.018932520593425	0.020	1.497	5	357	0.190	2.028

[a]Predictors: (Constant), Benefit
[b]Predictors: (Constant), Benefit, LogFinancialLeverage, ATECOGroup = Group 2, LogOperatingLeverage, ATECOGroup = Group 3, LogSales
[c]Dependent variable: LogDefaultSpread

Table 8.3 Anova

Model		Sum of squares	Df	Mean square	*F*	Sig.
1	Regression	0.003	1	0.003	7.020	0.008[b]
	Residual	0.131	362	0.000		
	Total	0.133	363			
2	Regression	0.005	6	0.001	2.426	0.026[c]
	Residual	0.128	357	0.000		
	Total	0.133	363			

[a]Dependent variable: LogDefaultSpread
[b]Predictors: (Constant), Benefit
[c]Predictors: (Constant), Benefit, LogFinancialLeverage, ATECOGroup = Group 2, LogOperatingLeverage, ATECOGroup = Group 3, LogSales

Table 8.4 Coefficients

Model		Unstandardized coefficients		Standardized coefficients			Collinearity statistics	
		B	Std. error	Beta	*t*	Sig.	Tolerance	VIF
1	(Constant)	− 0.277	0.001		−241.308	0000		
	Benefit	−0.006	0.002	−0.138	−2.649	0.008	1.000	1.000
2	(Constant)	−0.212	0.034		−6.223	<.001		
	Benefit	−0.011	0.004	−0.260	−3.156	0.002	0.398	2.514
	LogSales	−0.009	0.004	−0.173	−2.069	0.039	0.384	2.606
	LogOperatingLeverage	0.003	0.005	0.038	0.686	0.493	0.867	1.153
	LogFinancialLeverage	0.005	0.008	0.031	0.577	0.565	0.958	1.043
	ATECOGroup = Group 2	0.004	0.002	0.089	1.584	0.114	0.844	1.185
	ATECOGroup = Group 3	0.000	0.003	0.003	0.062	0.951	0.854	1.171

[a]Dependent variable: LogDefaultSpread

8.6 Concluding Remarks

The Italian benefit company (*Società Benefit*) is a new business model introduced by the Italian legislature in 2016, following precedents set by legislators in other jurisdictions. This model addresses the growing interest in the impact of business activities on the environmental and social context and moves beyond the historically predominant focus on economic-financial performance.

The model departs from shareholder primacy in favor of the two objectives of profit and common benefit that must balance each other. This approach not only safeguards the patrimonial and non-patrimonial rights of shareholders but also encourages companies to engage in social and environmental initiatives by revising the liability regime of directors.

The research explores a topic that has not been extensively covered in literature: the relationship between being an Italian benefit company and the risk of insolvency, as measured by the default spread. The issue is studied by using a statistical survey. To this end, two samples were selected: one consisting of Italian benefit companies and another of comparable Italian profit companies.

Specifically, by applying propensity score matching, three comparable profit companies were paired with each benefit company based on control parameters like ATECO codes, sales, operating leverage, and financial leverage, all indicative of company risk. After a descriptive analysis of both, the two samples were combined into one consisting of two groups: benefit and profit.

A log-log hierarchical linear regression analysis was performed, with the benefit company status (dummy variable) as the independent variable, the default spread as the response variable, and the control variables as mentioned above. Being a benefit company has the most significant impact on the default spread. The final result of the study is that lenders appear to perceive benefit companies as less risky than comparable profit companies.

The results of the statistical analyses confirm the research hypothesis and align with the prevailing literature, which recognizes the higher degree of sustainability, greater transparency of disclosure, and improved reputation of benefit companies as the primary reasons for their better reliability in the eyes of lenders.

The study also suggests promising directions for future research. Extending the data collection period and disaggregating the sample into sub-samples based on new parameters could provide deeper insights. These parameters could include the timing of when a corporation adopts the benefit status—either at the company's inception or subsequently—or involve a more detailed segmentation of existing parameters, such as sales and the ATECO code.

Such insights could help address the main limitations of the current research while contributing to our understanding of a phenomenon that is both recent and part of a significant shift in how environmental, social, and governance issues are perceived.

While numerous studies have investigated the impact of CSR policies on relationships with various stakeholders, few have focused specifically on the relationships with lenders. Therefore, this research not only provides insights specific to benefit companies but also contributes to the broader scientific discourse.

References

Alexander, F. H. (2020). Putting benefit corporation statutes into context by putting context into the statutes. *Business Lawyer, 76*(1), 109–150.

Angelici, C. (2017). Società benefit. *Orizzonti del Diritto Commerciale, V*(2), 1–12.

Austin, P. C. (2008). A critical appraisal of propensity-score matching in the medical literature between 1996 and 2003. *Statistics in Medicine, 27*(12), 2037–2049.

Baird, P. L., Geylani, P. C., & Roberts, J. A. (2012). Corporate social and financial performance re-examined: Industry effects in a linear mixed model analysis. *Journal of Business Ethics, 109*(3), 367–388.

Baudot, L., Dillard, J., & Pencle, N. (2020). The emergence of benefit corporations: A cautionary tale. *Critical Perspectives on Accounting, 67–68*, 102073.

Bauer, R., & Hann, D. (2010). *Corporate environmental management and credit risk* (December 23). Available at *SSRN*: https://ssrn.com/abstract=1660470 or doi:https://doi.org/10.2139/ssrn.1660470.

Bellavite Pellegrini, C., Cannas, C., & Dallocchio, M. (2023). Costo del capitale e valutazione d'impatto per le Società Benefit. In C. Bellavite Pellegrini & R. Caruso (Eds.), *Società Benefit, profili giuridici ed economico-aziendali* (pp. 61–73). EGEA.

Benedetto, U., Head, S. J., Angelini, G. D., & Blackstone, E. H. (2018). Statistical primer: propensity score matching and its alternatives. *European Journal of Cardio-thoracic Surgery: Official Journal of the European Association for Cardio-thoracic Surgery, 53*(6), 1112–1117.

Bianchini, M., & Sertoli, C. (2018). Una ricerca Assonime sulle società benefit. *Dati empirici, prassi statutaria e prospettive, Analisi Giuridica dell'Economia, issue, 1*, 201–220.

Blount, J., & Offei-Danso, K. (2013). The benefit corporation: questionable solution to non-existent problem. *St. Mary's Law Journal, 44*(3), 617–670.

Cao, K., Gehman, J., & Grimes, M. G. (2017). Standing out and fitting in: Charting the emergence of Certified B Corporations by industry and region. In A. C. Corbett & J. A. Katz (Eds.), *Hybrid ventures (Advances in entrepreneurship, firm emergence and growth)* (Vol. 19, pp. 1–38). Emerald Publishing Limited.

Capelli, I. (2020). La sostenibilità ambientale e sociale nelle politiche di remunerazione degli amministratori delle società quotate: la rilevanza degli interessi degli stakeholder dopo la SHRD II. *Orizzonti del Diritto Commerciale, 2*, 554–588.

Chava, S. (2014). Environmental externalities and cost of capital. *Management Science, 60*(9), 2223–2247.

Cian, M. (2021). On sustainable management and the powers of directors: A first start for deeper consideration. *Orizzonti del Diritto Commerciale, 3*, 1131–1148.

Codazzi, E. (2020). Società benefit (di capitali) e bilanciamento di interessi: alcune considerazioni sull'organizzazione interna. *Orizzonti del Diritto Commerciale, 2*, 589–627.

Codazzi, E. (2021). Scopo di lucro e di beneficio comune nel passaggio da società non benefit a società benefit. *Orizzonti del Diritto Commerciale, 3*, 1243–1290.

Cook, R. D., & Weisberg, S. (1982). *Residuals and influence in regression*. Chapman & Hall.

Cooper, E. W., & Uzun, H. (2015). Corporate social responsibility and the cost of debt. *Journal of Accounting and Finance, 15*(8), 11–29.

Corsi, C., Prencipe, A., & Boffa, D. (2020). Le Certified Benefit Corporation come modello di innovazione sociale. Un'analisi esplorativa degli elementi economico-aziendali emergenti dal contesto. *Quaderni di ricerca sull'artigianato, issue, 1*, 77–96.

D'Antonio, L., Johnsen, T., & Hutton, R. B. (1997). Expanding socially screened portfolios: An attribution analysis of bond performance. *The Journal of Investing, 6*(4), 79–86.

Damodaran, A. (2018). *The dark side of valuation. Valuing young, distressed, and complex businesses* (3rd ed.). Pearson.

Dehejia, R. H., & Wahba, S. (2002). Propensity score-matching methods for nonexperimental causal studies. *The Review of Economics and Statistics, 84*(1), 151–161.

Denozza, F., & Stabilini, A. (2017). La Società Benefit nell'era dell'Investor Capitalism. *Orizzonti del Diritto Commerciale, V*(2), 11–15.

Di Giulio, A., Migliavacca, P. O., & Tencati, A. (2011). Corporate social performance and the cost of capital: a meaningful relationship? In F. Perrini (Ed.), *Business ethics and corporate sustainability* (pp. 132–146). Edward Elgar Publishing.

Donaldson, T., & Preston, L. E. (1995). The stakeholder theory of the corporation: Concepts, evidence, and implications. *Academy of Management Review, 20*(1), 65–91.

Draper, N. R., & Smith, H. (1998). *Applied regression analysis* (3rd ed.). Wiley.

Drisaldi, R. (2022). La relazione di impatto delle società benefit. *Bilancio e revisione, 7*, 17–30.

El Ghoul, S., Guedhami, O., Kwok, C. Y., & Mishra, R. (2011). Does corporate social responsibility affect the cost of capital? *Journal of Banking and Finance, 35*(9), 2388–2406.

Eichholtz, P., Holtermans, R., Kok, N., & Yönder, E. (2019). Environmental performance and the cost of debt: Evidence from commercial mortgages and REIT bonds. *Journal of Banking and Finance, 102*, 19–32.

Everett, C. G. (2013). Measuring the social responsibility discount for the cost of equity capital: Evidence from benefit corporations. *The Journal of Behavioral Finance and Economics, 3*(2), 55–75.
Ge, W., & Liu, M. (2015). Corporate social responsibility and the cost of corporate bonds. *Journal of Accounting and Public Policy, 34*(6), 597–624.
Girerd-Potin, I., Jimenez-Garces, S., & Louvet, P. (2014). Which dimensions of social responsibility concern financial investors? *Journal of Business Ethics, 121*(4), 559–576.
Goss, A., & Roberts, G. S. (2011). The impact of corporate social responsibility on the cost of bank loans. *Journal of Banking and Finance, 35*(7), 1794–1810.
Hair, J. F., Black, W. C., Babin, B. J., & Anderson, R. E. (2014). *Multivariate data analysis* (7th ed.). Pearson.
Hoepner, A., Oikonomou, I., Scholtens, B., & Schroder, M. (2016). The effects of corporate and country sustainability characteristics on the cost of debt: An international investigation. *Journal of Business Finance and Accounting, 43*(1–2), 158–190.
Jones, T. M. (1995). Instrumental stakeholder theory: A synthesis of ethics and economics. *The Academy of Management Review, 20*(2), 404–437.
Jones, T.M., Harrison, J.S., & Felps, W. (2018), How Applying Instrumental Stakeholder Theory Can Provide Sustainable Competitive Advantage. *Academy of Management Review*, 43(3), 371–391.
Kim, M., Surroca, J., & Tribó, J. A. (2014). Impact of ethical behavior on syndicated loan rates. *Journal of Banking and Finance, 38*(C), 122–144.
La Rosa, F., & Bernini, F. (2022). ESG controversies and the cost of equity capital of European listed companies: the moderating effects of ESG performance and market securities regulation. *International Journal of Accounting and Information Management, 30*(5), 641–663.
La Rosa, F., Liberatore, G., Mazzi, F., & Terzani, S. (2018). The impact of corporate social performance on the cost of debt and access to debt financing for listed European non-financial firms. *European Management Journal, 36*(4), 519–529.
Maggi, D., & Rossi, P. (2022). La relazione di valutazione d'impatto: obbligo di deposito per le società benefit. *Bilancio e revisione, 1*(10), 1–8.
Magnanelli, B. S., & Izzo, F. (2017). Corporate social performance and cost of debt: The relationship. *Social Responsibility Journal, 13*(2), 250–265.
Menz, K. M. (2010). Corporate social responsibility: is it rewarded by the corporate bond market? A critical note. *Journal of Business Ethics, 96*, 117–134.
Moroz, P. W., Branzei, O., Parker, S. C., et al. (2018). Imprinting with purpose: Prosocial opportunities and B Corp certification. *Journal of Business Venturing, 33*(2), 117–129.
Mosco, G. D. (2018). Scopo e oggetto nell'impresa sociale e nella società benefit. *Analisi Giuridica dell'Economia, issue, 1*, 81–94.
Nori, G. M. (2021). La società Benefit un (nuovo?) mezzo per (non) fare impresa. *Rivista di diritto societario, issue, 4*, 787–813.
Oikonomou, I., Brooks, C., & Pavelin, S. (2012). The impact of corporate social performance on financial risk and utility: A longitudinal analysis. *Financial Management, 41*(2), 483–515.
Oikonomou, I., Brooks, C., & Pavelin, S. (2014). The effects of corporate social performance on the cost of corporate debt and credit ratings. *Financial Review, 49*(1), 49–75.
Palmieri, M. (2017). L'interesse sociale: dallo shareholder value alle società benefit. *Banca Impresa Società, XXXVI*(2), 201–237.
Parker, S. C., Gamble, E. N., Moroz, P. W., & Branzei, O. (2019). The impact of B lab certification on firm growth. *Academy of Management Discoveries, 5*(1), 57–77.
Rawhouser, H., Cummings, M., & Crane, A. (2015). Benefit corporation legislation and the emergence of a social hybrid category. *California Management Review, 57*(3), 13–35.
Richter, M. S., Jr. (2017). Società benefit e società non benefit. *Riv. Dir. Comm CXV, 2*, 271–285.
Riso, V., Tallak, M., Bracci, E., & Cantele, S. (2023). The transition towards benefit corporations: What are the roles for stakeholders? *Business Strategy and the Environment, 33*(2), 1–13.

Rossi, S. (2017). L'impegno multistakeholder della società benefit. *Orizzonti del Diritto Commerciale, issue, 2*, 1–12.
Schneider, T. E. (2010). Is environmental performance a determinant of bond pricing? Evidence from the U.S. pulp and paper and chemical industries. *Contemporary Accounting Research, 28*(5), 1537–1561.
Sharfman, M. P., & Fernando, C. S. (2008). Environmental risk management and the cost of capital. *Strategic Management Journal, 29*(6), 569–592.
Sjåfjell, B. (2019). Realising the potential of the board for corporate sustainability. In B. Sjåfjell & C. M. Bruner (Eds.), *The Cambridge handbook of corporate law, corporate governance and sustainability. Cambridge law handbooks* (pp. 696–710). Cambridge University Press.
Sneirson, J. F. (2019). The history of shareholder primacy, from Adam Smith through the rise of financialism. In B. Sjåfjell & C. M. Bruner (Eds.), *The Cambridge handbook of corporate law, corporate governance and sustainability* (pp. 73–85). Cambridge University Press.
Steurer, R. (2006). Mapping stakeholder theory anew: From the 'stakeholder theory of the firm' to three perspectives on business–society relations. *Business Strategy and the Environment, 15*(1), 55–69.
Taffari, G. (2023). Società benefit e relazione d'impatto: l'importanza degli strumenti di rendicontazione "non finanziaria". *Cooperative e Enti non profit, 23*(8–9), 18–23.
Toffoletti, L. (2022). La mancata attuazione dei benefici esterni nelle Società Benefit. Poteri di controllo di AGCM, legittimazione ad agire degli stakeholder e doveri fiduciari degli amministratori. *Osservatorio del diritto civile e commerciale, issue, 1*, 171–206.
Zoppini, A. (2017). Un raffronto tra società benefit ed enti non profit: implicazioni sistematiche e profili critici. *Orizzonti del Diritto Commerciale, issue, 2*, 1–11.

The manufacturer's authorised representative in the EU is Springer Nature Customer Service Centre GmbH, Europaplatz 3, 69115 Heidelberg, Germany. If you have any concerns regarding our products, please contact ProductSafety@springernature.com

Printed and bound by CPI Group (UK) Ltd, Croydon, CR0 4YY
30/09/2026
02225569-0001